PANZER ACE

PANZER ACE

The Memoirs of an Iron Cross Panzer Commander From *Barbarossa* to Normandy

Richard Freiherr von Rosen

Foreword by Robert Forcyzk
Translated by Geoffrey Brooks

Greenhill Books

*Panzer Ace: The Memoirs of an Iron Cross Panzer Commander
from Barbarossa to Normandy*
Greenhill Books

Greenhill Books, c/o Pen & Sword Books Ltd,
47 Church Street, Barnsley, S. Yorkshire, S70 2AS
For more information on our books, please visit
www.greenhillbooks.com, email contact@greenhillbooks.com
or write to us at the above address.

Publishing History
Richard Freiherr von Rosen's *Als Panzeroffizier in Ost und West* was first published by
Flechsig Verlag, Germany. This 2018 edition is published by Greenhill Books, London,
with a new foreword by Robert Forczyk.

CIP data records for this title are available from the British Library

ISBN 978-1-78438-266-7

Typeset and designed by JCS Publishing Services Ltd
Typeset in 10.5pt Caslon Pro
Printed and bound in England by TJ International Ltd, Padstow, Cornwall

Reprinted 2019

Contents

Translator's Note

The German ranks for the Panzer Arm appearing in this book had the following British Army equivalents:

Panzerschütze/Funker	Gunner/Radio operator
Gefreiter	Private, trained soldier
Obergefreiter	Lance-Corporal (non NCO)
Unteroffizier	Corporal (basic NCO grade)
Feldwebel	Sergeant
Oberfeldwebel	Staff Sergeant
Hauptfeldwebel	'Spiess' – Company Sergeant-Major
Leutnant	Junior Lieutenant
Oberleutnant	Senior Lieutenant
Hauptmann	Captain
Major	Major
Oberstleutnant	Lieutenant-Colonel
Oberst	Colonel

Following German artillery tradition, an abteilung was in general a formation of three fighting companies plus an HQ company and the usual range of support services. Its nearest equivalent would be a battalion. Typically an abteilung might have forty-five panzers.

A company at full strength might have around fourteen panzers and be composed of several platoons, perhaps four panzers per platoon.

The unit abbreviations used in this book in ascending order are:

PzAbt	Panzer Abteilung
PzRgt	Panzer Regiment
PzBrig	Panzer Brigade
PzDiv	Panzer Division

Foreword by Robert Forczyk

While there are many, many books about tanks in the Second World War, relatively few have been written by men who served as tank platoon leaders in that conflict. Two of the more memorable books in this category were Bob Crisp's *Brazen Chariots* (1959), about his service in 3 RTR in 1941, and Otto Carius's *Tigers in the Mud* (1960), about his service in Heavy PzAbt 502 in 1943–4. In armoured warfare, it is young tank platoon leaders who lead from the front, but unfortunately few of these men survived the war. Most accounts of armoured warfare were written by higher-level officers like Guderian or staff officers who did not actually serve on tanks at the small unit level. Consequently, *Panzer Ace*, written by Richard Freiherr von Rosen, is a welcome addition to the exceedingly short list of Second World War tank platoon leader memoirs. As a former Cold War-era tank platoon leader myself, I found *Panzer Ace* to be a gripping front-line account that amply brings to life the day-to-day responsibilities and challenges facing junior leaders at the spearpoint of mobile warfare.

The 18-year-old von Rosen entered the German Army (Heer) in 1940 and was trained as a tanker during the winter of 1940/1. His first taste of battle was as a gunner on a Panzer III medium tank during the opening stages of Operation *Barbarossa* in 1941. In his opening vignettes, the author details the intense effort that the Heer put into training its tankers, how tank crews were formed and vehicles provisioned for the campaign in Russia. I was surprised by the author's frank admission of widespread looting (and intoxication) by members of his battalion as they captured Russian towns and a rather casual attitude towards local security in occupied areas. In Bob Crisp's earlier memoir, he referred to similar proclivities as 'swanning about'. This is not how the Panzer spearheads are depicted in official histories, looting and drinking their way across Russia. On the other hand, the author's description of his crew's relentless quest to acquire creature comforts rings quite consistent with the behaviour of tankers from other armies. In von Rosen's unvarnished account, tankers are filthy, dog-tired and focused on simple tasks, like keeping the air filters clean. Combat was short and violent. In his first real action, the author's entire five-tank platoon was knocked out by concealed anti-tank guns and only eleven of twenty-five crewmen survived, after evading capture. However, tank units also suffered many non-battle casualties and von Rosen was injured in an accident in August 1941 and sent back to Germany to recover.

Von Rosen was certainly fortunate in missing most of the 1942 campaign in Russia and then being reassigned to the newly created Heavy PzAbt 502, the first German battalion equipped with the new Tiger I heavy tank. During his recovery, von Rosen received additional training and was commissioned as a Leutnant. In late December 1942, his unit was hurriedly transferred to southern Russia in response to the catastrophe at Stalingrad. It was in January 1943, on the frozen Kalmuck steppes, that von Rosen gained his first experience as a tank platoon leader. His unit, redesignated as Heavy PzAbt 503, conducted a fighting withdrawal back to Rostov, then to the Kharkov area. Armoured delaying operations are one of the toughest missions that a platoon leader can receive, and conducting it amidst a Russian winter was no small accomplishment. Afterwards, von Rosen describes the lead-up to Operation *Zitadelle*, the German offensive against the Kursk bulge, with interesting details about training and preparations. One of the author's most telling observations about Kursk was, 'we would discover that the Russian soldier we would face was no longer the man of 1941–2, but a soldier our equal in fighting efficiency and morale.' The detailed descriptions that von Rosen provides of tank combat during the Battle of Kursk are some of the best that I have read, rich with significant points that are often overlooked in other accounts. Not surprisingly, given the fierce Soviet resistance, von Rosen was wounded in action during the battle and again sent back to Germany.

After nearly a year away from the front, von Rosen returned to duty in June 1944 just as his battalion was transferred to France to deal with the Allied invasion of Normandy. Although Heavy PzAbt 503 played a major role in frustrating the British offensive known as Operation *Goodwood*, the battalion was eventually ground down by heavy losses. The author's descriptions of Allied artillery barrages and air attacks indicate how German Panzers could no longer operate in broad daylight, as they had earlier in the war. After the Allied breakout from Normandy, von Rosen managed to reach Germany, where his unit was re-equipped with the new King Tiger heavy tank. In September 1944, von Rosen was promoted to company commander. However, he notes how veteran tank crews had become a precious commodity and his former commander tried to pinch some of his best tankers from him. The Third Reich's manpower crisis was becoming acute and the author notes that the quality of the German NCO corps had begun to decline and that some of his replacements were far less effective than the soldiers of 1941–2. After a brief period of reconstitution, von Rosen's company was sent to Hungary in October 1944 to try and prevent the loss of Budapest to the advancing Red Army.

In Hungary, von Rosen found that even the King Tiger was challenged by the increased skill of Soviet anti-tank defences, noting, 'it was a grim feeling to be sitting in a Panzer, see a muzzle flash ahead and then wait for the hit . . . We could receive a hit so powerful that it stunned us all.' It is also amazing to read how the German high command foolishly employed the King Tigers on marshy terrain which put them at a clear disadvantage. On soft ground the King Tigers were easily mired and on one day von Rosen had five of his tanks stuck, which required retrieval under fire – a nightmare for any armour leader. The rainy autumn weather in Hungary seriously hindered German efforts to counter-attack Soviet breakthroughs and von Rosen's recollections of rain-soaked nights inside his Tiger are particularly poignant for tankers: 'One might think that a Panzer was watertight. On the contrary, water always found its way in. Because movement in the Panzer was very limited by how cramped it was, if it rained all day it was very unpleasant inside. Constant drips falling on your head or neck could drive you mad.' I had similar experiences during monsoon season in Korea in my M60A3 tank – long nights of water torture in tight spaces that one never forgets.

Von Rosen's final months in combat were a daily struggle to keep his remaining King Tigers operational, and he gives due credit to the efforts of his technical NCOs in the repair group. However, even skilled mechanics could not keep up with the amount of combat-damaged and broken-down vehicles, which reduced von Rosen's company to just a handful of operational tanks. Eventually, vehicle recovery became the primary daily mission, without which the company would have quickly disintegrated. Aside from weather and losses, the author also notes how the awful state of German infantry at this stage of the war – men he described as 'poorly armed and lacking any motivation' along with the lack of artillery or air support – prevented operational success. By late 1944, the Heer was no longer capable of conducting the kind of combined arms operations that had led to rapid success in 1940–1. Furthermore, the appearance of Soviet heavy tanks began to threaten even the King Tiger's aura of invincibility and he describes one occasion in January 1945 when four of his tanks were knocked out by concealed SU-152 assault guns. Von Rosen was wounded in December 1944 but remained with his company until severely wounded again in February 1945. At that point, he was fortunate in being sent to a military hospital in Bavaria, which fell in the American sector of occupation. Other members of his unit were captured by the advancing Red Army.

Like many German Second World War memoirs, von Rosen's tries to avoid political questions or reflection about the Nazi regime, but we get some glimpses in the final section of *Panzer Ace,* which covers the author's immediate post-war experiences. Von Rosen is sharply critical of the French occupation forces, while forgetting that millions of foreigners suffered under German occupation for four long years. He is particularly critical of French looting in Germany and the imposition of harsh food rationing, although Germans looted France and imposed equally harsh rationing. In the final section, the author also make it clear that he had a low opinion of Nazi politicians and, eventually, Hitler. Furthermore, he does concede that the Germans' defeat was due to their own mistakes and that he had unwittingly fought for a criminal regime – something not all German memoirs were willing to admit. Afterwards, von Rosen went on to serve twenty-two years in the post-war Bundeswehr and rose to become a Panzer-Brigade commander, but he does not cover this period, which is unfortunate. It would have been interesting to read how the author's wartime experiences influenced the training of his post-war tank units, although this is understandably a touchy subject even today in Germany.

The format of *Panzer Ace* allows the author to address a great many tactical details of interest to modern historians, such as what Panzer crews ate and their routine of daily life while on campaign. For modern tankers, it is also interesting to read about the difficulties of tank recovery in field conditions and the trials of keeping a functional radio net under combat conditions, which is harder than it seems. Von Rosen's memoir provides a valuable and frank first-person narrative of Panzer operations in the period 1941–5 which helps to dispel some of the 'gloss' put on by official histories. The result is a more honest appraisal of what it was like to be a successful small unit armour leader for four years of intense combat.

Author's Foreword

One is justified in asking why I have left it so late in life to publish my memoirs. After all, I wrote them years ago when my mind was clearer and I could refer back to my diaries and the many field post letters which my parents had kept.

I have written down my war experiences for my children and grandchildren since they found it difficult to imagine what someone born around 1922 had had to go through. They had known only freedom and security and were curious to find out how it had been for me.

When the Second World War began I was 17 and still at high school swotting Greek, Latin and Mathematics. At age 18 I was called up, and at 19 I had my first narrow escape from death in Russia. On my 21st birthday I led my platoon of four Tiger panzers at the Battle of Kursk, and exactly a year later I was aboard a panzer transport train for Normandy. Two days after my 23rd birthday I was released as a prisoner of war and returned home. That was my youth, a time of anxiety and great concern – more for my family than for my own life. Most of my contemporaries came through it, but many did not live to see the end of the war.

We went on the battlefield to protect the Fatherland, or at least we believed that was the reason. We spent little time pondering who had caused and begun this war and why. 'Prove yourself' was my motto, shared by many of my comrades in arms. Our parents had no say in the matter.

After I was called up I had the great fortune to be led by men who were first of all human beings and not just soldiers. I became an adult and they influenced my development. As I look back at my zealous youth, they were and remain for me models of the human and soldierly virtues. They placed their trust in me and showed me so by giving me responsibilities early on which were often matters of life and death. Without their help and leadership I would not have been able to master it all.

I dedicate this memoir to the memory of the seven men who still remain close today to this 90-year-old. I also devote this memoir to the panzer men of

3 Company/Heavy PzAtb 503 to whom I was a comrade although senior in rank. The bond of friendship has held firm to the present day.

Richard Freiherr von Rosen, March 2013

Franz-Rudolf Schultze. In 1940 Oberleutnant and course leader for PzRgt 35 officer aspirants. After the war he was the fourth military attaché to the West German Bundestag.

Hans-Detloff von Cossel. In 1941 Oberleutnant and commander of 1 Company/PzRgt 35. He fell in the summer of 1943 in the rank of Major commanding 1 Atb/PzRgt 35.

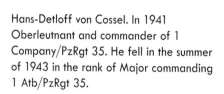

(left) Clemens Graf von Kageneck. In 1943 and 1944 Hauptmann and commander, Heavy PzAtb 503.

(below) Walter Scherf. In 1943 and 1944 Oberleutnant and later Hauptmann, commander of 3 Company/Heavy PzAtb 503.

Rolf Fromme. In 1944 Hauptmann, commander Heavy PzAtb 503.

Georg Graf von Plettenberg. In 1945
Rittmeister (Captain) and commander of
Heavy Cavalry Atb 4.

Nordewin von Diest-Koerber. In 1945
Hauptmann and last commander of Heavy
PzAtb 503.

1

The Second World War Begins

1939

15/16 Mar	Remainder of Czechoslovakia occupied: Reich Protectorate of Bohemia and Moravia created.
22 Mar	Former German territory of Memel annexed by the Third Reich.
26 Mar	Final Polish refusal of the German offer to clarify border issues.
31 Mar	Anglo-French guarantee of support for Poland.
23 Aug	German-Soviet Non-Aggression Treaty signed with secret protocol.
25 Aug	Anglo-Polish Pact of Mutual Assistance.
1 Sep	German attack on Poland.
3 Sep	Britain and France declare war on Germany.
17 Sep	The Red Army invades Eastern Poland.

As late as July and August 1939 we were at Oberbärenburg in the Erzgebirge as usual. Nothing was different on this visit from the previous ones. We went on many rambles with Mother, including into the Sudetenland, which had been annexed in October 1938, for example to the convent church at Mariaschein and into the Bohemian mountains. I myself had got to Oberbärenburg by motorcycle and used it to make quite a few excursions, visiting Saxon Switzerland and Dresden. I read the newspapers very attentively and listened every day to the news bulletins. Just as in 1938, the increasingly tense foreign-policy situation could be sensed everywhere.

The atmosphere became ever more oppressive in the second half of August. Air-raid sirens were tested and practice blackouts carried out, private vehicles requisitioned and reservists called up: all this pointed towards the impending conflict. We had entered the last ten days of peace. The radio broadcast endless military music and unflinching new reports regarding atrocities by the Poles against *Volksdeutsche*, with news bulletins with ever more dangerous threats sandwiched in between. Many of the reported attacks had been staged by the Nazis, such as the incident at the Gleiwitz radio station on 31 August, but others actually did happen. Whom should one believe? A typical comment by adults was: 'Without a miracle, war with Poland cannot be avoided,' or 'Once the harvest is in, it will start.'

On 23 August we breathed a sigh of relief. Shortly before, the unexpected had come to pass. Behind the backs of the Western Allies, the arch-enemies Hitler and Stalin had concluded a non-aggression pact. There was a secret protocol, hardly any knowledge of which had been made public, in which the Baltic States had been conceded to the Soviets' sphere of influence. Would this enable the calamity to be avoided at the last moment? Everybody prayed for it. On the afternoon of 31 August there was only one subject of discussion. The Reichstag had been summoned for the following day to hear 'a declaration by the Reich Government'. It was fairly clear what this meant. On Friday, 1 September everybody sat by their radio sets, my family too. Finally came Hitler's voice with the sentence announcing the disaster: '. . . since five forty-five we have been shooting back!' Now it was official: we were at war.

Depression reigned. What would we soon be having to face? The grown-ups remembered the awful war years of 1917 and 1918. The turnip and swede winter, the shortage of coal, military hospitals filled to overflowing, and so many families in mourning. Soon the radio announced the first measures: food ration cards, clothing coupons classified by age and gender, petrol rationing, travel restrictions, coal quotas, frantic activity – everything had already been prepared. In the years that followed we would have to have a blackout, have to hoard, have to evacuate. The only sources of information were the official Reich radio service, which broadcast reports prepared by the Propaganda Ministry, and the newspapers, controlled by the same body. Listening to foreign radio stations was not yet illegal, but for the most part their broadcasts in times of crisis did not provide the true circumstances affecting Germany. In any case their customary exaggerations condemned them as a non-credible source.

East Prussia had been separated geographically from the Reich since 1919, and the Reich's claim for an extraterritorial railway line and road across the Polish Corridor to connect with it seemed to me reasonable. Also that Danzig, which had been placed under a League of Nations mandate by the Treaty of Versailles, should be returned to the Reich. I found the claims of Polish atrocities against the citizens of German stock in the Polish Corridor and the province of Posen believable, while being dubious about the alleged Polish attack on the Gleiwitz radio station. To a certain extent there was little sympathy for the Poles, but a

February

M	T	W	T	F	S	S
					1	2
3	4	5	6	7	8	9
10	11	12	13	14	15	16
17	18	19	20	21	22	23
24	25	26	27	28	29	

future war against the Western Powers was considered a great danger and there was no possibility of avoiding it.

Even amongst my own generation there was little euphoria and enthusiasm for a war, but if the Fatherland was in danger then one had to make a stand and become involved. Whatever events had unleashed the war were irrelevant. Many believed secretly that it would be a short war ending with a quick victory. The very first special bulletins from Poland reinforced the hope that 'Once again the Führer was right'. Then two days later came the damper. It was Sunday, and Aunt Ina had heard on the radio that France and Britain had declared war on Germany. A local war against Poland was developing into a kind of world war, for Great Britain brought into the war the British Empire: Australia and New Zealand, India, and a few days later the South African Union and Canada. This did not look good.

I prepared for my return journey to Rastatt. Private journeys by car or motorcycle were forbidden and so I had to go to the Office of the District Administrator at Dippoldiswalde for an exemption certificate. I also received a docket allowing me 5 litres of petrol, enough to get me home to Rastatt. After breakfast on 9 September I set out, and spent that night in the panzer barracks at Bamberg, which I would enter fourteen months later as a soldier. The next day I arrived at Rastatt. I became a 'dispatch rider' for the military district and had a red corner stamped onto my number plate which showed my authority to use my motorcycle. Rastatt was in the so-called 'Red Zone' which was being evacuated. Women and children had already gone, and all schools and most businesses had shut down. The nearby Rhine Front was very quiet, the French idle in their Maginot Line, the Germans behind their Westwall. Only the big bridge at Wintersdorf had been demolished. Neither side wanted to fire on the other, and a friendly traffic existed across both sides of the Rhine. At least, that was how it was on the Upper Rhine (the end nearest Switzerland). In those days they called it the *drôle de guerre* (the 'Phoney War').

I made myself useful at home. The nightly blackout was strictly enforced. Slackness attracted a fine. Not just once did the neighbourhood warden hammer on the door and shout 'Blackout!' Not the slightest chink of light must be seen from outside. In peacetime air-raid and blackout practices had often been held, but these were not taken too seriously, one only bothered with the rooms being occupied at the time. But now it was part of everyday wartime life. Here was something I could do to keep myself busy. Wooden frames had to be made and covered with black paper to put over the windows in the evening. Makeshift solutions were no longer acceptable, everything had to be done for the long term. In time the system was perfected: black curtains for the bedrooms, while rooms with sliding shutters or blinds had only the air slits pasted over, these were checked from time to time. There was no longer any street lighting, the neighbourhoods were black as pitch. In train compartments only a dim blue light was permitted, while all road vehicles had to place a cap with a small slit over their headlights so that one could be seen by oncoming traffic. Even pocket lamps had to have a cover projecting the light down onto one's feet. Pedestrians wore phosphorescent badges on their lapels to avoid colliding. An air-raid shelter was set up in our cellar which in May 1940 offered us protection from French artillery fire.

From October 1939 I attended high school at Baden-Baden. There were just a few of us who met up each morning on Rastatt railway station. Mostly we did go to school but occasionally preferred to climb the Battert (a 570m hill on the edge of the Black Forest) or spent the morning in the reading room at the spa house. We were known to the people of Baden-Baden as the 'Westwall gypsies' and it was rare that any of us was absent. Our schools were re-opened on 7 January 1940 but closed again shortly afterwards: it was a bitterly cold winter and no coke was available for heating purposes.

At the beginning of February 1940 I submitted my application as a volunteer for the army officer's course, since that had always been my ambition. My papers were sent to the panzer troops. At the end of that month I was accepted as a volunteer and shortly afterwards passed the medical as 'fit for war duty'. At the beginning of July I attended for psychological testing at Stuttgart for two and a half days. This course was feared and the failure rate high, but I returned home with a feeling of confidence. Meanwhile the 8th grade scholars, amongst whom I had been transferred at Easter, had been informed officially that every one of them called up for military service would be awarded the *Abitur* (secondary school graduation certificate) 'if conduct and achievements in class justify it'. Accordingly from early summer 1940 most of my class had left, the majority to enlist voluntarily, some into the SS, after doing three months' compulsory labour service (with the Reicharbeitdienst, RAD – State Labour Service). On the other hand I was informed by the Military District Command that I could expect to be called up on 1 October. It seemed that my hopes were to be fulfilled. As an aspirant for an active officer's career I was exempt from the RAD.

The following series of events from the beginning of 1940 fundamentally influenced our outlook and morale.

Richard Freiherr von Rosen as an 18-year-old high school boy in October 1940.

Formal order dated 27 February 1940 from the Military District Command at Rastatt to the author requiring him to report at once to the local police in connection with his registration for call-up.

Wehrbezirkskommando
  R a s t a t t
Abt. IIc Freiw.

R a s t a t t, den 17.2.40.

Betr.: E r f a s s u n g

Herrn
  Freiherr v. Rosen, Richard
  Rastatt

Sie haben sich sofort bei der für Sie zuständigen Ortspoli -
zeibehörde unter Vorlage dieses Schreibens, zwecks Erfassung
zu melden.

a. B.
H a u p t m a n n

Letter dated 2 April 1940 from the Military District Command at Rastatt to the author's father, notifying him that his son's enlistment was expected to happen in the period up to 1 October 1940.

```
Wehrbezirkskommando                           Rastatt, den 2. April 1940.
      R a s t a t t .
Abt. IIc/Freiw.

Herrn
Amtsgerichtsrat
Freiherr von Rosen,
R a s t a t t .
Sybillenstrasse 7.

      Dem Antrag Ihres Sohnes Richard zufolge ist dieser heute
vom Wehrbezirkskommando Rastatt auf Grund der Bestimmungen für
den freiwilligen Eintritt als Bewerber für die Offizier-Lauf-
bahn des Heeres dem Ob.d.H. - HPA. - unmittelbar zur Einstel-
lung als Offizier-Anwärter in Vorschlag gebracht worden.
      Mit der Einberufung Ihres Sohnes ist bis 1. Oktober 1940
zu rechnen.
```

Letter dated 27 May 1940 from the Ludwig-Wilhelm High School, Rastatt, advising the author of the award of the *Abitur*, subject to conditions of conduct and achievements in class, for each 8th grade scholar called up for military service.

Notification dated 24 July 1940 to the author from the Military District Command, Rastatt, confirming the registration of his candidacy for the army officer's course, 'Orders for your call-up to follow in due course.'

The author's first field postcard home to his family in Rastatt, October 1940.

Members of the RAD at a crossroads near Rastatt/Baden where the von Rosen family lived for many years.

An early version of the Panzer IV as seen on a postcard available for soldiers to buy.

A Wehrmacht convoy passing through the town of Bamberg.

Panzerschütze Richard Freiherr von Rosen photographed in October 1940. The arm of service colour for the panzer uniform was pink piping along the edge of the collar, shoulder straps and collar patches. The triangle above the cockade on the field cap was also pink.

The Occupation of Scandinavia
1940

16 Jan	The Allies prepare for a pre-emptive military operation in Scandinavia.
27 Jan	Work begins to study plans for Operation *Weserübung* (the occupation of Denmark and Norway).
5 Feb	The Allied Supreme Command decides to send several divisions to Narvik.
7 Apr	British expeditionary force embarks.
7 Apr	Units of the German fleet sail for Denmark and Norway.
9 Apr	German landings at Kristiansand, Stavanger, Bergen, Trondheim and Narvik; Denmark is occupied.
14–19 Apr	Allied landings north of Narvik, and at Namsos and Andalsnes.
24 May	British Cabinet decides to end the Norwegian operation.
10 June	Norwegian armed forces surrender.

The Campaign in the West
1940

10 May	0535hrs: the German offensive in the West begins.
13 May	German troops cross the Meuse at Dinant and Sedan.
15 May	Holland capitulates.
20 May	German troops reach the Channel coast.
24 May	Panzer units halt short of Dunkirk on Hitler's order.
26 May	Evacuation by sea of Allied troops trapped at Dunkirk begins.
28 May	Belgium capitulates.
4 Jun	By this date, 338,000 Allied soldiers have been evacuated from Dunkirk.
14 Jun	Paris is occupied without a fight.
17 Jun	German forces reach the Franco-Swiss frontier.
22 Jun	Franco-German armistice.
25 Jun	0135hrs: war with France ends.

My mood after the initial military successes was almost euphoric. To have pre-empted the British in Norway was a master stroke. The Battle of Narvik was extremely dramatic. General Dietl defended the town for four weeks in the mountains between Narvik and the Swedish border with his force of Bavarian and Austrian mountain troops. He became a national hero. The British retreat from Norway at the end of May 1940 was seen as a clear indication of the superiority

of the Wehrmacht over them, at least in the air and on land. The unleashing of the
campaign in the West simultaneously with the operation in Norway was completely
unexpected and thus came as a surprise to the German people. The violation of
Belgian and Dutch neutrality was accepted as a necessity.

The German successes in the West were at first almost unbelievable. Every day
my father and I would advance coloured pins on a map to show the new front
line as reported by frequent special reports and the Wehrmacht bulletins. Our
radio was left on all day so as not to miss anything. At that time, at the time
of our national success, the Wehrmacht bulletins were always very credible and
unvarnished. It filled us with great satisfaction that the armistice was signed at the
same place (Compiègne), in the same railway carriage and with the same ceremony
as for the German capitulation in 1918. The previous shame was atoned for. Now
we could be very accommodating and generous in the armistice negotiations. Or,
in any case, it seemed that this should be so.

Over the next few days German convoys coming from France rolled endlessly
from dawn until dusk to their peacetime garrisons at Rastatt. They included the
Rastatt Infantry Regiment 111 and Artillery Atb 35. Great enthusiasm and relief.
Crowds waving and flowers – everything as it should be to welcome home a
conquering army. And there was I – still in school! I bought a map of England, for
now we were all sure that England was next. As we know now, we were mistaken.

Now my hour had come. On 18 October 1940 I received my call-up to
Pz ErsatzAbt 35 at Bamberg. My wish to serve with the panzers as an officer-
aspirant was to be fulfilled. The letter was waiting for me when I got home from
school at midday. My mother opened the door and led me rather ceremoniously
to the dining table, which lay prepared. She told me later how much she was
impressed by the happiness shining in my face as I read the content of the letter.
In accordance to my plan, I was now a soldier! No longer a dream but reality. After
lunch I cycled into town in order to tell as many of my classmates or acquaintances
as possible of my good fortune. 'But once you're trained, the war will be long over,' I
thought to myself. 'Maybe I might be a soldier of the occupation in France.' If I had
only suspected what was yet to come in the war and how many years yet it would
last! My father feared as much: the victories in Poland and France did nothing to
lessen his foreboding that none of our enemies would ever conclude a peace treaty
with Hitler. At that time it did not worry me what he said.

I went to school next day, took my leave of my professors and classmates and
reported my departure to the Director. Thus ended my schooling – longed-for,

but still very odd. I had five days left before my parents escorted me to the railway station and waved me off to Bamberg garrison. With an excited feeling in my stomach I reported to the officer of the watch at the panzer barracks. No 3 Company was expecting us, forty-one 18-year-old boys for training with PzRgts 35 and 36. Eight to a room, we stretched out and sized each other up: what kind of hotshots they were, with the girls, at sport or drinking beer. For me – apart from sport – this was virgin territory. All the same, I accompanied them to the canteen and drank my first beer. It tasted ghastly, but it was what men did.

Next day the life began in earnest. We were always on the go from six in the morning until curfew at ten, exercises and more exercises. A horde of instructors were let loose on us. 'Officer candidates? Well, we'll see about that!' I spent more time on the ground than standing up. For a change there was tuition, some weapons training ('Into how many parts can you dismantle a rifle?'), cleaning the barrack room, uniform or locker inspections, always followed by the check-up inspection. Yet all this crap even gave us pleasure. 'We are hard men, they will never force us under!' And the first song we learned was '*Es ist so schön Soldat zu sein, Annemarie!*' (It's so wonderful to be a soldier, Annemarie!)

After fourteen days at Bamberg we were transferred. I went with twenty of my co-recruits to our field unit, PzRgt 35 at Auxerre on the Yonne in France where we were assigned to an officer-aspirant's course. Our instructor was Oberleutnant Schulz, after the war a military attaché to the Bundestag. When he was around, our instructors suddenly became human. Otherwise we had nothing to laugh about. Two Obergefreite, auxiliary instructors, were extremely sadistic. This period was hellish because we were entirely at their mercy. Nobody dared complain because we were expected to be able to stand it. These primitive beings especially had it in for me because I was a 'von'.

After curfew one evening they roused us from bed in our pyjamas and made us crawl across the muddy village street where a herd of sheep had been in the afternoon. I lost my self-control. It was all because one of my colleagues had a drop of coffee in his field flask at room inspection. When the light was put out and we lay on our straw sacks in our filthy pyjamas, I drew the blanket over my head and howled in anger. I had never before imagined that men could be so foul. But my defiance also grew: 'Don't let it get you down, they must not have their victory.'

We were introduced individually to the regimental commander, Oberst Eberbach. He was very human, hearty and interested. I noticed by his questions and the manner of his leave-taking that he was well disposed to me. I was appeased.

At the beginning of December 1940 the regiment moved to the Rhineland. Our course was now held in the large hall of the Windhövel inn at Solingen-Höhscheid. The proprietress, Aunt Ella, was a determined personality who made sure that the instructors did not treat us too badly in our off-duty hours. From 13 December 1940 I was laid up in the military hospital at Wuppertal-Elberfeld with an infected foot, over Christmas and New Year too. When I returned to the course on 26 January 1941, panzer driving training had begun. That was a good time. We arranged it so that we always drove past the girls' high school with our Panzer I training tank during their long lunch break and did a lap of honour around the courtyard. We laid it on pretty thick, but unfortunately we never had leave and so there was no opportunity to return the sympathy shown us.

Our course ended on 6 February 1941. Another transfer was in the offing for the regiment, but before that we officer-aspirants were now classified as Fahnenjunker (officer cadets, senior grade) and spread over the eight companies of PzRgt 35. I went to 1 Company with Ekke Solf, soon to fall in Russia. The company commander was Oberleutnant von Cossel. We were lodged in billets in the village of Pattscheid near Opladen. Solf and I were taken into the house of Father Zimmermann, the local Catholic priest. We had a superb suite with bathroom and proper beds – long afterwards I kept in touch with him by letter.

In mid-February 1941 the regiment was transferred to the Cognac region of southern France: our 1 Company was in the small village of Marignac and received new recruits. Some of them were lodged in the village school. I was the Room Senior. A large room, thirteen beds with straw sacks, no locker, a water tap in the school yard: it was difficult to keep oneself clean. The commander and part of the company staff occupied a small château about a kilometre outside the village on a ridge affording a panorama over the countryside. Vineyards all around. We Fahnenjunker had to eat every midday in the company officers' mess. Really it was very pleasant to be with men who knew how to eat with a knife and fork and conversed in a cultured manner and to be served by orderlies.

For us this meant a shorter midday break involving washing, changing into uniform, a long run to the château, and after dining a long run back to change in order to present oneself promptly for the afternoon session. Woe betide us if we arrived late: 'Naturally, the gentlemen officer-aspirants.' Once a week it was Gentlemen's Evening at the château. The food was better, served with fine Bordeaux wines, a fire burnt in the hearth and we relaxed in soft leather armchairs. Oberleutnant von Cossel was pleasant, communicative, interested and humorous.

Recently a new recruit at Bamberg, von Rosen and a group of other officer-aspirants were transferred to Auxerre in France, where PzRgt 35 had been stationed since the beginning of November 1940.

The château at Senan near Joigny/Yonne served as their quarters. The author's rooms are marked with an 'X'. Recruit training was very demanding and lasted until 7 December 1940.

(left) On 13 December 1940 the author was admitted to the military hospital at Wuppertal-Elberfeld with an infected foot. With him in the picture are a fellow patient and two nurses.

(right) A game of chess with sisters at the military hospital. He was discharged on 6 February 1941.

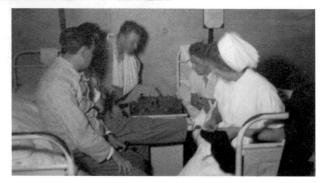

(below) The driving instructor explains the instrument panel and operation of the light panzer.

Panzer driving training at the end of January 1941 in Solingen. The training vehicle was a Panzer I chassis without the superstructure and turret.

The author, 'X' far left, with the group of corporals of the senior cadet grade in January and February 1941 at Solingen.

The author wearing the long Wehrmacht overcoat, warm enough for 'normal' winters.

The clergy house of the parish priest Father Zimmermann at Pattscheid/Opladen which served as the author's quarters, shared with a colleague. At the end of the senior cadet training course he was transferred to 1 Company/PzRgt 35.

Back on a train, mid-February 1941, this time to southern France. Sentries patrolled along the train at every halt. 'X' marks the author at top left of the open door.

The cattle truck floors were only covered with straw and the journey was anything but comfortable. Here hot refreshment is provided from a thermos.

The officers of 1 Company/PzRgt 35 were lodged at Château Gibeau. The château was surrounded by vineyards from which cognac was produced. The spring of 1941 was pleasantly warm, and one could sit outside comfortably in the château gardens.

(left) The senior cadets had quarters in Marignac/Gironde, a farming village.

(below) On Sundays, after dining in the officers' mess, the senior cadets were also permitted to use the comfortable armchairs in the gardens of the château.

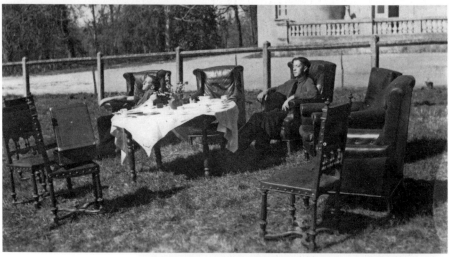

Leutnant König listening to gramophone records and enjoying the sunshine of southern France. He fell in July 1941 at the Stary-Bychow bridge.

PzRgt 35 returned to the Reich in April 1941. This photo was taken shortly before loading-up at Cognac.

The author, far left, with fellow members of the guard detachment.

Railway transport for Wehrmacht soldiers was often of the most primitive kind. The wagons were not fitted with toilets, resulting in this dangerous manoeuvre.

I was in his good books. The training schedule was now primarily panzer training with hardly any more discipline training and we had a lot of fun. Additionally I was no longer a recruit. I stood guard and also had duties as an auxiliary instructor.

In mid-March 1941 we were transferred to the Burgenland in Austria shortly after the Balkan campaign began. This came as a great surprise to all of us. The offensive resulted from the need to protect our Italian allies against the threat of defeat in Greece, their invasion not having been agreed beforehand with Hitler, and to prevent the British gaining a foothold there. Everything was settled so quickly, however, that we were not called for. At that time I was promoted to Fahnenjunkergefreiter (officer cadet senior grade, private soldier). Now I was a proper soldier. We spent a whole Saturday in Vienna, glorious! But it could not be repeated. Once again we were transported away by train; cattle wagons, straw, soot and filth.

The train rattled through the Protectorate of Bohemia and Moravia. Where was this train going? On 25 April 1941 my company arrived at the Warthelager, a large military training depot near Posen in the former Warthegau, now in Poland. It was a beautiful time of year, a glorious spring. On Saturdays and Sundays a company lorry drove into Posen. I always went if I was off duty. There I would meet my godfather Willy Seidlitz for a good meal. Every Saturday evening I went to the theatre or the opera, then caught the lorry for the 20km back to the camp. I also called on the Scheinpflugs, my friends from Oberbärenburg. Being from the Baltic States, the father had meanwhile landed up in Posen. I and my two friends played with model trains. As I was leaving, Frau Scheinpflug said to me, 'Your poor mother'. I believe that both her sons became soldiers – the war went on long enough for them to qualify.

In the regiment rumours were rife as to how things would turn out next. Either the USSR would allow us free passage into Persia or Iraq, from where we would break through to the Suez Canal, the Red Sea and Egypt. The Russians had placed a railway line and a highway at our disposal. Or we were to relieve Rommel. Nobody thought of an attack on the USSR.

The Balkan Campaign

1939

7 Apr	Italy occupies Albania.	

1940

28 Oct	Italian offensive against Greece begins.
29 Oct	The British occupy Crete.

1941

24 Feb	The British Cabinet decides to send an expeditionary force to Greece.
7 Mar	British troops land at Piraeus and Volos.
9 Mar	Italian offensive in Greece resumed.
16 Mar	The Italian offensive runs into trouble: Germany prepares a relief operation.
25 Mar	Yugoslavia joins the Tripartite Pact (Germany–Italy–Japan)
27 Mar	Military coup in Belgrade against the Tripartite Pact.
6 Apr	German campaign in the Balkans begins.
17 Apr	Yugoslav Army capitulates (344,000 prisoners).
6–27 Apr	Occupation of Greece.
21 Apr	Greece capitulates.
27 Apr	Athens occupied.
24–30 Apr	British forces in Greece (c.50,000 men) evacuated to Egypt.

By 1 May 1941 all elements of 4 PzDiv, of which our PzRgt 35 was part, had assembled in the Warthelager. A lively series of exercises began. Almost daily we drove short or long distances, great importance being placed on crossing swamps. It often happened that the entire company would bog down in swampy land and have to be pulled free by the heavy tractors of the workshop company. Great emphasis was also placed on anti-gas training. They kept telling us that we could almost count on gas attacks by our next opponents. My panzer was laid up for a longish period in the workshop: I spent half a day helping out there and learned a lot. After about five weeks the company had an inspection and emerged faultless. It had carried out all work asked of it, except for our panzer, which bogged down in a swamp. The regimental commander, Colonel Eberbach, shit on the driver from a great height for this. Besides panzer training we had many uniform parades, masked balls, etc. arranged by our 'Spiess', Hauptfeldwebel Klepzig. In this manner the seven weeks at the troop training depot passed by quickly. Now and again there was some talk of an operation against Russia.

In the final week of our training at Warthelager, PzRgt 35 received fifty new Panzer IIIs, of which eight came to our 1 Company. The company was now equipped with seventeen Panzer IIIs. Eleven had a 5cm gun, and six a 3.7cm gun: the two Panzer IIs each had a 2cm gun.

I had been in the rank of Gefreiter since March 1941 and became the gunner in a Panzer III with a 5cm 38 L/42 main gun and two co-axial 7.92mm MG 34s. The 22-tonne Panzer III SdKfz 141 had five crew: commander, driver, radio operator, gunner and loader. We carried loose with us one sub-machine gun, five Luger pistols and a quantity of egg-grenades and stick-grenades. The firepower of a single panzer was therefore impressive, besides which it was well armoured and fairly fast.

Oberleutnant von Cossel, our company commander, was 24 years of age and for me embodied the ideal type of officer – we would all go through fire for him. He came originally from the cavalry and influenced me with his very human manner of company leadership and dealings with the men. His bravery and calmness, even in critical situations, impressed me again and again. In every respect he was the model officer for me.

The final days brought us a lot of work. The new weapons had to be zeroed-in and calibrated, the gyrocompass installed, the panzer loaded up. It was extraordinary how much gear and equipment had to be put into a tank, and with proper handling it all fitted in. I sent my valuables home. The orders to roll could arrive at any time.

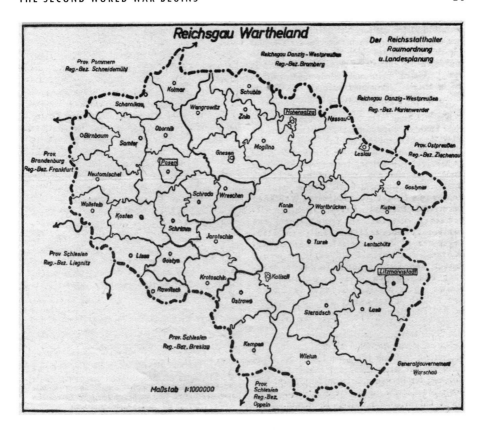

(above) After the Polish campaign, the administrative district of Reichgau Wartheland was created, its capital being Posen in the West. Warthelager was the training depot for 4 PzDiv of which PzRgt 35 formed part.

(left) A photo taken in March 1941 showing the author and the family with whom he was billeted in the Burgenland, Austria, not far from the border with Hungary

Oberleutnant Hans-Detloff von Cossel, commander of
1 Company/PzRgt 35. In 1941 this regiment was the
'armoured fist' of the Main-Frankish 4 PzDiv, whose
headquarters had been established at Würzburg in 1938.

Unteroffizier Pröbster on a rocking horse. Towing hawsers are
fitted to this Panzer III. The 4 PzDiv's insignia is on the glacis
plate near the driver's viewing slit, but is very difficult to make
out.

Group photo on a Panzer
III in Marz, Burgenland.
The author on the far left
with comrades Ekkehard
Solf and Fritz Fischer.

Burgenland/Austria, April 1941. The Panzer III numbered '114' in the foreground has the short 5cm gun. The author served as gunner aboard various panzers. The white bear near the turret number was the insignia for 1 Company. The other companies of I Abt (Major von Lauchert) each had a bear but in different colours.

Loading up. Equipment and personal belongings had to be stowed in the panzer. In the background tankers wait to refuel.

The panzers of PzRgt 35 were given a send-off from Wiener-Neustadt with bouquets of flowers. Looking to the future, spare sections of track are seen on the bow and front of the panzer.

The author visited Schloss Schönbrunn in Vienna on a Sunday excursion, end of April 1941.

The lake at Schloss Schönbrunn. Soldiers who had a camera took pictures which were then copied for their colleagues. Many copies of these photos have survived to this day.

Going towards the eastern border. The photo shows panzers of PzRgt 35 crossing a pioneer bridge over the river Warthe in the Warthelager troop-training grounds. This giant complex was set up in 1904.

Warthelager 1941: panzer and pioneer units of PzRgt 35 practise crossing the Warthe river in preparation for the campaign against Russia.

1 Company Panzer 114 camouflaged with birch branches. It is not known why the white bear insignia was painted both ahead of and behind the turret number.

(right) Travelling cross-country, Panzer 114 has become bogged down in swampy ground and is being dug free. At the right, driver Unteroffizier Braun looks away.

(below) The first objective of the attack at Kobryn has been reached without the company having had to fire a shot. Here the company is being refuelled in the Russian fuel dump at Kobryn.

(above) Having been topped-up at Kobryn, the panzers await new operational orders. The author, marked 'X', meanwhile enjoys the summer sunshine.

(left) Refuelling in the Russian fuel dump at Kobryn. In the foreground is Ekkehard Solf.

2

On the Eastern Front
(June–August 1941)

The Russian Campaign

1939

23 Aug	German–Soviet Non-Aggression Pact.

1940

14 Jun	Soviet ultimatum to Lithuania.
15 Jun	Soviets invade Lithuania.
16 Jun	Soviet ultimatums to Estonia and Latvia.
17 Jun	Soviets invade Estonia and Latvia.
26–28 Jun	Soviets invade Bessarabia and Bukovina.
12/13 Nov	Visit of Soviet Foreign Minister Molotov to Berlin (no agreement on respective spheres of interest).

1941

31 Jan	Completion of first invasion plan 'Barbarossa'.
27 Mar	Coup in Yugoslavia: Barbarossa postponed for at least three weeks.
5 Apr	Soviet–Yugoslav Friendship and Non-Aggression Pact.
22 Jun	0315hrs: Germany invades Soviet Union (without declaration of war).
22 Jun–10 Jul	Double battle at Bialystok and Minsk (300,000 prisoners taken).
2–15 Jul	Fighting on the Dnieper and Duna.
8 Jul–5 Aug	Battle for Smolensk.
1–9 Aug	Battle for Roslavl (author's first wound).
4 Oct	German offensive against Moscow begins.
5 Dec	Soviet counter-offensive begins.

At 1900hrs on 11 June 1941, the company moved out of the Warthelager for the nearest railway station and loaded up there during the night until 0300hrs. This was very difficult in the dark since there had to be a total blackout, but it went off without a hitch. The train began rolling towards dawn, steamed across Poland and pulled into Warsaw at 1900hrs. The city made a strange impression on all of us because there was no blackout. Lights were on in the tall buildings, in the tramcars etc. – something which we were no longer accustomed to after two years at war. At 0300hrs next morning we reached Siedlce, 70km from the German–Soviet border. At 0430hrs we began unloading the panzers, which took only half an hour because the ramps were extremely suitable for the purpose. At 0700hrs we set off for the border. On the dusty Polish highway it cost us half a day. For most of us, what we saw was totally new, although those who had been in the Polish campaign were already accustomed to it. The houses were all wooden with only a thatched roof. There were no brick buildings at all and the wells were quite peculiar. It was a preview of what we were to see later week after week in Russia. Even the small towns were built of wood. We especially noticed the many Jews here, identified by the yellow star.

Our readiness areas were precisely laid out, the endless great forests turned into one giant troop depot. Division after division lay here, completely camouflaged against air reconnaissance. The regiment lay in the Wohyn area: our 1 Company had its quarters in the middle of the forest. We lay there for four days, each crew putting up a tent. The weather was wonderful and we were occupied all day with technical duties, which in such an environment provoked a lot of fun. These woods were quite magnificent, all deciduous trees. The only bad thing was the many mosquitoes which bred in the nearby Rokitno swamps. After four days it began to rain so heavily that we were driven out of our tents and the personnel moved into a barracks 5km away where the company was given comfortable and above all dry quarters.

We brought up the panzers to a wood closer at hand, camouflaged them perfectly against aerial reconnaissance and carried out the duties of oil changing, weapons cleaning and, most important of all, the fitting of the new refuelling system using a petrol trailer. Each panzer had one of these two-wheeled trailers carrying two 200-litre barrels to be towed behind it, inside which was a pump for refuelling on the move. Before combat, the trailer could be released without difficulty from inside the panzer. The whole thing was found to be unsatisfactory, however, and was later discarded. It was a devil of a job to fit the system, but we succeeded.

On 16 June 1941 we loaded live ammunition, which took us all day. We had to ship aboard each panzer about 4,000 MG rounds and fill the ammunition belts with them, also around seventy HE and sixty AP shells and ten special shells. Pistol rounds, flares and hand grenades were also loaded and primed. The same day we were immunized against cholera. This was done twice before the operation. In the evenings I went from 3 Company with four men to 4 Company where Oberleutnant Krause gave us a brief introduction to the Russian language. Apart from writing the Russian alphabet we also learned some expressions useful on operations. I never understood anything else of it.

Towards evening on 18 June the commander assembled us to give notice that the operation would begin within the next few days. Then he notified our company of its first objective. We were to be the spearhead company and our orders were to move as fast as possible through thick woodlands with swampy marshes to the town of Kobryn, which was 60km the other side of the border. The strength of the Soviet forces at the border was not known for certain. Our leading panzer was 114 with Unteroffizier Pröbst as commander. We had mixed feelings now that we knew that in a few days everything which until then had been harmless fun would come to be in bitter earnest. In the evening the sentries were doubled in case the Soviets dropped paratroops.

The day of 20 June began with regimental roll-call: the entire PzRgt 35 was formed into a triangle for Oberst Eberbach to address us. He spoke grippingly and warned us about the Russians: 'You are going into a country in which the people live so primitively that you won't believe it. They don't even have proper toilets!' Possibly he spoke in this manner to calm our anxieties or to instil in us a feeling of superiority. In conclusion we remembered our fallen comrades on the battlefields in Poland and France, then returned to our quarters.

On the morning of 21 June we loaded all our personal belongings into the panzer: space was limited and it was no easy task. All panzers had a metal container behind the turret known as the 'rucksack' into which every crewman could stow a small travel bag, his overcoat and a few personal items. A second travel bag had to be given up beforehand and went with the divisional baggage train. At the rear of the panzer was a large wooden trunk for blankets, groundsheets and the like; there was also space in it for 'brochures', i.e. plunder. For that reason it was also known as the 'brochure trunk'. Almost every panzer had one. We fixed an empty ammunition box on the track cover, these were small wooden boxes with a good clasp and an interior lining of sheet metal for our rations. A wire was wound around the 'rucksack' and we hung our field flasks from it so that they were always ready to hand.

On the day before the invasion we received our special rations, for which we found space in the engine compartment and fighting compartment. They consisted of three tins of rice or vegetables, five small sacks of bread, three boxes of Shoka-

Cola and a miniature stove per man. This was in addition to our iron rations. None of it could be touched unless ordered.

Towards midday everything was ready. At 1600hrs the company assembled to hear the commander's brief address in his usual humorous style, then we were dismissed to our panzers nearby which had been towed out of the woods and lined up on the highway. Around 1700hrs the Abteilung HQ rolled past, and we followed, driving through Wohyn then onwards to Brest-Litovsk. Our destination was woods north of the town about 3km from the River Bug which formed part of the frontier at that point. On the way we drove past gigantic fuel dumps which the RAD had laid out within the vast forests: the RAD boys stood on either side of the highway watching us enviously.

At nightfall the drivers had the difficulty of driving in the dark. Now and again a short technical halt would be made. Meanwhile I slept on my gunner seat. It was a slow process, learning to sleep just anywhere. The seat was neither soft nor comfortable, and I was so tall that I could not sleep sitting upright. But in the end I did get used to it.

When I awoke at midnight I found that we had reached our readiness area. Individual panzers were shown to their appointed places, fuelled up, gun- and MG-barrels given a clean and drained of oil, all vehicles impeccably camouflaged, the tracks covered over and now it was serious. We were told to keep a watch for enemy aircraft. All jobs done, everybody stretched out and tried to sleep. If the codeword was given, the operation would begin at 0315hrs. If not, we would have to stand by.

The Operation Begins

22 June 1941: I had had a light doze. By 0300hrs on account of the tension and excitement nobody was still asleep. We got up and talked. Then, at precisely 0315hrs, the first rounds were fired. Our artillery batteries opened a crazy heavy fire from all sides on the Russian positions. Close by us was a 10.5cm battery. After a short while the morning sky had turned red, wherever one looked was on fire. The Soviets made no reply. After half an hour the firing ebbed somewhat, got stronger again and then almost ceased altogether. We could hear the rat-a-tat-tat of MG fire in the distance. Our infantry crossed the Bug and established a bridgehead. Towards 0400hrs the entire fighting force of the company was drawn up to hear

the commander reading the 'Führer's Order of the Day to the German Army of the East': 'The hour of the crucial test has now arrived for you too. Upon you lies the responsibility of saving the culture of Europe from Bolshevism.'

Our wheeled vehicles classified as 'Tross' (the rearward services) had not come up this far. A panzer company was made up of the panzer crews, the Kampfstaffel or battle component, divided up into the Gefechtstross, the combat train including the field kitchen, and Tross I and II. Tross I included the repair unit, ammunition and radio. Tross II was the wheeled Tross with the orderly room, motor pool, provisions, clothing, weapons and equipment, motorcycle dispatch riders, drivers, paramedics etc.

Our morale was excellent. Towards daybreak we received another delivery of field post, then waited for our orders to move out. Our infantry and pioneers ahead at the Bug river were not ready for us yet. During the early morning the infantry had established a bridgehead over the Bug without many losses and the pioneers were now at work erecting a makeshift bridge. They completed it around midday, and at 1300hrs my 1 Company received orders to move out.

As soon as we got into gear on the 'highway', the battle with the dust began. Without our issue of protective goggles we would have been blind. The convoys snaked their way from all sides onto our highway. We had priority everywhere, since we were the spearhead company of the panzer division. On the way there were several stops for congestion on the road. Here the first two German wounded, an Unteroffizier and a Gefreiter from SchützenRgt 12 of 4 PzDiv, spoke to us. Both had minor wounds and told us about the Russians' tactics. The infantry had found it very difficult to make progress on the other side because of the swampy terrain.

Towards 1500hrs we reached the makeshift bridge over the Bug. The river here was about 150m wide. We had to wait for over an hour because the bridge had been damaged by the weight of troops passing over it. At about 1630hrs the company finally crossed it and now we were on Russian soil. A slug of cognac, and on we went. Soon we saw the first prisoners, escorted by infantry. They had good uniforms, the mud on it providing good camouflage. On the Russian side it was very marshy and we had to take care not to bog down. We got through without a hitch: the company formed up and we set off in good order at a decent pace, first through woods already cleared by the infantry and littered with Russian equipment. They had pulled back very hastily. After about 5km a halt was called to give the Abteilung a chance to form up. The Abteilung commander, Major von Lauchert, came forward to us.

No 1 Company was now given another three Panzer IVs (with a 7.5cm gun and two MGs) and got ready for the drive to Korbyn: on the way enemy resistance was to be expected. Our spearhead panzer was commanded by Unteroffizier Pröbster, then came Leutnant König and the 1 Group vehicle with the company commander, followed by three Panzer IVs, our hard nuts to crack, II Platoon, the Light Platoon and finally III Platoon.

Behind us rolled 2, 3, and 4 Companies, then II Abteilung. Other elements such as anti-tank guns, pioneers, artillery etc. had been attached to our regiment and as a whole within the division formed the assault group 'Eberbach', named after our regimental commander Oberst Eberbach. He had already been awarded the Knight's Cross in France and at the end of 1941 was only the second officer of the Panzer Arm to receive the Oak Leaves for the outstanding successes of his assault group. Our task now was to force our way as deeply as possible into enemy territory. At dusk that first night we set off at about 2100hrs and headed into the unknown.

At first we crossed open country. Behind a hedge I saw my first dead Russians. The sight of it never gave me pleasure to the extent that I had imagined it would earlier. We assumed that the enemy would be positioned behind every clump of woodland and found it incomprehensible that he had not prepared his defence in those areas of territory ideal for it. The spearhead panzer reported all details to the commander by radio. Every panzer had at least a receiver, a large number of them a transmitter also. The convoy followed a woodland trail through the thickest area of forests: of the enemy there was no sign. Slowly night came. Our morale was sky-high.

I sat behind my weapon, but the night was black as pitch and since I could see nothing through the sight I had a sleep, as did my loader, Gefreiter Äschlimann, whose peace was always difficult to disturb. Following the changeover our new commander, Feldwebel Volz, stood in the turret and maintained contact with the driver, Gefreiter Jentscheck, via the intercom system.

In the darkness the commander had to give steering directions to the driver, for on such a dark night and with the tremendous dust being kicked up, the driver could see very little through his viewing slit. Getting out during a short rest, one would sink ankle-deep in the fine sand. We proceeded on narrow forest tracks with few halts, the leading panzer maintaining constant radio contact with the company. Towards midnight we reached the major Brest-Litovsk Rollbahn without having met any enemy.

This Rollbahn was the road to our destination. Rollbahns were shown on Russian maps, of which we had reprints, as autobahns. They bore not the slightest resemblance to a German autobahn. They were simply ordinary paved highways, a great rarity in Russia. We had now arrived amongst the great swamps known as the Pripet Marshes, and if one left the road left or right one sank into them. It was eerily silent. Construction machinery stood along the roadside; the Russians had therefore been busy developing the Rollbahn towards the western frontier. After about an hour, at 0230hrs we got underway again. The morning of 23 June was already dawning.

Now we made fast progress, except for frequent halts whenever we came to one of the endless bridges over the swamps which the Soviets had been upgrading to take the weight of their heavy tanks. We had to go around all these bridges. At the first villages, what we found particularly striking were the portals at the entrance and exit, scanty frames with latticework still adorned with fir from 1 May, at the centre a tiny picture of Stalin. In the centre of the village would be a pulpit for addressing the populace. We saw the same thing repeated in all villages and towns. The local people were entirely well disposed to us, bringing butter and eggs to the panzers. The whole village would turn out and stand to the left and right of the road, waving to us vigorously, and they hurried up from the most remote hamlets. The sun rose ever higher and by 0900hrs we could make out in the distance the silhouette of Kobryn, and within a quarter of an hour we reached its first houses.

That night the company had advanced 60km, a remarkable achievement bearing in mind the early heavy going and interruptions. To our chagrin 3 PzDiv had got to Kobryn before us, and was already continuing along the Rollbahn. This division had had two permanent bridges readily available for crossing the Bug and so unlike ourselves had not had to wait for pioneers to build a pontoon bridge before they could set off. We were therefore a little depressed that we now had to follow behind 3 PzDiv.

We parked our panzers in a large garden, camouflaged them well, of course, and attended to minor defects. There was no petrol yet, it was said to be coming up soon. Rich pickings were rumoured and the commander detached a Panzer II to loot a large warehouse. I reported myself out for a light-hearted stroll through the town. I had left my pistol in the camp and noticed suddenly that there were no other German soldiers in the vicinity but instead some very shady types. When these began to get unpleasant I retraced my steps to more inhabited areas of the town, where I came across armed soldiers breaking open a street kiosk. I left with a giant sack filled with cigarettes and soap for the company, where it was all shared out fairly. Our panzer got thirty bars of toilet soap. Other colleagues brought in similar plunder. At midday we received permission to open a box of the special rations.

Just as we started eating we got the order to refuel and roll. We drove across the market square past a giant plaster statue of Lenin flanked by two Soviet tanks. As we discovered, every town had at least one statue each of Lenin and Stalin, sometimes even the two of them seated together on a bench. We crossed the suburbs to reach the railway goods yard which hosted a huge fuel dump. Here we took what we needed: oil canisters for air filters and engines, water canisters, very important because of the heat, and many other useful items. Then we refuelled from gigantic barrels. The primitive Russian refuelling installation caused us a number of problems. After the whole company had fuelled up we found a spot nearby for sharing out the plunder: shirts, briefs, underwear, blankets, sleeping bags, cooking utensils, Party badges, trousers, boots, etc. The company had also come across a case of butter and some big Dutch cheeses: we had no bread and so ate cheese spread with butter, which tasted marvellous. We were quite happy to make do in the circumstances.

Towards evening we drove across town again to the Rollbahn. Ahead, 3 PzDiv was in action. Russian tanks had attempted to attack the town but came to grief with much bloodshed and we soon saw the pitiful remains. No 1 Company had orders to secure the area 10km beyond Kobryn. As it grew dark we were at readiness in a small wood and camouflaging up, but after half an hour, just as we finished, another order came for us to do the same thing in another position. Meanwhile night had fallen, black as pitch, and we noticed fires all around us. As we got closer we saw that these fires were from burning wrecked tanks which had been finished off by 3 PzDiv. Towards midnight the company put up at a farm: II Platoon was responsible for security, the rest of us could get some sleep.

I took some straw from the barn and slept behind my panzer, nicely warm near the engine, stretched out in my stolen sleeping bag. Reveille was at 0400hrs: ten minutes later the company moved out. Each morning was the same, everything had to be done pretty damned smartly. Washing and coffee were luxuries and had to be forgotten. What with the dust, which mixed with the oil and sweat, we looked like pigs. Our uniform was no longer black but a filthy grey.

It was not far to the Rollbahn, where an indescribable sight met our eyes: one burnt-out Russian tank after another, some with great shell holes, some destroyed

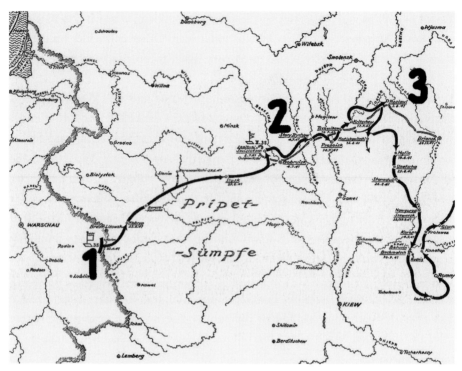

The route followed by PzRgt 35 (as part of 4 PzDiv) from 22 June 1941 at the Bug river (1) via Stary-Bychow (2) and approaching Roslawl (3). On 3 August 1941 the author received a serious injury and was returned to Germany for treatment. From Roslawl, 4 PzDiv bore south.

The citadel of Brest-Litovsk, somewhat to the east of 4 PzDiv's crossing point, was taken with heavy casualties on 29 June 1941.

A standard 4 PzDiv truck on a supply run at Kobryn. To the right is an abandoned Soviet T26-A. Note the Soviet star on the mudguard.

At Kobryn, as everywhere else in the Soviet Union, the ubiquitous statue of Stalin was to be found, here at the town centre in a park surrounded by a star-shaped flowerbed.

Kobryn, 26 June 1941.
Experts look over
abandoned Soviet tanks
and tractors. On the right-
hand side of the photo
is an 18-tonne recovery
vehicle, the bear insignia
indicating it belongs to
I Abteilung.

This unconventional T-26A
light tank had a 37mm
gun in one turret and
an MG in the other. The
white arrow on the door
of the building points
towards the command
post of 1 Company: the
letter 'C' stands for 'von
Cossel'.

PzRgt 35 motorcycle
riders were given this
blockhouse as their
quarters.

During the fighting farm buildings were continually set on fire, robbing the civilian owners of their livelihoods.

In 1941, 4 PzDiv formed part of Panzer Gruppe Guderian, all its vehicles being marked with a 'G' as here on a Kfz 15 car. In the background is a 'Krupp-Protze' artillery tractor.

(left) Groups of Soviet prisoners, some with their hands up, approach German panzers on a highway.

(below) In woods near Bereza this Panzer IV received a hit in the ready ammunition and was totally destroyed.

Ahead of the wrecked Panzer IV is a Russian T-26 Model 1933 with cylindrical turret and 45mm gun.

A column of Soviet prisoners being escorted to the rear by a motorcycle and sidecar. Behind, German panzers follow. At the left of the picture German infantry stand watching.

This 1-tonne tractor of PzRgt 35 has been hit, the rear section being burnt out.

(top) A Russian 45mm anti-tank gun, the crew of which fought to the last. Motorcycle troops and vehicles of 4 PzDiv drive past the scene.

(centre) A Russian T-37 amphibious tank abandoned on the Bereza–Kartuska Rollbahn. The MG has been removed: in the background a Panzer III of PzRgt 35.

(right) Panzer 114 commanded by Unteroffizier Pröbster in woods. A pit was dug and the panzer parked above it. Even the tracks were earthed over. This provided the crew with a safe refuge overnight.

The woodland refuge of these men of I Abteilung HQ/PzRgt 35 is a standard refuelling truck with trailer.

Panzers and lorries of PzRgt 35 advancing, the crews, except for the driver, sitting on the hull.

Faster vehicles, marked with 'G' to indicate Panzer Gruppe Guderian and trailing a cloud of dust, overtake a panzer column.

Division commander General von Langermann in the passenger seat of his Kfz 15 car with the 4 PzDiv pennant above the forward mudguard. His vehicle is escorted by motorcycle dispatch riders, half-track radio vehicles and other escort units.

A heavy artillery Abteilung advancing. The huge 13m-long barrel of a 24cm gun is being drawn by an 18-tonne tractor. Another tractor can be seen ahead. The gun, dismantled into its component parts, was distributed over six carriers. In the right of the picture civilians inspect a broken-down lorry.

A 21cm mortar of a heavy artillery Abteilung advancing along a well-made road. The mortar was dismantled into two parts for towing by 12-tonne tractors.

A typical scene during the 1941 advance. Panzer 114 with its fuel trailer. Great distances were covered in the first months of the Russian campaign. An MG at the ready against air attack, and branches for camouflage, protect the panzer and its crew.

A group of civilians during a halt in a village. Initially German troops were received as their liberators from Bolshevism.

Oberleutnant von Cossel,
commander of 1 Company,
receiving a report from
a motorcyclist. In the
background a panzer of
2 Company.

(above) A 1 Company
panzer with the white bear
insignia.

(right) A 1 Company
panzer crew stowing
equipment in the
'rucksack' behind the
turret.

Packs of captured better-quality Russian cigarettes. The ordinary Russian soldier 'rolled his own', crumbs of Machorka in newspaper.

A panzer crew stretched out on a groundsheet, enjoying a meal.

A round of skat being played on a panzer hull in an area obviously free of the enemy.

Orders for a Panzer III. A couple of the men have camouflage netting over their helmets. This was rarely seen in the summer of 1941. Barely visible on the mudguard of the Kfz 15 is the insignia of 4 PzDiv.

A variety of vehicles passing through Baranovichi below a thick pall of smoke.

(above) 1 Company attacks Baranovichi airfield.

(left) Aircraft burning everywhere. In the foreground the short 5cm gun of a Panzer III.

(below) A Russian Martin bomber on the Baranovichi airfield. Hangars and buildings can clearly be seen in the distance.

This Russian Yak-1 fighter stood on its nose during landing, damaging the propeller blades, and then fell back onto its undercarriage.

A Panzer III of 1 Company/PzRgt 35/4 PzDiv (right) meets a Panzer III of 3 PzDiv to complete an encirclement.

The wreck of a Soviet 155mm field howitzer at a roadside, the body of a Russian gunner lies under the chassis. This efficient gun was produced in large numbers by the Russians.

Two Panzer IIIs of 2 Company on sentry duty at the edge of a wood being resupplied ammunition from a Panzer I ammunition carrier seen a little behind them near the small spruce trees.

Behind the hill with the small spruce trees, Russian prisoners await onward transportation. Behind them can be seen the rear of a Panzer III. A lorry of II Abt Staff/PzRgt 35 stands ready.

by our aircraft in low-level attacks. On that morning alone we saw the tanks of at least a full armoured division. In addition there were guns of every calibre, field kitchens and other military equipment. It was really difficult to take it all in. The great marshes lay either side of the Rollbahn; one needed to be careful not to stray off the highway. We kept going flat out until about 1000hrs and then stopped for the rest of the day. These long runs were wonderful for everyone but the drivers. We had rustled up a piece of leather upholstery for the rear of the panzer and sat on it as if it were a sofa – in the crazy heat constantly holding our field flasks – and gazed through our goggles at the wreckage of the Russians. If one felt hungry, a slice of bread thickly spread with butter did the trick. Those were the finest hours for the common soldier.

From 1000hrs we got the vehicles in order, cleaned the air filters, very important in this heat for, with a breath of wind, dust would get into the carburettors and the engine would not run properly. After that our time was our own. First we had a good look at the Russian equipment: naturally their tanks interested us most of all. We ate, slept or wrote as the mood took us. A Fieseler Storch flew above the Rollbahn, keeping constant watch. Prisoners arrived in small groups, sent back from up ahead. They seemed to be Mongolian for the most part. Some wore civilian clothing, contrary to the rules of war, but were instantly recognizable as soldiers. When darkness fell, we set off again and drove through the night. I slept wonderfully on the hull at the rear of the panzer.

At first light I was awake again, the same scene right and left of the highway. Towards 1000hrs the order came for the company to secure a bridge against ground-attack aircraft. We soon reached the said bridge and took up position. It was not a very favourable spot for us since there was no cover anywhere. Camouflaging a panzer in the open was very difficult. An 8.8cm Flak battery had come up to protect the bridge against air attack and was very close to us. It was being hinted that the Russians would do anything to either capture the bridge or destroy it. There was a lot of work to be done on our vehicles, for after such a long run everything had to be checked over.

We worked on the tracks, air filters and weapons were cleaned, we fuelled up etc., all of which took up a lot of time. I was just about to have a wash for a change when the Flak suddenly opened up. We saw six bombers at very high altitude quickly turn tail under fire, but they came back a quarter of an hour later and scarcely had we recognized them than their bombs exploded in the midst of the Flak position, though without causing any great damage. The Flak was very accurate and soon a bomber was plummeting earthwards. It roared ever faster towards the ground, where it exploded. On the way a wing became detached and spun down slowly like a flaming torch. That was the first of the many aircraft that I saw shot down. After another thirty minutes another wave came. We saw the bombs drop and explode between the widely spaced panzers. Our chief radio operator, Gefreiter Hildwein, was wounded with a splinter in the knee. Until then we had watched without taking cover, this was all new to us. The commander now gave the order to dig foxholes beneath the panzers. We hacked out a large, square hole, tossed down blankets and then the panzer was driven over it for cover. If another air raid came, we would all crawl under the panzer and be safe to some extent. One would hardly believe the monkey-like rapidity with which we abandoned the panzer and got under it on such occasions. That morning there were six Russian air attacks, in which they lost three aircraft to Flak and our fighters.

Because of the immense plague of mosquitoes we made a small fire and played cards. I lost twenty Reichsmarks. But what did money matter any longer? The amounts being bet sometimes went as high as 200 Reichsmarks. Then gambling was forbidden, thank God. For the rest of the day we had quiet, and not even at night were we disturbed.

Next morning, 26 June, we went to alert status, but nothing happened. Waiting for the first real engagement with the enemy began to get on our nerves. Towards 1100hrs the order came to get the vehicles ready. In great haste everything was

loaded aboard and stowed. Barely a half hour later we moved out, down the
Rollbahn again just as on previous days. Around 1500hrs we suddenly received
orders to go to battle readiness.

The weapons were loaded and freed. We were to attack an airfield to the left of
the Rollbahn and secure it for the use of Mölders' squadron. Soon the company
bore left off the Rollbahn along a narrow woodland track. Here the dust was
appalling and despite our tight hatches it still filtered through the cracks into the
interior. This made it very demanding for the drivers, who literally drove into a
grey fog with no sight of the vehicle in front. Through my gunsight I could also
make out nothing. It was amusing to ask ourselves what would happen now if
the enemy attacked: nevertheless, calm and composed, we headed ever onwards
into the unknown for 20km. On the way we came past our artillery which had
the airfield under fire. All safety catches were now off: at any moment we might
encounter the enemy. Suddenly the wood cleared and the great airfield lay before
us. Everywhere were Soviet aircraft either burning, or already smouldering wrecks.
The Mölders fighter squadron, coming in at low level, had done its work well.
There was no sign of the enemy. The company formed a battle line and brought
the edges of the woods under fire on the assumption that the Russians might be
hiding there. Then it grew dark and we withdrew from the airfield, cleaned the
weapons, ate and slept.

27 June 1941: reveille was at 0230hrs. Nevertheless we awoke refreshed. At
0245hrs the commander told us of the day's attack. The company was to make a
feint across the airfield and then operate against the nearby town of Baranovichi.
The other companies and II Abteilung would make a wide sweep to break down
any resistance. As soon as we moved off at 0300hrs, alert status was ordered. We
spread out at high speed in all directions to clear the airfield, ran into some marshy
undergrowth and had to make a detour. This led us past a large fuel depot which,
as we found out later, was heavily mined. Some of our vehicles came very close
to running into the minefield. The Russian artillery fire was so accurate that we
suspected they must have a spotter nearby: their shells fell fairly close and every
time one exploded we would involuntarily duck our heads even inside the panzer.
We guessed that the observer was in a water tower, fired on it and tested our
weapons at the same time. A success: the enemy artillery ceased fire. We set off
again towards the town which was close by. In a meadow we passed eight brand-
new AA guns, probably never used against us, a welcome capture. We were ordered
to bombard the town, but then the order was cancelled because 2 Company had

already entered it. When we reached the town limits we went straight in, the streets were empty. Our panzer got stuck in a hole, and only the skill of our driver managed to get us free: meanwhile the company had gone on ahead. We drove through the town frantically in search of the company, but in vain: the enemy was expected to appear everywhere, a very unpleasant situation. After some time we re-established contact by radio: the company had driven through the town and kept going until they had halted at a patch of woodland from which they received fire. The company had replied with the MGs and silenced the enemy. The MGs of our panzer were not totally trouble-free, being new and not yet zeroed in. At the first opportunity we would have to rectify this.

By radio came the report that the advancing 18 PzDiv was already in our vicinity. This meant that the encirclement of Bialystok was complete. The company turned about and returned to the town, where relatively little damage had been inflicted. We stopped in the town centre: each panzer had to have one man to keep guard on it while the rest of crews could go 'organizing'. Soon we found a warehouse with hundreds of crates. All were forced open with the bayonet and anything useful taken away: wine, mineral water (especially important in the heat), chocolate, chocolate-creams, sweets. Soon every panzer had a few crates, and beaming faces everywhere. The crews bartered between themselves and so each man got what he wanted. I found some bottles of a very good liqueur. Meanwhile 18 PzDiv rolled past us in the city without the chance to stop. My, were their faces long. It seemed laughable how they drove through town in full fighting order, protected on all sides, while we had been here quite some time and moved about completely freely. Further searches had revealed a clothing store from where anybody could have shirts, socks, briefs and ladies' clothing for making scarves. There was no more washing clothes, anything dirty was thrown away and replaced by something new. To cap it all my tank commander, Feldwebel Volz, had discovered four giant barrels of beer, and our panzer kept one. Now we drank the whole time even when on the road. Soon we had no idea where to stow all our loot. This was not at all in accordance with good order and military discipline and after three hours in the broiling heat we turned about, drove back across the town, where the populace was now daring to venture out on the streets, and an hour later we reached the airfield, sighting our first fighters circling overhead. Mölders wanted to land here. Dead Russians lay everywhere, but as strange as it may sound nowadays, we only slowly grew accustomed to the sight. We kept driving for about half an hour until a halt was called in the shelter of some woodland.

The mosquitoes plagued us so infernally that we made small fires everywhere, but these were not much use. We worked on our panzers through the midday hours, my MGs were calibrated by the armourer or at least he had a try. Finally came a delivery of field post, though I got nothing. In the evening we slept together near the panzer. Tomorrow was my birthday. Often I thought of my family. How were they really getting along? In our filthy uniforms we were a seedy-looking crowd, not a clean spot anywhere, our skin grey with dust, the pores black. If one rubbed a hand over the skin it left little black rolls and the fingerprints stood out. Everything was sticky, filthy and stank. Nothing could be done about it. If only we had some water for washing. Or a bath. Such thoughts were best left aside.

At 0100hrs we were awoken suddenly and informed we were moving out. This was not easy in the darkness. I remembered in passing that this was my 19th birthday. We got rolling again, everybody half asleep. After two hours a halt, day was breaking. Now we could get back to sleep. In the morning I wore my new Russian underwear for the first time, the dirty ones were simply thrown away. That was what we always did. Finally we could wash a bit: each man got a quarter-bucketful of water. Before washing it was brown and after . . . My loader, Walter Äschlimann, went off on a hunt for poultry and came back after some time with a chicken he had shot. We cooked it in our washbucket. I was just getting the fire going and the chicken was almost ready when suddenly I heard a shot and Äschlimann tipped over from the panzer. While cleaning his pistol he had shot himself through the stomach, a clean through-and-through although it looked fatal. A motorcycle rider brought the Abteilung doctor and an ambulance ten minutes later. After emergency dressings were applied he was taken off to the main dressing station for an operation which saved his life. Our mood was now very low, my birthday joy forgotten and nobody wanted to eat the chicken. I was assigned another loader and around midday we got under way again.

The dust made us suffer terribly again, our throats were dry, our eyes smarted. Even the protective goggles were not totally effective for dust found its way through every tiny crack. Around 0400hrs we got back to the Rollbahn of our previous advance and now we headed east. Some panzers had gone into the workshop for repair, a number having damage caused by the Russian petrol and oil. Thus the company's numbers were reduced.

At the sides of the Rollbahn always the same picture of endless material wreckage – was everything being destroyed? Our tankers overtook us on the way and we were refuelled during a rest stop. Then darkness fell and with it came another difficult period for the drivers. I stood up in the turret and gave our driver his instructions through the throat microphone while the rest of the crew slept. The journey was very tiring: in the dark one had to keep the sharpest possible lookout. So on it went until 0500hrs next day.

Upon arriving at the town of Sluzk we rolled in straight away. On the outskirts the Russians had built a sports stadium in the Bolshevist-Roman style. The figures had a blue face, otherwise everything else was white plaster. The columns were painted blue from top to bottom: also not forgotten were the statues of Lenin and Stalin, never absent. We stayed for half an hour in the town while a shop was ransacked but to our disappointment it had already been thoroughly plundered. Then we moved on with a dreadful rattle over the miserable paved streets. In the town centre was a large square surrounded by Party buildings. Dead centre stood a very large pulpit painted with a relief of the October Revolution on the front face, left and right of it stood statues of proletarians and over everything at the rear towered a larger-than-life statue of Stalin. Loudspeakers were fitted at every corner. The public assemblies were held here. We also saw, as later in other places, banners stretched across the street which probably said, 'Workers of the World Unite' or something similar. The town centre was almost undamaged, but other neighbourhoods were totally gutted, probably torched by the Russians themselves. From the giant fields of rubble to our right and left only chimneys and great iron stoves poked through.

We sped along the Rollbahn (we could make 40kmph on the road) until 0600hrs and stopped at a small village to work industriously on the panzers, the most important thing as ever being to clean the air filters of dust. This took two hours and then the 'Spiess' brought out a large number of big boxes containing several thousand looted eggs. Anyone could help himself. I boiled a hundred for my crew and packed them in an empty ammunition box together with fifty raw eggs. For myself I used twenty eggs to make an omelette which I ate alone. I had no fat and so it was quite hard. The consequence was frightful stomach ache and I vomited the whole thing up. At midday we set off once more. I lay on the rear of the panzer hull, miserable and suffering and had to use the floor hatch several times. It took three or four hours to reach the airfield where Mölders' squadron was to be found. Then we settled down quietly. This was a major disappointment, for 3 PzDiv was ahead of us on the Rollbahn and we wanted to be the leader, wanted to show what we could do. Soon, however, we would have the chance, for at midday the commander's panzer, the 'Hundred-er' (i.e. panzer number 100) broke down with engine damage and had to go into the repair shop. Oberleutnant von Cossel now took over our panzer, bringing with him his loader, Schütze Hofweber, who was up to the mark. Feldwebel Volz, previously our commander, now became our driver. Hartmann remained the senior radio operator. Thus I held the position of gunner in the panzer of the company commander, which I considered a distinction. Yes, I was proud to have this prominent place. Towards evening Russian aircraft approached the airfield, our fighters went up to intercept them and eventually shot down seven. The fighters circled continuously above our panzer. We felt a mood of great enthusiasm. In the night the mosquitoes pestered us dreadfully.

On the morning of 30 June, the usual camp regimen. Not until the afternoon did we finally get on the Rollbahn, hoping for a decent encounter, but irritatingly often we found the highway totally blocked. Sometimes three convoys would all be heading in the same direction alongside each other. Overtaking was impossible. We found out that II Abteilung had been given another mission in which they had to bear away left from the Rollbahn and attempt to overtake 3 PzDiv on their left flank. All so that we could finally see some action. It was very depressing to be always following 3 PzDiv. In the evening we stopped in a small village and had to stand guard along a section of Rollbahn. In the twilight we changed the oil over a ditch then camouflaged the panzer in a garden.

At 2345hrs the sentries awoke the whole company, and we assembled in order to congratulate our commander on his 24th birthday at midnight. Bottles of champagne and cognac were produced and did the rounds. The commander made a brief speech of thanks while some of the advanced sentries fired a salute. By 0100hrs we were all asleep again: we had to be rolling by 0500hrs and in the morning it was always cool. We were to follow II Abteilung. In the course of 1 July we approached the Beresina. The Beresina in White Russia was a very special river for me. I remembered the fate of Napoleon and the expanses of Russia which now lay before us. Would we go down the same path? Was it also do or die for us too? When, how and where would I re-cross this river westwards? Napoleon had reached Moscow in an incredible triumphal procession before the great catastrophe overtook the Grande Armée. These and similar thoughts preoccupied me very much in those days, and we had not yet received our baptism of fire.

At the Beresina our force had apparently run up against stiff resistance. Battalion Hofmann was supposed to establish a bridgehead there but had come up against a Russian armoured train. No 6 Company came to their aid. Now we drove left off the Rollbahn and crossed a bridge which the Russians had wanted to set afire during the night. Some of the tracks had become boggy from heavy downpours. The sky did not look all that promising today either. The panzers had to tow the motorcycle riders and lorries through the worst muddy parts. We kept going all day, passed the town of Svisloch at midday and reached the Beresina half an hour later. A kilometre from the river we saw a Russian tank platoon, totally wrecked. The two bridges over the Beresina were still intact. The Russians kept trying to establish a bridgehead on our side of the river but had been ripped to shreds by the quadruple Flak placed here. The panzers would be crossing the river by the great railway bridge with planks laid between the rails. Our I Abteilung made a halt in a small patch of woodland with a 15cm howitzer battery beside it. The battery began firing towards evening. We set up a huge tent made from our tarpaulins behind our panzer and made ourselves as comfortable as possible.

In the night it rained torrentially and the water entered the tent from all sides because the trench around it had not been dug properly. We sat with our bottoms in water. One after another we awoke and got hastily into the panzer, which was far too narrow to accommodate five persons sleeping. We were very cold and our bones ached from sleeping upright. Nothing is worse than being soaked through, dog-tired, frozen and having to sleep awkwardly. Sleep comes for a short while, then one starts into wakefulness.

Towards morning the weather changed. We dried ourselves and our things in the warm sunshine. Then to mark the commander's birthday retrospectively we had a picnic in a fine spot nearby. The whole crew lay on blankets around a primitive table. We served ourselves butter, bread, eggs and pork chops, and fabulous French red wine, a personal gift from the commander. Our mechanics had brought a pig on their motorcycle together with frying pans from a nearby town. The meat was cut into equal portions and soon everybody was frying for we had more fat than we needed. Small petrol fires flamed everywhere – at the time we had plenty of fuel. We lazed all day waiting for the order to pull out. In the evening the opportunity came to tune in for the news – reports of enormous successes being made by our troops! We were really proud to be part of it. If only I could have news from home. The best time of all was when the field post was distributed. When night fell we were still seated on our panzer and Hans Graupel played some tunes on his accordion which left us all dreaming of home. We hoped that the next few days would bring us our first engagement.

The Operation at Stary-Bychow

We set off very early on the morning of 3 July 1941. The going was extremely poor as a result of the continual rain and we made hardly any progress. Our drivers had to call on all their know-how: we had to tow wheeled vehicles through the morass since they could not proceed otherwise. Finally we got to some good roads and headed for Bobruisk, the crossing-point over the Beresina. Unfortunately we still had not succeeded in overtaking 3 PzDiv by our detour. There was a real race on between 3 and 4 PzDiv towards Moscow. We still followed on their tail. On the road there were huge numbers of dead Russians and horses: a foul stench surrounded them. After driving through the town at midday we crossed the Beresina by means of a bridge built by the pioneers. At this point 3 PzDiv branched off to the south, leaving the Rollbahn free for us. During a short halt the Abteilung commander, Major von Lauchert, came forward to order 1 Company to lead the regiment to the Dnieper by way of Mogilev. Oberleutnant von Cossel took command with our panzer and we headed into the unknown at a fast pace. No Russian troops were to be seen, apparently preferring to withdraw without offering resistance. When we arrived as the first German troops in a Russian village, we would mostly be greeted with gifts of bread and salt, and women and children would stand at the roadside waving to us. Were we liberators? We believed we had to free their people from Bolshevism.

Around 1800hrs we reached the Druth, a tributary of the Dnieper. The wooden bridge of the Rollbahn had been destroyed, having been set on fire a short while previously as we saw by the still-smouldering wooden beams. We exchanged fire with Russian infantry on the other bank and then it all fell quiet. Our Light Platoon with Panzer IIs had been sent out to scout for a place nearby to ford the river, and now our regimental commander, Oberst Eberbach, came forward to us to see for himself why we had stopped. Suddenly an officer from Divisional HQ arrived on his motorcycle to give Eberbach new orders from Division. We were no longer interested in Mogilev, the new objective was the bridge over the Dnieper at the town of Stary-Bychow. Quick glance at the map, distance about 50km. 'Cossel, that is your objective!'

A place to ford the river was found about 700m upstream, but it presented difficulties. We began the amphibious crossing before dusk. Some panzers sank down halfway across, the water was so deep that it came in through the driver's hatch. The bank on the far side was very marshy and many panzers sank in over the running wheels. It required substantial effort to pull them free. Thick woodland stretched almost to the river bank so that we had only a small strip for movement. Finally, long after it had grown pitch dark, our first three panzers reached the Rollbahn on the far side while the main body of the company was still struggling in the swamp and morass.

We waited for morning on the Rollbahn, from where we were to begin our advance. I was up all night on watch together with the gunners of the other two panzers, we lay with machine-pistols in cover in front of our vehicles. That we were almost head-to-head with the Russians we noticed at first light, and we took them prisoner. They were glad that for them the war was over.

4 July 1941: Reveille for the company was at 0230hrs. At this time the other elements of the company had reached us plus a platoon from 4 Company sent as reinforcements. It had been a busy night for them too, helping bring all the panzers across the ford and swamp. The commander called us together and told us our assignment: 'Stary-Bychow and the Dnieper bridge. We leave in 15 minutes.' No time for washing or breakfast, and no coffee either because the field kitchen had not been able to follow us over. Our engines were warmed up, the spearhead vehicle moved off, the advance was rolling. Spearhead vehicle was the leader of I Platoon, Leutnant König, followed by Feldwebel Schneider's panzer, then the commander, in whose panzer I was gunner. Behind us came II and II Platoons, the heavy panzers of 4 Company's platoon and at the rear our Light Platoon.

It was very cool on that glorious summer's morning, but in the panzer itself it was stifling and muggy. While the two leading panzers kept going with hatches closed, the loader and I sat with the hatches open, the commander standing in the open turret. We kept a close watch on the Rollbahn and the woods to left and right. It seemed likely that the enemy would have hidden himself in them and that he was bound to make an attempt sooner or later to halt our advance. Then the woodlands on both sides were replaced by fields of tall corn. The spearhead panzers made a brief stop to observe and suddenly enemy fire was raining down on our panzers. Never in training had I got inside and closed the hatch so fast. Our spearhead was shooting at two anti-tank guns blocking the road. These guns were quickly silenced though the Russian infantry kept firing, but they had nothing which could penetrate our armour. We pressed on, leaving the rearguard to mop up the resistance. For us the race to the Dnieper bridge was the important thing. We had to reach it with all speed and surprise the Russians before they could demolish the bridges vital for our advance.

We came to a fork in the road where according to the map we had to bear right off the Rollbahn to follow tracks and paths across fields to get to Stary-Bychow. After 2km we reached a small stream with marshy banks which we crossed quickly by means of a wooden bridge. In our keenness to keep rolling, at first we failed to notice that the bridge had given way with the sixth panzer on it. This separated the company into two parts. Five panzers had crossed the water, the rest had stopped at the wreckage of the bridge. A simple detour around the spot was not possible here, and a place to ford had to be looked for. This would take time while our only chance of success lay in taking the enemy by surprise. Oberleutnant von Cossel therefore decided to press on with the five panzers in an attempt to reach the objective. We stepped up the pace, for a long stretch of track remained to be covered ahead of us. In the panzer with the hatches shut it now got so hot that the loader and I fell asleep on our seats due to fatigue: the previous night I had not slept a wink. The commander let us sleep and did not wake us until he saw the town of Stary-Bychow on the horizon. We assumed that the town with the bridge over the Dnieper would be defended, but were mistaken. The Russians had not expected that we would turn up here today: the German main thrust hitherto had been towards Mogilev, much further to the north.

Our five panzers, actually a laughably small strike force, pushed on fast towards the town. The terrain was open and easy to observe. Suddenly we came to an anti-tank ditch which formed part of a complete ring around the town, though at some places it had not been finished, and here we could cross over. We continued in single file without making contact with the enemy. The peace made us feel ever more uneasy, for sooner or later Ivan was bound to notice us coming and react! In such uncertain situations the effect on the nerves is always especially great until the moment when the enemy chooses to reveal his presence by opening fire. Then one finally knows that one has to fight, and against whom, and the nervousness dissipates. I kept watch through my sight whose telescopic effect was very powerful. The first houses were now to be seen clearly and there was movement. Vehicles, lorries and horse-drawn carts. After another 100m we came to another anti-tank ditch laid out parallel to the first one. And now the Russians responded. They let us get within range and then opened up with heavy anti-tank guns from prepared positions. By the muzzle flashes there were various sites, the shooting poor from all of them. We replied with round after round of HE. This second ditch was also incomplete and had gaps. We got through and now, ignoring their fire, headed flat out for the first houses and into the town.

People ran, took cover, fled. We forced our way through and got to the town centre, a marketplace crammed with horse-drawn carts, military vehicles, lorries and crowds of people all intent on getting to the bridge over the Dnieper at all costs.

It was a complete madhouse. Preparations had been under way to evacuate the town but we arrived unexpectedly early. Our two spearhead panzers looked for the access road to the bridge, a lorry, loaded up with barrels of spirit, got between them and our panzer. I fired a round into the cargo and at once the vehicle burst into flames. We swerved wildly through several streets, sweeping them clear by our presence alone, until the spearhead pair found the road which sloped down to the bridge. We stepped on the gas for the last 100m and saw it before us – intact! Here too the area was teeming with fleeing Russians, soldiers and civilians. By radio the commander informed Abteilung that our five panzers were in the process of crossing the bridge and would establish a bridgehead on the far side. That was the last message from us which Abteilung could make out. Whatever got in our way now was simply run down. Right and left of us the Russians jumped over the railings into the river – chaos reigned.

After reaching the other bank we made a short halt in order to survey the terrain. From the end of the bridge the road ran towards a high embankment, either side of the road was bushy but looked very marshy. About 2km away was a second bridge over either stagnant water or a tributary of the Dnieper. It was not shown on our maps. The commander radioed the last panzer to remain on the bridge and stand guard.

He wanted to press on to the second bridge with the four panzers in order to prevent it being blown up too. We had no time to bother ourselves with what lay behind us and what was happening. We hoped that Major von Lauchert with I Abteilung would be following on our heels and watching our backs, but it turned out quite differently. I Abteilung was still far behind us and in the afternoon was held up in the streets of Stary-Bychow and forced to fight hard. It was hours before they got to the Dnieper. We knew none of this, nor did we know that at the Dnieper the Russians had set up a defensive position, the 'Stalin Line', with which they were hoping to finally stem the German advance. Artillery and anti-tank gun emplacements were at all favourable points for crossing the river, and especially at the bridges, where they had installed deep-layered field fortifications. Infantry trenches and observation posts up to the river banks overlooked the territory near the river like a spider's web. The Russians had

On the outskirts of Bobruisk, German 15cm howitzers in open order fire on identified enemy targets.

The ruins of Bobruisk. The western part of Russia suffered greatly from the effects of the fighting.

A snapshot of Major Meinrad von Lauchert, commander, I Abt/PzRgt 35/4 PzDiv. He was awarded the Knight's Cross on 8 September 1941.

Soldiers still confident, always advancing.

A Panzer III of 1 Company at a pause for observation. Behind it a barn burns.

The railway bridge over the river Beresina at Svisloch where the PzRgt 35 spearhead had to turn back on 1 July 1941. Despite the wooden supports to hand the bridge remained unfit for panzers. On the other bank is a Panzer III of 5 Company without tracks. Not until conversion work on the bridge was completed later was the main body of PzRgt 35 able to cross. A 3.7cm Flak on an 8-tonne tractor provides anti-aircraft defence.

Stukas dive-bombed the permanent way close to the railway bridge and put a Russian armoured train out of action.

The Commander-in-Chief, Panzer Gruppe 2, Generaloberst Guderian, being shown the situation by Oberst Eberbach and a staff officer. Eberbach commanded PzBrig V, which fought alongside PzRgts 35 and 36 of 4 PzDiv.

Oberst Eberbach at high speed in a Kfz 15 auto. He was awarded the Knight's Cross in 1940, and on 31 December 1941 received the Oak Leaves.

Oberst Eberbach and another officer remain at the table after the conference and midday meal.

A staff conference at the highest level during the rapid advance of 1941. In the photo: (1) Generaloberst Guderian, (2) General von Langermann, (3) Oberst Eberbach, (4) Major von Lauchert, and other officers.

Passing through light woodland near Bobruisk after rain – a foretaste of the later period of mud. In the foreground a Panzer III with 3.7cm gun, in the background on the right a lighter Panzer II.

The crew of Panzer 114 after finishing work. Greasy handprints can be seen on the trackguard.

Panzers had countless lubricating points which had to be serviced with a grease gun. The equipment had a foot pedal for forcing the grease through the tubing.

The spearhead of PzRgt 35 crossed the Beresina over a pontoon bridge at Bobruisk. In the background the wrecked railway bridge.

Panzer IIs roll down to the pontoon bridge erected by pioneer units. On the left horizon the partly demolished railway bridge can be seen clearly.

The pontoon bridge built by pioneer units consisted of multiple sections and had to be assembled according to the width of the river. These bridges were masterpieces of the pioneer bridge-builders' art and during an advance or retreat were often the only means of crossing bodies of water.

Panzer IIs and the II Abteilung command panzer rolling down to the pontoon bridge at Bobruisk.

After leaving Bobruisk a 2 Company panzer stops by a crashed Me 109F. Such wrecks by the wayside were popular sights.

A shot-down Russian Sukhoi Su-2 fighter-bomber, a Type soon to be replaced by the feared Ilyushin Il-2 'Sturmovik'.

The crew of Panzer 53 look down with misgiving as this panzer loaded with a motorcycle but lacking the MG and gun covers heads across the Drut.

The waters of the Drut close dangerously high over the bow of this Panzer III but seconds later it has firm ground beneath its tracks.

A 2 Company panzer stuck fast on the river bank and having to be towed free.

This half-track ambulance is being borne across the Drut on a ferry of rubber dinghies, the danger of the vehicle bogging down being too great.

A Kfz 15 auto of 1 Company being loaded on the rubber-dinghy ferry. Russian prisoners who helped out in the building of the boarding stage look on with interest.

In comparison to a half-track, a Kfz was much lighter to transport. In the background the wrecked wooden bridge over the Drut.

(above) Panzers of 4 PzDiv roll into Stary-Bychow.

(left) The Russian Orthodox church at Stary-Bychow, on the right an abandoned Russian civilian car.

(below) This abandoned Russian lorry in front of the church at Stary-Bychow served as a roadsign for 4 PzDiv units. Vehicles of 17 InfDiv are seen rolling past it later.

Motorcycle units of
4 PzDiv during a halt in
Stary-Bychow.

A photo from the magazine *Die Wehrmacht* which published a special report about the fighting for the bridge at Stary-Bychow. Naturally no mention was made of the panzer losses. To the right of the central plume of smoke was where the panzers of von Cossel's advanced detachment were destroyed.

Three of the wrecked panzers of von Cossel's advanced detachment blocking the embankment road. This photo was taken after the recapture of the embankment by German troops.

A post-war sketch showing the bridge before it was blown up by the Russians. Legend, arrow left, 'Town of Stary-Bychow on the left bank', arrow right, Damm = embankment.

These original sketches with captions by the author were prepared immediately after his rescue.

(**below**) Seen from the Russian side. Captions, reading down:

X = Destroyed section of bridge.

'Dnieper, starke Strömung' = Dnieper, strong current.

'Hier fanden wir Schutz...' = Here we found cover from artillery fire.

'Pfeiler der gesprengten Brücke' = Pillars of the wrecked bridge.

'Hier fanden wir das Boot...' = Here we found the boat. From here I came under Russian fire.

(**opposite, top**) Key: 1. My wrecked panzer (bottom of roadway); 2. Three panzers immobilized close together; 3. Hole in which we hid; X. Here I met the commander; Dotted line back to 3. my route after abandoning the panzer.

(**opposite, centre**)

'Gang in den Bunker . . .' = Passageway into the bunker entrance through which we crawled.

'Hier ungefähr . . . ' = Here approximately was our command post.

'Unser Fluchtweg' = Our line of escape.

'Böschung, Brücke' = Slope, bridge.

'Fluss' = River.

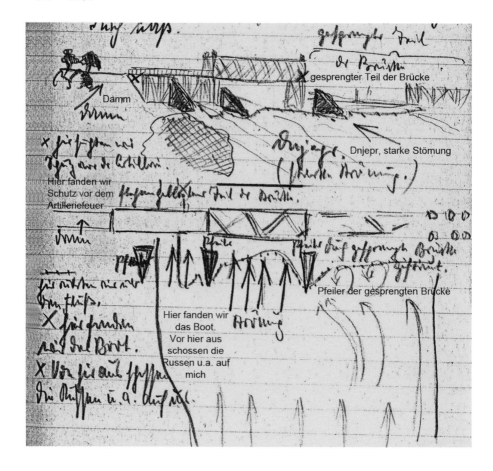

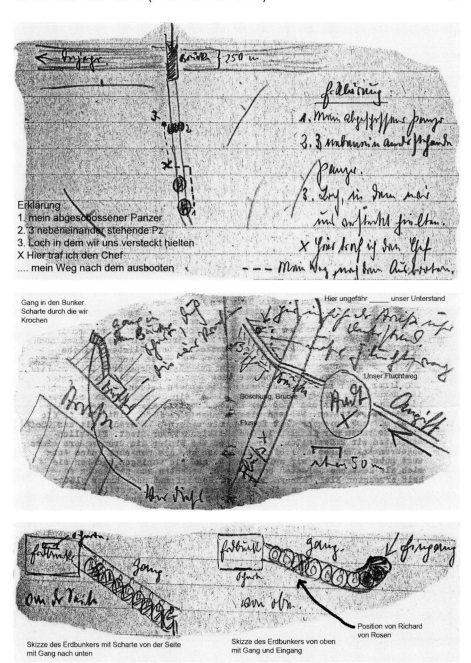

Erklärung :
1. mein abgeschossener Panzer
2. 3 nebeneinander stehende Pz
3. Loch in dem wir uns versteckt hielten
X Hier traf ich den Chef
.... mein Weg nach dem ausbooten

Gang in den Bunker.
Scharte durch die wir
Krochen

Hier ungefähr _____ unser Unterstand

Unser Fluchtweg

Böschung, Brücke

Fluss

Position von Richard
von Rosen

Skizze des Erdbunkers mit Scharte von der Seite
mit Gang nach unten

Skizze des Erdbunkers von oben
mit Gang und Eingang

(above, left) Sketch of earth bunker with firing slit at side and corridor down.
(above, right) Sketch of earth bunker from above, showing corridor and entrance.
'My position'.

German infantry resting on the banks of the Dnieper by the damaged bridge now passable only by a narrow catwalk. There was still no other means of crossing.

A good view of the fully preserved eastern part of the bridge. Pioneers are already at work building a temporary replacement.

At last the later vehicle convoys can proceed to the far side of the Dnieper over the pioneer bridge erected left of the wrecked bridge.

A long convoy of wheeled vehicles makes its way to the pioneer bridge, enabling the advance to proceed.

According to the sign, this pioneer bridge built between 16 and 18 July 1941 had a weight capacity of 16 tonnes, and was therefore unsuitable for the regiment's heavy Panzer IIIs and IVs.

In this photo the ice deflectors can be seen around the bridge pillars. The anti-tank PzJg Atb/17 InfDiv is seen crossing here.

Two photos of Major von Lauchert's command Panzer III. Lauchert was commander of I Atb/PzRgt 35/4 PzDiv and was known as the 'Bear Leader' because of the bear symbol used by his Abteilung.

A 4 PzDiv convoy in Stary-Bychow, July 1941.

Oberleutnant von Cossel (in the long greatcoat) informing his men of the events on the bridge embankment and the escape. Leutnant Burkhard is second on the left.

Oberleutnant von Cossel informing officers of the panzer regiment of the failure of the operation to capture the bridge at Stary-Bychow in a surprise attack.

The graves of panzer crewmen who fell on the bridge embankment.

A funeral service in a woodland glade for members of 4 PzDiv.

Grave of Leutnant Richard König.

Grave of Panzerschütze Sigismund Breu.

The Abteilung surgeon
by his Kfz 15 doing
paperwork.

Other graves on a hill, in the background comrades waiting to move out.

Tributes on fresh graves.

A 1 Company panzer
crew enjoy a rest break
on their Panzer III.

brought up everything available to defend the river. As we discovered later, the
Russians had installed sixty-five anti-tank guns to defend the road at the Stary-
Bychow bridge alone.

Therefore after crossing the bridge we stopped briefly while the commander
radioed his orders to the other panzers, and then all hell was let loose. Anti-tank
guns to the left of us, anti-tank guns to the right of us, and we were on a raised
road served up on a platter. 'Artillery emplacement two o'clock,' the commander
shouted to me. I swivelled the turret to the bearing and fired shell after shell.
The Russian positions had been camouflaged outstandingly well. I could only
judge by the muzzle flashes from where they were shooting, and I was at a loss
as to where I should concentrate my own fire because they were all around us.
Suddenly there came a deafening metallic explosion – direct hit on the front
of the panzer. 'Artillery left!' shouted Feldwebel Volz, our driver. I whirled my

traversing wheel like crazy to bring the turret to the new position. I could hardly see anything through my gunsight and so opened my side hatch to better judge my trajectories by eye although this decreased our protection. The air shimmered with heat, making everything in the optic hazy. We received two more hits on the front, but they bounced off, the armour held. I was firing round after round quite automatically, as the casing was ejected the loader put the next into the breech. There was no time for reflection and the real danger was that when it got serious we would be hardly conscious of it, so fixated were we on the enemy.

I saw Leutnant König's spearhead panzer turn around and pass us on the way back to the bridge. The second panzer, Feldwebel Schneider's, did the same. Had they both lost their senses? Now our panzer was the leader. That neither got far, but came to a stop a short distance behind us, was something of which I was not aware. From my seat I could only see forward through the optic or to my left through the open hatch while the commander could see 360° through his viewing slit. There was no way back for our panzer because the other two blocked the road and we could not pass either side since we were on a raised embankment. I have no idea how long we held out there stationary, shooting and receiving hits. Five minutes, ten? Looking back, it seemed an eternity. Suddenly the rear of our panzer was burning fiercely. What the cause might be could not be determined in the situation: was there a fire in the engine compartment or had some petrol canisters been hit? Whatever the reason, not only the stern was ablaze but the surrounding area too. 'Everybody out!' the commander shouted and almost in the same second I tumbled out through my hatch, fell into the flames and then rolled down the high embankment, finishing up below in the undergrowth. Stumbling and crawling, I attempted to head for the bridge, but there was practically no cover and so I became a target for the dug-in infantry everywhere. Bullets whistled around my ears and I saw the little fountains of earth around me as they burrowed into the ground. Of the commander and other crew members there was nothing to be seen. I was alone.

Automatically I scrambled back up the embankment, was across the road with a single leap and rolled down the embankment the other side. Here I lay low at first in order to catch my breath and dared scarcely raise my head so as not to offer them a target again. Then I saw the commander and Feldwebel Göhrle both crawling on all fours towards me. The commander had a wound through the arm and was clearly in pain. I lay beside him in the mud, and the men of other panzer crews, who had all abandoned their vehicles as we had had to do, crept up to us, the somewhat taller grass still not offering much cover. I drew my pistol, which I had loose in my trouser pocket, and from nervousness or the desire for self-preservation fired blindly towards the Russian positions. The commander said only, 'Stop that and save your ammunition!' An anti-tank shell exploded between the two of us: the Russians had spotted our small group from their positions. We had to get away from here, difficult with Russians all around. Now they came out of cover and we saw for the first time where their positions were. For them the fighting was over and they began hunting us down. Almost unarmed, all we were for them was prey. We set off at a crawl for the bridge, using every small hump in the ground for cover. Unteroffizier Plötscher, crawling ahead, suddenly found a hole which led inside the bottom of the embankment and was big enough for a man to crawl in. Plötscher had now disappeared and we others followed one behind the other to this hole, crept inside and were suddenly invisible to the Russians. Only Feldwebel Göhrle kept going to the bridge. I do not know what became of him, whether he was killed or taken prisoner.

The hole was the entrance to a small tunnel which after a metre underground rose steeply upwards into an earth bunker. Of this we were not aware at the time. In the tunnel it was pitch black. At first we just sat cowering in a line, not daring to go on since we feared that Russians would be in the bunker. It seemed that this was therefore the end of the road for us. Our own troops were far away; we were in the middle of the Russian positions. None of us thought we had a hope, although it was not expressed in words. We were all dumb, helpless, apathetic. Only one thing was clear to me: I was not going to be a prisoner of the Russians! Now I took stock of those who had succeeded in fleeing here: besides Oberleutnant von Cossel, Unteroffizier Plötscher and Unteroffizier Vetter, the two Obergefreiters Turbanisch and Ostwald and the Panzerschützen Markgraf and Hofmann. All those named sat in the dark tunnel behind me: in front of me were Panzerschützen Renner and Büchner.

Now a Russian civilian appeared and collapsed in front of the last two named at the entrance to our gallery. He was wounded, bleeding and moaning pitifully. With this racket he was bound to make the Russians aware of us. We shouted to Renner and Büchner, 'Shut his mouth or kill him!' or something like that. This was not so easy to do and from my position as third from the rear in the row, I could do nothing. It was in any case too late. What we could not see was that the Russians, after leaving their trenches, had begun systematically combing the terrain in order to find the panzer crews. They advanced in a chain, as if beating for game. Some of them were at our panzers, others heading directly for the hole. And next came harsh shouts: '*Rucki viyersh!*' (Hands up!). The wounded civilian crawled out of the hole on all fours and now I saw the Russian boots. '*Davay' Davay!*' (Quickly, Quickly!)

I could not see the hand movement which went with it, but Büchner and Renner crawled out of the entrance and went towards the Russians with hands raised and were received with a wild uproar. The man behind me laid his hands on my shoulders as if to restrain me. Those were seconds I shall never forget as long as I live. Incredibly, the Russians did not bother to see if any other Germans were in the tunnel and neither, as was their custom, did they toss a hand grenade into the entrance. If they had done so I would have thrown it back and if a Russian then crept into the entrance I would have shot him dead with my pistol which I held ready. I still believe it today, our situation was so desperate I would have done for the lives of us all. And so what saved us?

In those dramatic seconds, a German fighter aircraft swept over the Russian position and began raking the ground with MG fire. The Russians took cover and had to endure several attacks. Their interest in us was diverted by having to think about their own safety. We sat in the tunnel, each preoccupied with his thoughts, one apathetic; the others anxious and nervous. I had to keep my nerve, not to fail, these were my only thoughts, if at first totally wild and confused, to pull myself together and not let the others affect me.

Unteroffizier Vetter took over security at the entrance to the gallery and I crept forward to von Cossel, who whispered to me how he had survived getting out of our panzer. At the moment I got out, and our loader Hofweber was about to use his hatch to escape, the panzer was broadside on, mortally wounding Hofweber. It had been a terrible thing to hear his cries, but he was beyond help. I had got out of the panzer only a split second before. He did not know how our driver, Feldwebel Volz and the radio operator Obergefreiter Hartmann had fared. We did not see them again. (Volz became a prisoner of the Russians and was held at Smolensk, from where German troops released him when taking the city ten days later.)

I also discussed captivity with von Cossel. It was self-evident for us that we did not wish to fall into Russian hands alive. I had passed my pistol to Unteroffizier Vetter and requested the commander, should it come to it, first to shoot me and then himself. These words may seem unlikely to today's reader but I clearly remember saying them. Cossel gave me a thoughtful look but said nothing. I am sure he would not have done it.

Already ninety minutes had passed under the ground in our tunnel, and no sign of our comrades of I Abteilung who could have rescued us. If the rifle fire of the

Russians outside flared up from time to time, then each time we hoped that it was to defend against a German attack. But we were always disappointed. Where were our troops? Had they given us up for dead? I do not recall who was the first to do it, but we conquered the last 5m of the gallery and came into a small bunker which was built at road height directly into the crest of the embankment. It was about 2 x 2m and high enough for us to be able to sit up. The ceiling consisted of a layer of thick beams covered over above by turf, although we did not know that then. In the embankment slope the bunker had a shooting or observation split from where one had a view from a certain height of the Dnieper foreland and the Russian defences.

There were eight of us here. We were more on top of each other than beside each other. We covered the entrance into the bunker from the tunnel with a jute sack found in the bunker. This gave us the feeling of being a bit more closed off: in any case they would have to come up the gallery and remove the sack to find us. Maybe it was just an illusion, but at the time it was a great psychological help.

Now that we took a breather we could sum up our miserable plight. Unteroffizier Vetter sat with my pistol at the bunker entrance, ready to kill any Russian who tried to come up the tunnel. I lay directly by the firing slit observing the terrain in which the Russian positions and some well-camouflaged snipers could be made out. Behind them the broad and sluggish Dnieper flowed. On the other bank one could see some of the houses of Stary-Bychow. There was no life on the streets, not to mention German soldiers. For our commander the situation was particularly difficult: his wound hurt and we had no dressings pack with us. All had been left behind in the panzer.

Now and then a round exploded, an MG fired, and Russian voices were calling out to each other, coming nearer. We listened intently. Little remained of our already faint hopes of rescue now. The Russians were directly alongside, we heard their steps dragging in the grass, then they were overhead and stood there. The earth below their feet must have sounded hollow to the Russians, for one of them stamped a couple of times and earth trickled down around us as the ceiling and walls shook. Their voices grew excited, had we understood Russian we could have understood every word. Slowly they moved off. Today miracles by the dozen! We did not know yet if they had discovered us or if we had got away with it again. As a precaution I closed up the window with earth so that even on a closer inspection they would see nothing in the dark interior. Obviously it made our hiding place darker, but in a way it calmed our nerves. With our bare hands we dug depressions in the ground so as to lie more comfortably. It was all purely for the sake of self-preservation: the work gave us something to concentrate on and kept up our hopes of rescue.

The Russian firing grew livelier. Now their artillery joined in and the heavy shells roared into Stary-Bychow: we could not see this, but guessed it was the target by the distant explosions. A very heavy vibration caused sand to trickle down again from the ceiling and walls. What was that? Certainly not artillery. 'The Russians have blown up the bridge,' somebody said. This was bad news. Our last hope that our comrades could come and get us was gone. We talked in whispers, trying to rustle up encouragement. It was oppressively hot in the bunker, outside the sun stood high. We had been here five hours and had no water. It was fairly clear that no help would be coming our way today. We heard the Russians coming again and lay there apathetically. We could hear their steps distinctly in front of our bunker, then again on top of it. They were still searching for wounded and German panzer men in hiding, but our wrecked panzers interested them more than our dungeon. Probably it would be too filthy a job to crawl through the narrow tunnels. Soon we heard much shouting and loud bargaining from over there: we assumed they were in the panzers and sharing out what we had left behind, which included my camera and all my personal belongings. Hours later they were still arguing. For us the minutes were endless. The air in our bunker was very depleted, some of us had the desire to cough, often the best will in the world could not prevent it. Each of us reacted differently to the situation. I had to visit the empty tunnels frequently with diarrhoea.

After a long period of silence, the shooting suddenly resumed. Apparently the Russians had set up an MG on the road right above us and were firing it in short bursts, at what we could not be sure. Now and again between the bursts we heard an MG34 fire. This was a German gun, we all heard clearly its trusty noise. But who was firing it? Then we realized it was the Russians using an intact MG recovered from one of our panzers. Our nerves were in shreds: sometimes the shooting stopped, only to resume closer or further away. It continued like that the whole afternoon. I kept telling myself that we had got through the strong Stary-Bychow defences and across the river without losses. I had not been wounded, not even afterwards when we lay in open ground almost without cover. We had found this hideout and so far the Russians had failed to winkle us out. But after coming this far, would rescue be impossible?

This could not be. During the war I had never learned to pray and firmly believed that I had a special protection. I told this to myself repeatedly. Oberleutnant von

Cossel was much troubled by his wound. We talked about the possibility of leaving the bunker and swimming across the river but had decided it was hopeless. The Russians had positions everywhere and we had no information about their posts and sentries. All we knew for sure was that the MG above our heads occasionally fired short bursts. Furthermore there was bright moonlight and almost no cover in the ground we would have to cross to get to the river. So the operation was out of the question. We still had the hope that perhaps next morning, after they had had time to prepare, the German attack across the Dnieper would succeed and our comrades would fetch us out. We also hoped that the bridge might still be usable for getting across. Outside it had grown dark, the moon hidden by cloud, most of us were dozing with exhaustion. One or other had to be shaken awake if he snored too loud or spoke in his sleep. In the quiet of the night every sound carried. Again we heard footsteps approaching. Not even the night brought us peace. The steps came nearer but strangely no person. Now the noise was overhead, the sand trickled down from ceiling and walls, there was a moo-ing and then we knew that the visitor was a cow quietly grazing. We could hear the Russians talking quite clearly: we assumed they would still be in our panzers. The commander sent me down to the tunnel entrance to establish what was up. I stayed there about an hour and saw by the lights from inside our panzers that the Russians were still rummaging. Horrified, I thought of our secret code books, which would now be in Russian hands. I also saw two sentries on the road almost above our bunker. The moon was out from behind the clouds and I could see the Dnieper shining like a silver band. From time to time a flare was sent up on the other side. Were our people meanwhile in Stary-Bychow? It grew deadly quiet again, except for the irregular breathing of my comrades. It began to get light, but very cold. Soon it was daylight again, and my stomach continued to torment me.

5 July 1941, 0400hrs: the most favourable time for a German attack. Not a sound. We thought we could hear panzer engines in the distance, but nothing happened. A German aircraft flew past overhead. 0500hrs. All quiet, and now it began to dawn on us that we were not going to be rescued today. Our disappointment was unrestrained. The Russians above kept coming and going, and the longer the day went on the clearer it became that we were going to have to take things into our own hands. We discussed leaving the bunker in darkness to get down to the Dnieper and swim across. This was our last and only chance. At midday there was tremendous heat. We could tolerate hunger, but the thirst was a real torment. The tongue stuck to the gums, our feverish eyes stared. Abandoned to our fate, yet

the thought of possible escape in the evening helped us keep it together. We had either to try it, or give in. Through the firing slit we looked at the ground we would have to cross. We guessed there would be Russian sentries near the river banks but could not make them out. And what would be on the other side of the Dnieper? Were German troops there?

Now we discussed the details of our escape. We would leave the bunker through the firing slit. It would have to be enlarged. We drew up the order of departure and set the time for 2200hrs, by when it would be dark. Because the Russians had gone over the ground time and again in the search for us, we assumed that they would not be expecting Germans to be hiding among their positions. Perhaps their sentries would be less alert and watchful now that the front had been quiet for thirty-six hours. That would be our chance. We talked ourselves into believing it. We would crawl along the embankment to the bridge and river, about 250–300m without cover.

The day passed as slowly as the previous one. Occasionally German artillery fired on the Russian positions, and the shells exploded very close by. If just one had hit our bunker that would have been the end of everything. The tension rose towards evening and manifested itself in some problem or other. One man suddenly became hard of hearing, another urinated without pause, a special chapter in itself. Thank heavens some of the men wore jackboots, which were handed round for urinary purposes: of my own problem I have already written. I think I must have gone eight to ten times in that thirty-six-hour period and there couldn't have been much left in my intestines, for I had not eaten for two days. The evening came, oppressively sultry, a storm was brewing. We had expected it, and towards 2000hrs it began to break, not much rain, but the sky was overcast. Tonight the moon would be hidden. We saw this as a good omen. Towards 2100hrs the commander gave me the sign and I cautiously began to enlarge the firing slit with a table knife. Slowly but surely it progressed until the opening was large enough for a man to force his way through. We made the last preparations, removed our footwear so as not to betray our presence by the scraping of iron. We also removed our black panzer jackets since they made crawling difficult. The commander repeated that we should not worry about him, even if he could not go on. This was something we ignored: to leave our commander behind – never!

Ten minutes left to 2200hrs. The cloud cover began to break up, bathing everything in bright moonlight. A cloud passed now and again. Now we had no time to lose: we had to go irrespective of whether the situation was favourable or not. A thin layer of mist lay across the meadows. Obergefreiter Ostwald was scheduled to leave the bunker first. He was too keyed up and had to make three attempts to get through the window. Then the commander followed and I was third. I stuck my head out and saw the commander creeping down the slope. It was a strange feeling, knowing that only a few metres above us was Ivan. I gave myself a heave and followed the commander as quietly as possible. Now that the die was cast it was all the same to me. I pressed my head as close as I could to the ground. The grass here was very short, but was longer further ahead and offered a bit of cover. I caught up with the commander, but of Ostwald there was no sign. He must have chosen another route to the one agreed upon. Unteroffizier Plötscher with Markgraf and Hofmann came up next. Where were the rest of them? Unteroffizier Vetter and Turbanisch?

We crawled onwards through the grass, working our way metre by metre to the foot of the embankment. Suddenly there was a metallic sound to the left of us. It sounded like a Russian machine-gunner handling his weapon. We could see nothing, but the sound was distinct, as though he were constantly reloading. We heard suppressed voices. It was possible that a sentry had discovered us but his weapon had jammed. We lay pressed to the ground and waited. I was now ahead with Markgraf, the others behind me. We awaited our fate, one shot was enough to rouse the entire Russian trench system. In such a case we would attempt to reach the river in great leaps and bounds and without regard to cover. Our chances would be poor. Meanwhile it was probably midnight now. All at once something hissed, there came a dull report and a strong wave of pressure from the blast. Lumps of earth rained down. German artillery was giving the Russian positions harassing fire, and we would have to make our way through it.

The Russians must have drawn their heads in, this being the only way to explain why they failed to see us. It gave us a chance, but it was also not pleasant to lie in our own artillery fire. We heard the distant boom-boom of the guns. After a few seconds the shells would hiss over and explode around us. Using the artillery fire we crept forward faster on all fours for the river. We recognized the bridge and saw that on the Russian side it was undamaged from the bank to the middle of the river: the remainder had been blown up and collapsed. The wreckage lay in the river and on the foreshore the other side. Near the river the terrain was fairly undulating with here and there a low bush. We reached the bridge: the first goal had been achieved. Suddenly Markgraf noticed a rowing boat down in the water, hidden in the rushes. I didn't believe him at first, but then I saw it. Now I was perhaps a little incautious.

I was not taking the Russian sentries into account any longer. With a few jumps I reached the boat and tried it out. The oars were aboard. At once something hissed over and only a few metres away a tall plume of water rose up. I lay flat in the boat for better cover, then realized that the wooden hull was not safe enough, jumped out and sought the others.

Unteroffizier Plötscher lay in the reeds near the bridge. Clothing lay around him and I asked where the commander was. He pointed out across the water and said that the commander wanted to swim to the other shore to contact the German sentries and if possible fetch help. The problem with that idea was that we still did not know who held the other shore. At precisely that moment an enormous column of water fell over us, the first of many. Instinctively the remaining four men, Plötscher, Markgraf, Hofmeyer and myself, fled to the standing part of the bridge. Directly under its roadway we had some protection, and also against being seen. We cowered close together. About every twenty seconds a shell came over and I took note of the fall of shot, either into the water or the bank. We heard shell splinters tinkling down on the bridge: it was a really bad situation to be in. The other shore was brightly lit, and we watched a house burst into flames immediately after being hit. All at once, from either side of us, some tracer was fired towards the far shore: the Russians must have noticed something, for we saw that they were concentrating their fire on the central bridge pillar. Dear God, that might be the commander! There was nothing we could do to help. MG fire was returned from the far side. The whole place was in uproar. The artillery kept firing on our location: we had to get out of there.

Without much thought we rushed to the rowing boat. Plötscher sat at the oars, Markgraf and Hofmann lay flat in the boat and I pushed it away from the bank and jumped in. We got tangled in some telegraph wires hanging down from the bridge and were held fast. When Plötscher finally worked out how to extract us with the oars, we were sucked into the current and swept away: finally he got it right and stabilized the boat. Slowly we made progress against the current: we had to row under the bridge upstream, for downstream below the bridge we had seen an MG nest. When we got to the first pillar we got tangled with the telegraph wires again and it required a great effort to get free. I pushed the boat away from the pillar against which the current was forcing us and now we had some cover behind the great ice deflector in front of the pillar in the river. Next we had to row across the current to the ice deflector of the next pillar. Plötscher rowed with all his might and came close to the next pillar. Here the Russians must have seen the boat

– there was no doubt this time because they fired at us and sprayed the water with bullets. We thought at first that the shooting came from the far bank, that maybe it was Germans firing under the mistaken impression that we were a scouting party. Therefore we shouted as loud as we could, 'Kameraden, don't shoot, Germans!' We repeated it three times, and here was another miracle, for the Russians stopped shooting. We were now in cover behind the second ice deflector and from here the boat reached calm water. There we suddenly heard a weak voice close by calling, 'Plötscher, Plötscher'. That was the commander!

We reached the other bank quite quickly, I sprang out of the boat and waded in shallow and then breast-high water, holding to the beams of the wrecked bridge, towards where Cossel was holding tight along a beam and staggering towards me. He was totally done for. The two of us got to the far bank easily and stretched out in a depression that gave us all-round cover. First we paused for breath. Five of us had made it across the Dnieper safely. We were all completely exhausted and could not believe that we had succeeded in escaping. We had no idea where our comrades Vetter, Turbanisch and Ostwald were.

Our next move was to get away from the riverside to the high bank. This needed great caution in case the German sentries, who must have been posted somewhere in these parts, opened fire on us. With Plötscher I crept along the waterfront in search of another resting place for the commander, since we could not stay so close to the river. By daybreak we had to be away. After a short while, the commander came crawling up on all fours with the other two, and we all needed another longer rest before the final stage. I remained with Cossel while the others crawled off to find the German sentries. The Russians must have noticed this for they set up an MG in midstream on the still-standing part of the bridge and fired some tracer in our direction. We kept our heads down until it was over, and then I crawled slowly onwards with the commander, whose wound was causing him very great difficulty. At the end of the bridge the wreckage was strewn everywhere and so gave us at least a chance of some cover.

Plötscher had gone alone along the road which led up steeply from the river bank to the town as far as the first houses. He waited for us to come up and together we crept along the street, one man behind the other, always looking for cover, passing the gaps between the dwellings with leaps. At the highest point of the road, about 150m away, a barrier of boarding blocked the view. When it got light, all the enemy side could be seen from here. We were about to go around the barricade when one of us saw a German sentry. He was not very alert, for he had failed to notice our arrival. From cover we called, 'Sentry!' The man, totally surprised, raised his rifle: we allowed ourselves to be seen and recognized, and shouted, 'Don't shoot!' We approached him with our hands up and would have given him a hug but the commander admonished him instead for not spotting us.

The sentry brought us to his unit and the duty officer had us taken in his Kübelwagen to the Regimental HQ of PzRgt 35 which lay in a wood outside Stary-Bychow. We arrived there at 0400hrs. Oberleutnant von Cossel went slowly to the regimental commander's Kübelwagen where Oberst Eberbach was asleep in the seat. Cossel opened the door, Eberbach woke up: 'Cossel!' and the two men fell into each other's arms. It was incredible: we still could not grasp that we were saved. Soaked through, without jacket or shoes, hair unkempt, we stood before the regimental commander. The whole HQ was awoken. Dry underwear and greatcoats were brought, a flask of cognac did the rounds and from the kitchens came hot broth and chicken.

We were told that two days previously, Leutnant Burckhardt and four men had come back when the bridge was still intact. Four hours after us Unteroffizier Vetter appeared, having swum the Dnieper further downstream. Turbanisch drowned in the attempt, of Ostwald nothing further was known. Thus altogether eleven men of the original twenty-five had made it back. Much later I discovered that Feldwebel Volz, our driver, and Unteroffizier Ostwald had been released after ten days' captivity when Roslavl was captured.

Oberleutnant von Cossel initially remained at the regimental command post, while the rest of us were returned to our companies towards 0600hrs where we received the warmest welcome. The news had spread like wildfire. First we ate, then towards 0800hrs the whole company fell in for the commander, who made his appearance virtually in rags and a thick dressing. He took his leave of me and was flown to the Charité hospital in Berlin, from where it was hoped he might return in a week. Oberleutnant Rosshirt commanded the company until Cossel's actual return a fortnight later. The rest of us slept for a whole day, having so much sleep to catch up on. On the orders of the regiment, Unteroffizier Plötscher and I collaborated in writing a report which seventy years ago set down the essentials: the events of the time burnt themselves into my memory.

We were given fresh uniforms and I went to Leutnant Burckhardt's panzer as his gunner. The wagon was in good working order and so did not require much attention. We rested. I received my birthday mail which had arrived meanwhile. My parents sent me a packet containing a watch. My first!

A little later we moved out and had another look at the route we had taken on the morning when we occupied Stary-Bychow. We went on stand-by again in a wonderful wood on the edge of town. We made ourselves at home and had everything we needed except water. We were to lay here until the attack over the Dnieper was resumed. The divisional motorcyclists were right forward at the river. Elements of Mölders' fighter squadron were at the airfield. Caravans, tents, field beds, radios, they had it all. If they needed beer or anything else, a Junkers transport aircraft brought it up. We had the greatest difficulty keeping ourselves and our clothing clean with the little water available. We were as filthy as pigs. We opened out our groundsheets near our panzer, wrapped ourselves in a blanket and slept. We had no complaints. The time passed doing nothing and we enjoyed our lives, which had hung by such a thin thread. In the evening I was informed of my promotion to Unteroffizier with effect from 1 July for courage in the face of the enemy. It came so suddenly I could hardly believe it. The lieutenant organized a bottle of champagne, and we sat around a camp fire near our panzer and drank together.

The following morning my promotion to Unteroffizier was announced before the assembled company. In the afternoon I was accepted officially into the Corps of NCOs and in the evening had my first watch as orderly NCO. It was absolutely quiet except for a Russian bomber which made a low-level pass directly above us. I kept glancing at my shoulder straps to make sure that the lace was still there as I did my inspection that night.

On 10 July 1941 the division began its attack across the Dnieper, not this time as a surprise blow but after substantial preparation by artillery and the Luftwaffe. At 1100hrs that day I had to report with my Dnieper comrades to the regimental commander. We were awarded the Iron Cross Second Class, Leutnant Burckhardt and Unteroffizier Plötscher the Iron Cross First Class. I was proud, and the day brought another surprise: at midday the Abteilung ordered that Leutnant Burckhardt and we four, who had come back with Oberleutnant von Cossel, were to proceed to Stary-Bychow in order to cross the Dnieper with the first troops and look over our wrecked panzers. A group of the pioneer platoon with a rubber dinghy was assigned to us. We drove through Stary-Bychow on two light tractors following our earlier route of advance and halted about 150m above the bridge position. There were Russians on the other side of the bridge, and we witnessed a low-level attack by two Me 110s on their trenches while the first men of our infantry regiment worked their way through the bridge wreckage to the far bank. Soon they had gained a foothold and the first prisoners came over. Now we climbed across the bridge too and reached the far bank. Left of the road the first thing we found was the corpse of Leutnant König, recognizable only by his uniform, a ghastly sight which shook me to the core. We continued our search and found our dead comrades scattered near our panzers, on the road and in the river meadows. First my loader, the young Hofweber. He was terribly injured and must have suffered in agony until the *coup de grâce* which the Russians undoubtedly gave him. Then Krompert, Lindenberger and Stössel. These were still seated in their panzer, where a direct hit had torn off Lindenberger's head. Further on lay Gerlsberger and finally we also found Hans Ebersberg, who had pluckily covered the way back for his comrades and while doing so received a fatal wound in the stomach. They had wanted to take him with them, but he requested that they leave him there, and write to his parents when they had the chance. This was the worst thing of all in the whole campaign: to see comrades with whom one had sat in the panzer, or to whom one was a friend, in such cruel circumstances – mutilated and decomposing, almost beyond recognition.

I went to my panzer and found some items which were still usable, but the Russians had taken most of it, and all articles of value. Meanwhile a man had come from the Propaganda Company and he took snapshots of us in all possible positions. I had another look at the hole in which we had hidden and marvelled that we had got out alive. Towards evening a company arrived which had been called up by a motorcycle dispatch rider. We dug graves for our comrades and buried them there in the simple soldierly way. Why did they have to die and I survive?

Breaking through the Stalin Line

In the early hours of 11 July we were ordered to make ready to cross the Dnieper and continue east. This gladdened our hearts. Towards midday we set out from the Stary-Bychow airfield. On the way down to the river, we observed seven victorious aerial duels within an hour, which naturally went down well with us all. Around 1500hrs we crossed the bridge which the pioneers had erected across the Dnieper. Previously we had made quite a few halts to prevent bottlenecks. Now the bridge was under Russian light artillery fire. The accuracy was poor but nevertheless it was not very comfortable to be on the bridge watching the shells explode all around us in the water. We moved on quickly and crossed a second, longer bridge. The Russians had a view of the entire road and kept us under constant bombardment.

Soon we got to a wood devastated by artillery and rockets. A large anti-tank obstacle blocked the road and the countryside off the road was mined but the pioneers had cleared a path for us and our infantry now occupied the terrain. We drove down the big Rollbahn eastwards for about 20km and then left it for a small village where we spent the night. The Light Platoon was deployed to secure our flanks while we others first had to search the houses for Russian soldiers in hiding.

Early next morning we set off again. Our panzer had engine trouble and was running too hot. If one opened the radiator cap all the water gushed out, and so we had to keep refilling it. The problem was the right-side fan, which had stuck and could not be got going again. Towards midday we came under rifle and MG fire from a wood where we had intended to rest. Therefore we could not dismount, and so set fire to the wood.

Around 1500hrs our 1 Company was ordered to advance. Nobody knew exactly what the problem was. We were ordered to battle readiness and fifteen minutes later arrived in open country where we received anti-tank gun fire which was falling too short. We could see the muzzle flashes and fired back but without visible effect. Unteroffizier Wieser, who left the panzer, was wounded in the foot by a shell splinter. Thereupon Oberleutnant Rosshirt sent two Panzer IIIs forward to clear the way for us. Feldwebel Dreher was hit and killed, the crew got out but Markgraf was lightly wounded. They all managed to reach the other panzer, if fairly exhausted. A further frontal attack would achieve nothing and so with elements of 3 Company we detoured around this wood with its thick undergrowth and a field of wheat. Soon we caught sight of the Russian anti-tank guns and came under fire. We crossed a trench without loss and, rolling forwards at a fast pace, forced the Russian gunners to pull back, their two guns being rendered useless by a hand grenade in each barrel.

Now we received more heavy anti-tank fire and could not identify from where it came; two panzers were hit. Our losses were becoming too heavy and the order came by radio, 'Cease fire, secure, turn back.' We carried out the order, comical though the situation appeared to us. The panzers turned about and the Russians fired into our rear. The company took the same way back. On the way we attempted to take in tow Feldwebel Dreher's wrecked panzer, but this failed. We cleared it out completely and took anything of use with us. At dusk we reached the wood in which the Abteilung lay. The other companies had also had losses. Immediately upon arrival we tanked up and re-ammunitioned. Our panzer was running so hot that the carburettor caught fire, although it was quickly extinguished. In any case we were not going to be able to move again until the mechanics got the fan working.

Next morning it was planned to repeat the attack but after this was cancelled the maintenance crew turned up. Towards 1000hrs it was reported that the Russians were advancing on our wood. All available panzers were formed up and sent out to a meadow from where they fired all they had. The Russian artillery knew their targets and so we too were obliged to seek refuge under our panzer now and again. The Russians attacked in waves so that the situation occasionally looked very threatening. Our panzers began to run low on ammunition and so we had to belt ammunition the whole time at the side of our non-operational panzer if not lying in the muck when shells began to fall nearby. This went on all day. In the afternoon our panzer was repaired. Towards evening came the report that the commander of 2 Company, Oberleutnant Rachfall, had fallen. His tank had run over a mine, he had had to abandon the vehicle and so fell into the hands of the Russians. My panzer was now drawn into the defensive line which pushed up closer to the Russian positions in the darkness. Overnight there were no events to report except for some houses being set on fire: Oberfeldwebel Walowsky of 3 Company was wounded by a Russian who crept up to his panzer.

At first light we pulled back a little. Two 8.8cm Flak guns had arrived and were excellent and on target. Now the Russians could come. They fired shrapnel and got a direct hit on the observation post but there was nothing else to report. At midday we were relieved, the panzers were brought back to form up and then headed cross-country towards Propoisk. This time II Abteilung was ahead of us. As on all previous advances we had a grim struggle against the dust. The terrain was lightly undulating and not easy to monitor, with clumps of woodland here and there. Towards 1600hrs a long halt was called and the order given for battle readiness. The panzers were well camouflaged in a copse. We refuelled and took on more shells. I got the gun ready myself, cleaning and draining the barrel. The field kitchen brought up hot food for a change. We all sat around the panzer, the 'Spiess' was there too, and we chatted about this and that. We were still feeling the effects of the very heavy fighting of the last few days, and so our talk was not particularly optimistic. But moods changed often and the next day we would probably be thinking the opposite.

We had been held up by a damaged bridge over a stream. This had been repaired by the pioneers, and our Abteilung now led the way forward, 1 Company in third place. II Abteilung was well ahead of us all and had pushed up near the town of

Propoisk, but the attack had been held back until next morning on account of the late hour although we ourselves kept rolling. Soviet fighters circled above us without attacking. A halt was called once it was fully dark. We went into thick woodland. Great discretion was called for; the Russians were lurking everywhere along the Rollbahn. They could work their way up to a panzer and lob in a Molotov cocktail. It was something tried against us by the Russians for the first time here but fortunately for us not on this occasion.

15 July 1941: A few men stretched out on the rear of the panzer slept for fifteen minutes. We could hear firing ahead: II Abteilung was on the move again. We set off at 0130hrs. Scarcely had we exited the wood than we saw on our right a burning German armoured scout car. The Russians had brought up a 105mm gun somewhere nearby and were shooting directly at us. A house in the vicinity was burning, illuminating everything with a ghostly light. All around was deepest night. We increased the distance between the panzers and drove flat out across the danger area. All hatches were tight shut, the driver floored the gas pedal. The explosions sounded strange so close to the panzer; through the sight I saw a brief flash at each impact and shell splinters would fly against the panzer armour. We were happy to get through it. It was simply impossible to make out where the gun was. Soon after we came to a village still occupied by the enemy. We received fire from every house, but nothing to worry us. Rifle bullets whistled around our turret. I had to admire the motorcycle infantry of our reconnaissance platoon. They had no protection at all, but just drew their heads in and kept as close as possible to the side of the panzer. They got through all right here, but later suffered dreadful losses.

From ahead we were told that II Abteilung had entered Propoisk and held the three important bridges behind the town intact. These bridges, about 400m long, crossed a small river in a valley and were of all-wooden construction. The valley was overlooked by the enemy, but the panzer division went through the middle of them, and left them on left and right for the following troops to mop up.

Dawn had begun to be visible in the east when we drove into the town. First we stopped on one of the main roads and severed the telephone wires with wire-cutters. Then the company was divided up across the whole town in order to secure its most important points. Here and there the first fires broke out. The Russians set fire to everything in their retreat. Our panzer stood with another for two hours on security. The crew of the other panzer rooted out twenty Russians from a house: they threw down their weapons and surrendered. Towards 0800hrs we formed up in the town again. Unteroffizier Mendeletz's panzer, just come out of the workshop, ran over a mine while passing a demolished bridge. Nobody was hurt but the drive wheel at the rear was done for. Leutnant Burckhardt took our panzer to tow him in. Meanwhile I went with my loader into town to look over the shops, but found nothing much worth having. We spent a while rummaging in a Russian mixed-goods store which sold everything from furniture to underwear and toys, naturally all cheap Soviet stuff. When our panzer came back, Burckhardt hadn't been able to tow Mendeletz, and so we loaded aboard a 20-litre barrel of some cheap alcoholic drink and set off to join the company. It was no easy task to find it, and we cruised the streets for a good half-hour. The population would have been around 15,000. Because the buildings were all wooden, it had started to burn everywhere. After half an hour we ran the company to ground at a fuel dump on the edge of town. Two men armed with a pistol and hand grenade got out from each panzer to search the place. It was found that the barrels and tanks were empty. The company now received orders to secure the town against attack.

The situation was approximately as follows: our panzer was the most advanced, with a potato field ahead of us. The Russians had dug an anti-tank ditch 200m in front of us. The panzer itself stood in an abandoned gun emplacement, and so therefore we had a good field of fire. There were shell casings and cordite bags lying everywhere. We stretched out in the sun and tried to catch up on lost sleep. Suddenly, Leutnant Burckhardt saw a head appear behind a row of potatoes. He pointed it out to me without making a fuss. I went at once to my gunner's seat and traversed the gun slowly. The Russian made no move. I fired an HE shell which could not have missed. The whole affair seemed peculiar and so the Light Platoon was sent to investigate. It turned out that between our panzer and the anti-tank ditch in the potato field in front of us was one infantry slit trench after another. One could not do very much from the panzer and so the Light Platoon got out and we fired at everything that moved. With hand grenades and pistols they cleared all the slit trenches one after the other so that by midday it seemed that the job was finished except for the occasional find here and there. Wrong again: suddenly there appeared close to our panzer from a large, previously undiscovered trench fifteen men and a commissar. When we opened fire on them, they put their hands up. The crew wanted to disarm them, at which the commissar threw some egg-shaped hand grenades at us and they all disappeared into their bunker again. A hand grenade of our own which we tossed in was returned at once. The next hand grenade killed the commissar and the rest of them surrendered.

Relative calm returned until the evening. Another unit, motorcycle infantry, I believe, took over the security. Previously we had set a nearby village alight with gunfire in order to illuminate the surrounding terrain. While doing this a shell burst in the barrel of the commander's panzer, rendering it useless. Because our panzer was in the best condition, Leutnant Burckhardt was replaced by Oberleutnant Rosshirt as commander. The former commander's panzer went to the weapons workshop.

In the previous weeks of fighting the company had had several breakdowns due to engine failure and was down to its last five Panzer IIIs. Russian oil and petrol and the long-distance runs had taken their toll. We drove through the burnt-out remains of Propoisk and together with other I Abteilung companies secured ourselves against Russian attacks in a tall cornfield. One man per panzer had to stay awake and so towards midnight I could finally turn in. Packed into a sleeping bag with a blanket on top I had a wonderful sleep in the corn until 0200hrs when we were awoken again. All of I Abteilung formed up in order to follow II Abteilung, which had meanwhile reached Kritshev and secured a bridgehead there. That morning it rained torrentially so that we had to shut all the hatches tight and try to sleep during the drive. After 25km an order came, probably by radio, and the entire Abteilung suddenly had to turn around, drive back through Propoisk and park in a wood. By now the weather had improved somewhat. There was much to do aboard the panzer, always the same: clean weapons etc., all of which took up a lot of time. The right-hand fan had stuck fast again so that the same work had to be undertaken as a few days previously. Once this was finished one could have a quick wash and shave or lay out on a blanket and sleep. To have a meal in peace once in a while was a boon. The wood had wonderful strawberries and, eaten with sugar, which we never lacked, they tasted quite excellent and moreover contained the vitamins so sadly missing from our diet.

So, towards 1500hrs the following day the order came to 'Make ready' and a little later the Abteilung moved out and crossed the three great bridges beyond Propoisk. First we drove 35km on the Rollbahn, went through Chernikov and then left the road to the right and came to a halt in woods 23km from Kritshev. Here, so we were told, we would have several days' rest. We put up a tent near our panzer and had a glorious sleep. Our people brought a pig and over a small fire I spent three hours making wonderful roast pork. It tasted just like home cooking: the only thing missing was the potatoes, so we had to make do with bread.

Meanwhile Leutnant Burckhardt had driven to the workshop to check on the panzers there. We simply had to increase the numbers, and so he went there to see

(**above**) Along churned and rutted woodland tracks, the units struggled forward. Motorcycle infantry with sidecar often had to get off and push. An 8-tonne tractor with 2cm quadruple Flak is in the act of overtaking them.

(**left**) A military ambulance and motorcycles with sidecar passing the panzer men. In the background a vast convoy of vehicles.

The body of a fallen German soldier in a canvas shroud being conveyed to a burial ground by horse-drawn wagon.

The same cortège passing along a dry woodland track. Notice the dust rising behind vehicles and troops on the march.

German military cemetery of InfRgt 394/3 PzDiv in the Propoisk woods. Birch trunks and branches were used for this purpose for ease of working.

The Russian campaign of 1941 caused greater losses than were initially expected.

Oblt. Krause mit Lt.Lange am
27.7.41 in früher Morgenstun-
de am selbstgezimmerten Tisch
an der Rollbahn sitzend zwi-
schen Tscherikoff und Kritschew.
Lt.Lange wurde bald darauf ver-
wundet.

Oberleutnant Krause with Leutnant Lange in the early hours of 27 July 1941, seated at a makeshift table on the Rollbahn between Cherikov and Kritshev. Lange was wounded shortly afterwards.

Otto Steppert and Heinz Böswillibald posing on a powerful 122mm (mislabelled as 17.2cm on the photo) Russian gun captured near Cherikov in July 1941. The muzzle is blocked by a shell jammed nose-first into it.

Russische 17,2 Kanone bei Tscherikoff
im Juli 1941
Otto Steppert und Heinz Böswillibald

Watching the fighting from a safe distance, nearby a wrecked Russian T-26 light tank.

(left) Panzer III 112 at Rhyskovka. The gunner can be seen at the open turret hatch.

(below) PzRgt 5 forming up across endless fields for the attack on Roslavl at the beginning of August 1941.

Snapshot taken over the short 5cm gun of a Panzer III. On the horizon, targets are on fire.

(left) A seriously damaged Panzer IV, with shell damage on both sides.

(below) A Russian 'anti-tank, anti-aircraft gun' dug in on the flat battlefield west of Roslavl. Well-camouflaged guns of this type with good penetrative power caused the German panzers heavy losses.

The workshop platoons and companies had their work cut out for them. Here a new engine is being installed in a panzer chassis. The wear and tear through operational use, dust and sand was enormous.

This Panzer III was penetrated by three hits through the front armour. The driver and radio operator of a 1941/42 German panzer would have had little chance of surviving such damage inflicted by a T-34 or a 76.2mm anti-tank gun.

Two Panzer IVs hitched up to a broken-down Panzer III to tow it to the road.

Side view of the collapsed wooden bridge and damaged Panzer III in which the author received his hand injury near Roslavl on 3 August 1941.

Overhead view of the author's Panzer III after it slipped off a collapsed wooden bridge near Roslavl on 3 August 1941. The swastika on the turret is for aircraft identification purposes. After his hospitalization, the author never returned to this company.

(top left) Oberleutnant Hans-Detloff von Cossel was the author's company commander. He had already been awarded the Iron Cross First and Second Class in 1939.

(top right) Von Cossel was decorated with the Knight's Cross on 8 September 1941.

(right) Von Cossel in panzer uniform. He fell on 22 July 1943 as commander of I Abteilung/PzRgt 35 and was awarded the Oak Leaves posthumously.

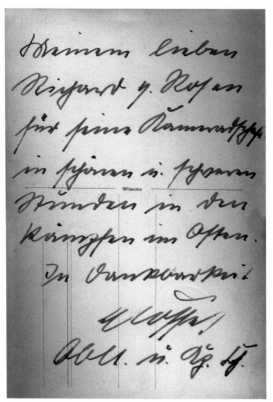

(left) On 3 August 1941, on taking leave of the wounded author, Detloff von Cossel wrote him this dedication on a postcard: 'To my dear Richard von Rosen, for his comradeship in the best and worst hours during the fighting in the East. In gratitude, von Cossel, Oberleutnant and Company Commander.'

The commander of I Abteilung/PzRgt 35 with which the author served was Major Meinrad von Lauchert, who together with Detloff von Cossel also received the Knight's Cross on 8 September 1941.

Von Lauchert was awarded the Oak Leaves on 12 February 1944 in the rank of Oberstleutnant.

A certificate issued from Supreme High Command HQ on 30 July 1941 and signed by Walther von Brauchitsch, Army C-in-C, in which he presented to Major von Lauchert, Commander I/PzRgt 35 'My special recognition for his outstanding achievements on the battlefield at Ryshkovka on 12/13 July 1941'.

Im Namen des Führers
und Obersten Befehlshabers
der Wehrmacht

verleihe ich

dem

Gefr. Richard von ROSEN
1./ Panzer-Regiment 35

das
Eiserne Kreuz 2.Klasse.

Div.Gef.St. ,den 9. Juli 19 41

Gen.Major und Div.Kommandeur
(Dienstgrad und Dienststellung)

(above) Immediately after the events on the bridge at Stary-Bychow, 'In the name of the Führer and Supreme Commander of the Wehrmacht' the author was awarded the Iron Cross Second Class on 9 July 1941, the certificate being signed by Generalmajor von Langermann.

(facing page, bottom) During his service with PzRgt 35 up to 3 August 1941, the author had no experience of the Russian T-34-76 tank, newly arrived at the front. In this interesting photo of a wrecked example one can see clearly the robust rear drive wheel without gear rim. The rolling wheels met upright teeth in the track plates, which caused the tank's characteristic audible 'Clack-clack-clack'.

Edi Achatz

Unteroffizier Eduard Achatz was one of the veteran panzer men in PzRgt 35. He was taken prisoner by the Russians at Stary-Bychow. His diary inspired the author to write his own war memoir

In an act of great devotion to duty, Unteroffizier Hugo Plötscher rowed the author and many other colleagues across the Dnieper to safety, preventing their capture by the Russians.

The tension and emotional stress of the events at the Stary-Bychow bridge have visibly matured the author at age 19. This photo shows him as an Unteroffizier after he had already left 1 Company/ PzRgt 35.

The author in a hospital ward listening to the latest Wehrmacht bulletins telling of the advance on Russia.

August 1941: On the way to the military hospital at Greiz/Thuringia from Russia. This time not in a cattle truck but from the look of it a first-class railway compartment.

Some willing German Red Cross nurses. They were known as 'Karbolmädchen' – 'Karbol girls' – after the disinfectant of the same name.

The senior surgeon of the Greiz military hospital, Stabsarzt Dr Schuldt.

Fetching the mail for comrades. The author (right) carrying a basket of post with a comrade. There was plenty of time to write to one's loved ones from hospital.

Dienststelle 38o19 c   O.U.,den 3.9.41.
Abt.IIb   - Az.22/41.

Betr.: Verl.Auszeichnung.
Anl. : ein Pz.Kpf.Abz.
        eine Besitzurkunde.

                    Herrn
                    Erich Frhr.v.R o s e n ,
                    Rastatt in Baden,Sibyllenstr.7.

            In der Anlage übersendet Ihnen die Dienststelle das

Ihrem Sohne Richard verliehene Panzerkampfabzeichen in Silber mit Besitz-

zeugnis.Da die Lazarettanschrift Ihres Sohnes hier nicht bekannt ist,konnte

ihm die Auszeichnung nicht übersandt werden.

            Einschreiben gilt als Empfangsbescheinigung.

A notification from Service Centre 38019c dated 3 September 1941 stating that 'Enclosed herewith the Service Centre sends you the Panzer Assault Badge in Silver with certificate awarded to your son Richard. Since we do not have the military hospital address for your son, the award could not be sent to him. Registered letter serves as confirmation of receipt.'

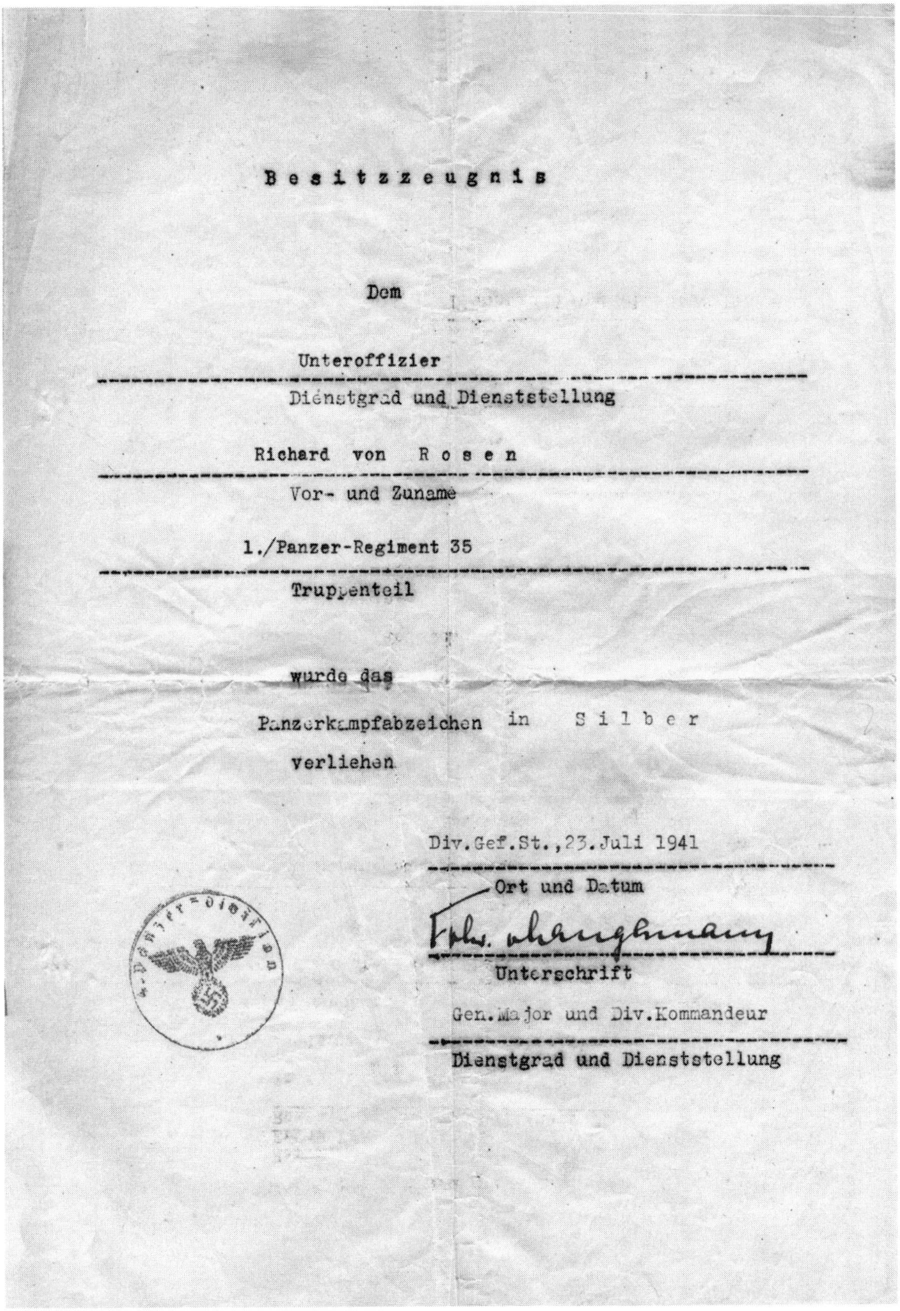

Besitzzeugnis

Dem

Unteroffizier
_____
Dienstgrad und Dienststellung

Richard von Rosen
_____
Vor- und Zuname

1./Panzer-Regiment 35
_____
Truppenteil

wurde das

Panzerkampfabzeichen in Silber

verliehen

Div.Gef.St.,23.Juli 1941
_____
Ort und Datum

Fhr. Langermann
_____
Unterschrift

Gen.Major und Div.Kommandeur
_____
Dienstgrad und Dienststellung

The certificate of the award of the Panzer Assault Badge in Silver made to the author on 23 July 1941 and signed by Generalmajor Langermann. Divisional HQ having run out of these certificates, they were simply typed up in the orderly room.

Dienststelle 38019 c
Abt. Ia   -   Az.31/41.   O.U.,den 5.9.41.

Betr.: Privatsachen Ihres Sohnes Richard.
Anl.: eine Aufstellung.

                    Herrn
                    Freiherrn von Rosen
                    Rastatt/Baden,Sibyllenstr.7

        In der Anlage übersendet Ihnen die Dienststelle eine
Aufstellung über die bisher noch bei der Dienststelle befindlichen Pri-
vatsachen Ihres Sohnes Richard.Die Gegenstände wurden am 25.8.41. mit
Lkw.nach Deutschland gebracht und dort an Ihre Adresse weitergeleitet.
        Es wird gebeten,den Empfang zu bestätigen.

                    Heil Hitler!

                    Oberleutnant u. Komp.-Chef

A letter from Service Centre 38019c dated 5 September 1941 to the author's father enclosing a list of his son's personal belongings which were 'brought by lorry to Germany on 25 August 1941 and sent on from there to your address. Confirmation of receipt is requested.' The serious omission of the greeting 'Heil Hitler!' on the letter of 3 September 1941 is remedied on this letter.

for himself and bring back as many as possible to the company. On the Rollbahn troops of our division rolled by unceasingly. There was a lot of heavy artillery in particular which we thought would be for the bombardment of Moscow. In the afternoon I bathed in nearby water, the first time I had had a proper wash in the entire campaign. We were black as soot from dust, filth, oil and powder smoke. Our bodies were grey, the pores black. Dust clung to hair and beards.

All the next day there was nothing to report. The barber came to shear us, the tailor and cobbler also paid us a visit. Both were overwhelmed with work. That day those of us who had been involved in three attacks were awarded the Panzer Assault Badge although we did not receive it until much later because Division had run out of them. In the evening at 3 Company a concert with the regimental band for the birthday of the Abteilung commander was scheduled, but towards evening came the order for battle readiness. No information was forthcoming as to why; we had been promised several days' rest here. Later we discovered that the Russians had recaptured the Rollbahn in our rear and surrounded the panzer pioneers who had camped on it. We moved out at 1900hrs, 3 Company in the lead. The spearhead vehicle was that of Leutnant Hohnstätter who had been in charge of our course in the Warthelager. Beyond Chernikov we crossed a bridge which was under observation by the Russians so that every time a panzer arrived on it a shell would explode nearby. The bridge was hit several times, but was quickly repaired. Towards ten that evening the spearhead vehicle got through to the panzer pioneers without opposition and relieved them. They had protected themselves by laying mines on the road, and these were soon removed. The advance was resumed: on the road it was pitch dark.

Wounded and Back to the Home Front

In this chapter I have reported in my own words on the opening days of the campaign in the East as I experienced it as a gunner in a Panzer III. I have described the Stary-Bychow operation particularly extensively, since it opened all the doors to my future career. As we came to realize in the fighting around the Propoisk bridges, the struggle was now becoming fiercer. Our panzer spearheads forced their way forward along the Rollbahns without concerning themselves about the enemy they left behind to their left and right. On 3 August 1941 Roslavl was taken. Other units were ahead of us and we detoured around the town in order to remain on the heels of the enemy as his principal pursuer. I was in the spearhead panzer, and we stepped up the pace so as to maintain contact with the retreating Russians. It was hot in the interior and we drove with the side hatches open. A wooden bridge on the outskirts of Roslavl failed to take the weight of our fast-moving panzer, collapsed and we plunged off it. It was only a minor mishap, but three fingers of my left hand were crushed by a falling beam. I was given an emergency dressing and taken to the main dressing station before being conveyed over 100km to the nearest railway station in a swaying field ambulance with seriously wounded men. The station installations were being repaired while the tracks were being changed from the Russian broad gauge to European gauge. Even if they managed 30 to 50km a day, the line remained quite a distance from the nearest front. Ammunition and fuel were the principal commodities being brought out from the Reich, and the trains returned there with the wounded.

After seven days on a train – initially in a goods wagon on straw, then from the Polish border in a hospital train – on 11 August 1941 I arrived at a military hospital in the heart of Germany at Greiz in Thuringia. A fine doctor saved me from having to have the three fingers amputated. They were pierced at the tip and stretched for six weeks in extension bandaging. On 12 August my mother came from Oberbärenburg, followed a few days later by my father, who was taking a cure at Bad Oberschlema. By the beginning of October 1941 the wounds were well healed, the fingers just a little stiff, and I was discharged to the Panzer Reserve Abteilung at Bamberg.

I received fourteen days' convalescent leave, my first leave as a soldier. It was wonderful to be at home again and with pride I showed myself in town in the black panzer uniform with the Iron Cross. My father took me to his reserved table with his boon companions; it did me good to know that he was proud of me.

Back at the Reserve Abteilung in Bamberg I was given a Korporalschaft (sixteen recruits) to train. Since I had only spent a few days in a barracks with its very rigid daily programme, this duty was totally strange to me. I was much more a '*Frontschwein*' than a strict disciplinarian [Translator's Note (TN): In both World Wars a *Frontschwein* was a soldier who had served at the Front and been awarded the Iron Cross Second Class and the Wound Badge]. Therefore I had some difficulties. At New Year I had another six days free of duty and went home.

3

My Quiet Time in the Reich (February 1942 – January 1943)

On 25 February 1942 I reported as officer-applicant for the course being held in Berlin at the Panzer Troop School, Wünsdorf. The tutor attached to my class was Hauptmann Wollschläger of PzRgt 35, a close friend of my former commander von Cossel who knew of the events at Stary-Bychow. Therefore Wollschläger was well disposed towards me. I enjoyed the course although it was three months' slog, day and often night, under observation by countless instructors, senior NCOs and officers who judged whether one was 'up to the mark'.

I led the only infantry night exercise of the whole group of candidates (four classes), which brought me much praise. As a panzer man I had little knowledge of the infantry but spending the Easter holidays with my cousin Bernhard Schöne, a Hauptmann in the infantry, at his home in Berlin, he knew by heart not only the opening situations and the course of the exercise but also all orders I had to give as its commander. My personal contribution was that at the beginning of the exercise I had to hammer home as intensively as I could to the assembled group the particular significance of red, green and white flares to begin, end or suspend the exercise, and repeat myself over and over again. My course colleagues considered that I had treated them as being stupid and in the 'beer newspaper' at the end of the course composed a poem which ended: 'You Prussians always lay down the law, thoroughness will win the war!' (or words to that effect). I believe that in all my commands, even in the post-war Bundeswehr, I was similarly thorough (even pedantic) and never asked too much of my subordinates.

At the end of the course on 1 June 1942 all the candidates paraded on the exercise ground at 0900hrs. We were all promoted to Fahnenjunkerfeldwebel (officer cadet senior grade, sergeant rank). Then the best of the course were announced. I was completely surprised to be called forward first and received the prize for best in my class. After the ceremony we sat in our rooms sewing the sergeant's star on our uniforms. At 1100hrs we had to parade again, and now in a rather solemn ceremony 70 per cent of us were promoted to Leutnant. As the best in platoon my effective date was not 1 June 1942 but 1 February 1942 so that I had several months' seniority over my colleagues. The junior lieutenant's uniform hung in the locker: four weeks previously we had received our uniform purchase warrant and could now have our uniforms tailored. All active officers provided their own uniforms, receiving a one-off clothing payment and a monthly clothing allowance. Now we had to order jacket, long trousers, riding breeches, boots, greatcoat, cap, dagger and, if one wanted, a sabre. This had kept us and the tailors very busy in the next few weeks.

The following morning at 0700hrs buses arrived to transport us to the Sportpalast to hear an address by Hitler. The place was packed with all men from the Army, Luftwaffe and Kriegsmarine promoted to the equivalent rank of junior lieutenant with effect from 1 June 1942. We had to wait four long hours until the event began at midday. I was not impressed either by the 'entry' of the Führer, the introduction by Göring, nor Hitler's speech. The jubilation ordered was more mechanical than emotional. Although this was the first time I had seen Hitler in the flesh I was not stirred, I was simply happy to have achieved my first career goal, for there had been some stumbling-blocks even at Wünsdorf. In the evening, colleagues and I celebrated our promotions in the Hungaria Bar near the Gedächtniskirche until my train to Rastatt left at midnight. Eight days' 'operational leave'.

Subsequently I had to report back to the Panzer Reserve Abteilung at Bamberg, where I hoped that PzRgt 35 would soon request me. There was no rush, however, for the Abteilung liked to hold on to its young officers for several months in order to have youthful instructors. First of all I had to provide basic training to the recruits of 3 Company. This was pure infantry business. I say again: I liked nothing in the whole infantry bag of tricks. I could attempt to provide training which was more human and intelligent than what the barrack wallahs served up. I found the unnecessary grinding-down which I had myself experienced repugnant.

In Bamberg at that time a company had been formed as part of a new panzer battalion which was to be equipped with the newest German development, the Tiger. They were still at the prototype stage, but wonderful things were predicted of them. Weighing 58 tonnes, an 8.8cm gun, thick armour: almost a life assurance. The commander of this forming company was Hauptmann Lange, who was at liberty to choose his future personnel from the Reserve Abteilung. He asked me in the mess one day if I was interested. I was fixated on my old regiment, however, and wanted to go back to von Cossel, and so firmly declined his very interesting offer. But Lange had a hotline to the Army Personnel Bureau in Berlin and a few days later my transfer came though: to 2 Company/Heavy PzAbt 502. At the same time the formation of this company was moved from the barracks at Bamberg to the Fallingbostel troop depot on Lüneburg Heath. I arrived there at the end of June. Advanced detachments were also coming from other panzer garrisons so that in a short time Heavy PzAbt 502 was up to full strength in personnel in all its companies.

Our 2 Company had seven officers, and some Panzer IIIs for its Light Platoon but still no Tigers. As 'the youngest' I had to take over infantry training, for soldiers had always to be kept busy with something while we had no panzers. It was my task to provide four hours of purely theoretical instruction in shooting every week. It was not so developed then as it is today and after a while I ran out of things to say but somehow I stayed the course without looking a fool. My talks were certainly not dynamic and I confirmed to myself that I was better at the practical side than the theoretical.

From 21 July to 20 August 1942 I was in the military hospital at Bergen/Fallingbostel with volvulus and had to undergo a similar operation as the one two years before at Rastatt. I had convalescent leave until 30 September and spent it very pleasantly at home.

Meanwhile 1 Company had received their Tigers and the entire Abteilung bar 2 Company was transferred to the Leningrad front. There the first operational deployment of Tigers took place under very unfavourable circumstances. A crazy order was given for them to attack over a log road in heavy swamplands. Equally crazy was the intention of the Abteilung commander, Major Märker, to transfer 2 Company to the Abteilung on the Leningrad front even though it had no Tigers, and thereby complete the formation of PzAbt 502. The necessary order arrived at 2 Company and caused Hauptmann Lange, inferior in rank to Major Märker, no end of displeasure. The Abteilung had no fixed accommodation, being in the midst of woodlands, and so the company would have to excavate its own earth bunkers.

Hauptmann Lange sent me as a courier to the Abteilung on the Leningrad front in order to inform the commander orally that Lange was not disposed to carry out the order to transfer 2 Company, and also put it in writing. I took the most careful note of Lange's language so as to convey the message with the same urgency and brevity to Märker. I took the front leave train via Berlin for the three-day run to Krasnovardeisk, the last station on the German railway line near the outskirts of Leningrad. Major Märker let me make my report, but when he heard that

2 Company was not going to be transferred he interrupted me in a fury, repeated his order and threw me out of his bunker, not without having ordered me first to return forthwith to Fallingbostel in order to relay this order to Lange.

Thus I was at the Leningrad front for two hours and now returning to the Reich, this time a five-hour run in a convoy of lorries passing through dangerous partisan country, then a flight (my first ever!) in a Ju 52 from Pleskau to Riga. I had six hours there free to do some sightseeing, then caught the front leave train to Berlin. Hauptmann Lange laughed when I described Märker's reaction. He went to the telephone and spoke to the Army High Command in Berlin. Result: 2 Company was not transferred. We stayed at Fallingbostel.

In December 1942 rumours were rife that 2 Company would eventually be incorporated into the Waffen-SS because the PzRgt/SS-Leibstandarte *Adolf Hitler* was to receive an additional Tiger company. Since the reservoir of experienced panzer men in the SS at this stage of the war was not so large that an operational unit could be formed quickly, somebody remembered our 2 Company, which was at that time separated from its Abteilung at Fallingbostel. What could be better than simply to transfer this company of experienced panzer men into the SS, then the issue of Tiger panzers would follow much more quickly because SS units got preference in all matters of supply and equipment. The rumour was therefore based on a certain logic and there had been similar cases. Those who would have been affected were not consulted but thank heaven it did not come to that. Meanwhile the situation on the Eastern Front had come to a head. Two Soviet Army Groups had met up at Kalatsh after a wide pincer movement and encircled the Sixth Army at Stalingrad.

The panzer barracks at Bamberg in October 1941.

The author was not present at the front for the harsh winter of 1941. The photo shows gunnery training at the panzer firing range.

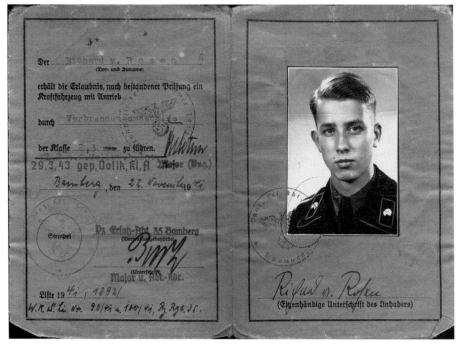

The inside pages of the author's driving licence. This replaced the original lost at
Stary-Bychow.

This grey type of driving licence made of layered cloth lasted into the 1990s.

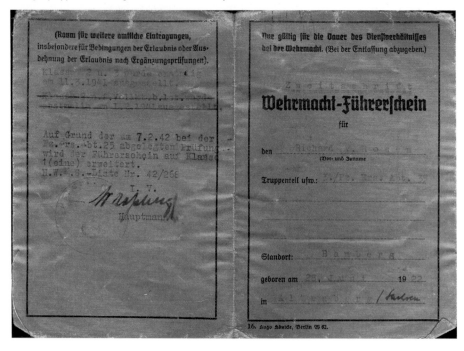

Hauptmann Wollschläger was the author's platoon leader on the officer selection course at the Panzer Troop School, Wünsdorf.

Hauptmann Wollschläger firing a carbine at 100m range standing.

Officer candidates at Wünsdorf. Like the author they were mostly of corporal rank with front experience.

Training panzers at Wünsdorf: far left a Panzer I, centre a command Panzer III with 3.7cm gun and frame aerial, behind it and to the right other Panzer IIIs with the short 5cm gun.

Setting off for an exercise in the countryside, here on a Panzer III with the short 5cm gun. The hull MG was removed for this exercise.

A Panzer III with a 3.7cm gun. The tactical symbol of the panzer troops, the rhombus, carries the suffix 'OAL' for Officer Applicants' Course.

Additional armour plates were riveted to this Panzer III but it remained hopelessly inferior to the Russian T-34 and from now on was only used for training purposes.

Hauptmann Wollschläger (centre with officer's cap and Knight's Cross) with officer-aspirants from II Platoon in which the author also served.

Group photo of the Inspection at Potsdam, April 1942: A = the author B = Hauptmann
Wollschläger C = Heigl.

Signatures on the reverse of the group photograph: 1 = Horny; 2 = Reinhard; 3 = Huber; 4 = Grauert; 5 = Desch; 6 = H. Pampel; 7 = W. Hellmann; 8 = Schoffer; 9 = Pavel; 10 = Langer; 11 = Ellenberger; 12 = Graf; Helldorff; 13 = Bergnet; 14 = Karl-Heinz Jammerath; 15 = Meents; 16 = Behrens; 17 = Kaut Otto (German Cross in Gold); 18 = Pamme; 19 = Helmut von Speil (German Cross in Gold); 20 = Jerney; 21 = Günther Löffler; 22 = R. Birkel; 23 = von Brockhausen; 24 = H. Schwarz; 25 = Horst Fortun (Knight's Cross and German Cross in Gold)

With Hauptmann
Wollschläger in Potsdam.

The author (far left) with other course participants near pioneer pontoons, spring 1942,
Wünsdorf.

Colleagues on the course
with the author.

Unteroffiziers Pamme
(left) and Graf Helldorff.

The author (right) with colleagues during an exercise discussion.

The author at rest during training, spring 1942.

The motto is 'Enjoy the spring sunshine': the hand-grenade throwing stand, Wünsdorf, spring 1942.

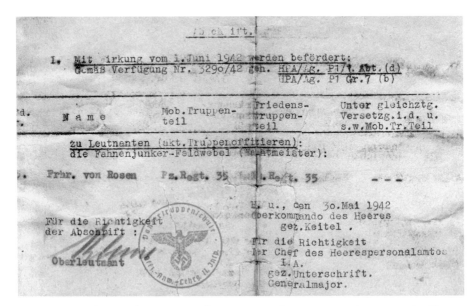

Entry in his *Soldbuch* (ID/paybook) confirms the author's promotion to Leutnant with effect from 1 June 1942.

The prize for best in class for II Platoon at the Panzer Troop School, Wünsdorf, was awarded on 29 May 1942 to the author. The note reads: 'For good performance during participation on the 9th Officer Applicant Course.'

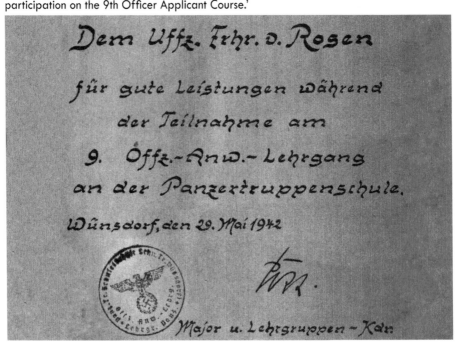

On 1 June 1942 the author was promoted to Fahnenjunkerfeldwebel (officer cadet senior grade, sergeant rank) and a few hours later to Leutnant.

Panzer IIs and IIIs arrayed in orderly columns on the large barrack square at Bergen/ Fallingbostel.

Dividing off for duty at Fallingbostel, 1942. In the centre in panzer uniform is Gotthold Wunderlich.

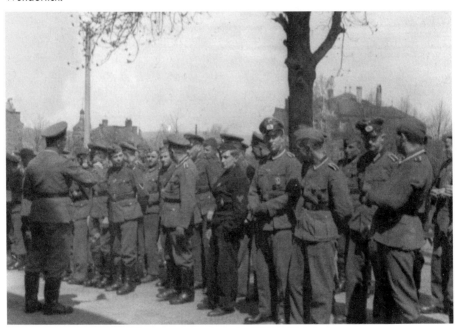

(left) Obergefreiter Edgar Elsner in front of a Panzer III bearing the insignia of a mammoth for Heavy PzAbt 502. The two forward MGs have not yet been mounted.

(below) Gefreiter Wunderlich (left) in front of a Panzer III with the long 5cm L/60 gun in September 1942. However, 2 Company later received the Panzer III-N with the short 7.5cm gun.

The mammoth insignia was even displayed in the accommodation block at Fallingbostel. At the window Oberfeldwebel an der Heiden, at the door Feldwebel Haase.

Commander, 2 Company/Heavy PzAbt 502 Eberhard Lange, awarded the German Cross in Gold on 13 May 1942.

In 1942 Oberleutnant Scherf was platoon leader, 2 Company/Heavy PzAbt 502, but is seen here in the summer of 1941 with officers recently awarded the Iron Cross Second Class.

Autumn 1942 at Fallingbostel. Platoon leader Oberleutnant Scherf announces a new duty arrangement.

Shortly before the departure for Russia at the end of December 1942, the first Tigers arrived from Kassel at 2 Company. Here a new Tiger, direct from the factory, with camouflage netting.

Ju 52 transport aircraft on a wintry airfield. The author made his first flight in such an aircraft.

4

Back to Russia (January–May 1943)

Eastern Campaign 1942/43
Army Group South
1942

28 May	Battle of Kharkov.
7 Jul	Conquest of the Crimea.
23 Jul	Capture of Rostov-on-Don.
19 Aug	Beginning of German attack on Stalingrad.
21 Aug	German flag raised on Mount Elbrus in the Caucasus.
19 Nov	Beginning of Soviet counter-offensive at Stalingrad.
20 Nov	Russians break through Romanian Fourth Army.
23 Nov	German Sixth Army surrounded (300,000 men).
12–21 Dec	German relief offensive.
22/23 Dec	Hitler vetoes breakout by Sixth Army.

1943

25 Jan	Stalingrad pocket split into northern and southern parts.
31 Jan	Southern pocket under Field Marshal Paulus surrenders.
2 Feb	Northern pocket capitulates.
14 Feb	Rostov evacuated.
To Mar	Winter defensive battles in the Mius-Don region.
5–16 Jul	Operation *Zitadelle*: last German offensive in the East.
5 Aug	Russians recapture Orel.
7 Sep	Stalino given up: loss of the Donetz Basin.
23 Oct	Soviets break through to the Lower Dnieper.
6 Nov	Soviets advance on Kiev.

Stalingrad was one of the greatest disasters in German military history, but it was not the only defeat of strategic dimensions: in November 1942 US troops had landed in strength in Morocco and Algeria: at the same time Rommel had been forced to retreat westwards with his army after El Alamein. These three events, together with the collapse of the U-boat war in the spring of 1943, were the military turning points of the Second World War. The war could no longer be won.

We were now to head to the Stalingrad front to take part in the relief offensive – as an independent company! While our Heavy PzAbt 502 was tied down on the Leningrad front in the north, we were attached to Army Group Don. As an independent company we needed additional signals, supply and workshop units which otherwise only existed in the Abteilung organization. What happened next was a masterpiece of organization by Army High Command. Within two days we received from all parts of the Reich a supply, transport, workshop and tank recovery platoon. The equipment came from one direction, the personnel from another. Within days the company grew from around 150 men to 500. At the same time the new Tigers came from the Henschel works at Kassel, a total of nine between 21 and 26 December. One Tiger for the company commander, two platoons each with four Tigers and a light platoon with eight Panzer IIIs made up the fighting component of the company. Each platoon had two officers, I was half-platoon leader in Oberleutnant Scherf's I Platoon. This generous allocation to the Tiger company would not last long, however, for coming events reduced the number of officers and we received no replacements.

When one reads all this, perhaps it is possible to imagine what feverish activity consumed us in those days. The first railway transport left Fallingbostel station on 17 December 1942. On 24 December I was sent with a lorry and two men to a Saarbrücken foundry to fetch ice shoes for our panzer tracks. Christmas evening I spent in a tavern at Echternach, where they prepared for us a hare which we had run over in the street. I telephoned home and so had contact with my parents. People today will hardly understand how difficult this was then. One could not dial a trunk call. At that time in most towns one could dial a number direct, but a trunk call had to be connected up from one exchange and often through various others. This could easily take hours. A call could be booked as 'urgent', but then it cost double: the 'blitz' call was ten times dearer. In the latter case one could be connected within ten minutes. Probably my call unsettled my parents more than it pleased them, for they might have thought that I was calling from the front, from the place being most mentioned in the army bulletins: Stalingrad.

On the drive back along the Cologne–Hannover autobahn I relieved the exhausted driver during the night. There was thick fog, the headlamps were blacked out, so I saw virtually nothing. Driving was such hard work that I fell asleep for a few seconds. The lorry left the road and mounted the verge, the radiator colliding with a large signpost. The radiator withstood the impact but a mudguard was crushed inwards and the windscreen cracked. Now the cold kept us awake. On 26 December I got back to Fallingbostel in the early morning and got a rocket from the commander for the damage to the lorry, but before we began loading up, the workshop had repaired it.

My transport left Fallingbostel at five in the morning of 28 December 1942. In the cattle truck this time was a round iron stove and fuel for it. It was beautifully warm sitting right in front of it. Thank heavens there was a stop now and again when the steam locomotives (there were only stretches of electrified track in Bavaria and Saxony) had to stop for water and coal. Then one stretched one's legs and food would be served from the field kitchen lorries. Some people played marathon skat (I once played for twenty-four hours non-stop and lost a fortune), others dozed or slept. This kind of railway journey was certainly neither full of new things to see nor comfortable. If the train halted along an open stretch of track for signals, this would be used as a toilet stop, since there were no facilities on board. And this all in deepest winter. When the signals changed, the locomotive whistle blew and then generally the driver would allow enough time for trousers-up and scrambling back aboard. While on this subject I would mention that if there was a long run without a stop naturally this could be very unsettling and the business had to be conducted at the open door of the wagon. If the running board was icy, or the night was dark, or a tunnel came up suddenly, it was a dangerous operation but we quickly became used to it.

Although we were categorized as '*Blitztransport*' and had priority over all other traffic heading East, the journey went on for days. On New Year's Eve the train reached Gomel in White Russia. Here we had to change the panzer tracks. Our normal tracks were too broad for rail transport on central European stretches and so there were special wagons for Tigers which had the narrower 'Tiger tracks'. The changeover was done at Gomel. In the bitter cold and with the iced-over ramp it was difficult work for the crews. We did not see the New Year in and so it was a New Year's Eve I shall never forget. Three days later we arrived at Rostov-on-Don. The railway buildings and platforms were crammed with nervy Romanian soldiers, a stoic mass, few carrying weapons. They looked like an army on the run. German railwaymen advised that the Russians had broken through the Romanian lines again and now there was no end to their panic. The railway people said we should sit in our panzers for the rest of the journey. The Russians could break through anywhere and suddenly appear on the railway line. So we did what they said. The panzers were manned so that we could defend ourselves should it become necessary. It was bitterly cold in the panzer. It did not seem to us that we were setting out on a bright and joyful war despite the Superpanzers we had brought along.

On 6 January 1943 the train reached our destination at Proletarskaya on the edge of the Kalmuck steppe. Previously we had passed through Manytsch, the geographical border between Europe and Asia. That evening the entire company was assembled to be told that we were now attached to 17 PzDiv. Next morning we set off on a ten-and-a-half hour drive to the Kuberle sector, our future operational area. We formed part of PzRgt 39 and would work together with Panzer Company Sander of the regiment. It was steppe warfare with no fixed front on either side. Our objective was to seek out and destroy the enemy.

The operation began on 8 January 1943. It is not my intention to describe it even though I remember it well, but what happened straight away was something I had never experienced before. Towards evening on the first day we had to beat off an attack by Russian infantry supported by tanks. We were on fairly elevated ground and could see over the terrain before us for miles. In the distance I saw the black dots of an immense army of ants making its way towards us. Between them were larger black points: tanks. Two Russian infantry regiments, about 4,000 men with armoured support, were attacking us. We let them approach, destroyed the tanks and then went for the infantry, which began to dig in hastily. They were brave, one has to give them that. We couldn't force them to retreat and as darkness fell we pulled back because they would not leave their positions. In the action report it stated that we wiped out about 1,000 Russians. We lost a Panzer III which, without our being able to prevent it, as if intentionally, had headed ever deeper into the Russian lines and suddenly disappeared into the haze. We never heard from the five-man crew again. Furthermore we had three wounded and had to tend to Leutnant Forkel, who had a broken arm. We spent the night in the open, but never again: the temperature fell to -30ºC. In future the last operation of the day would be to occupy a village to spend the night in. If the Russians got there first, we attacked and ejected them. In that respect the Russians were no different from us. There were not too many villages in the steppe and so one had to make sure they were preserved and not destroyed. The owners would sleep on or around the stove, we on the floor or under the table. They were friendly people, the Kalmuks. Naturally they were suffering because of the war. Next day Leutnant Tauber fell. He was outside the panzer and was hit by small-arms fire.

We had many problems with our Tigers. They were new and had hardly been properly tested. We also had the impression that a lot of the problems could be attributed to sabotage at the production stage. Therefore we were fighting on two fronts, against the enemy and against technical difficulties. Our workshop had its work cut out to mend the damage.

Corps ordered that the battleworthy panzers of the company, three Tigers and seven Panzer IIIs, were to be placed under the command of Oberleutnant Scherf of 16 InfDiv (mot). We were then involved in several actions with long stretches of countryside in between. On 14 January the three Tigers were ordered to proceed west to Kamarov to relieve 16 InfDiv (mot) and then return to the company at Proletarskaya. The Panzer IIIs remained under the orders of Division. The relief of 16 InfDiv was more difficult than at first thought because a ridge with a strong Russian anti-tank position blocked the way. The three Tigers exchanged fire with the anti-tank guns, but there were more guns than we had previously identified. We received hits. Suddenly over the radio a shout from Scherf to me: 'Have shell damage, you take over!' I was perplexed. I had never been in such a situation before. Now it was up to me to take out the enemy guns. I reacted at once and radioed, 'Understood. Out,' and without further reflection: 'Rosen to 224: anti-tank gun on the ridge ahead. Go!' Naturally we never used names over the radio, but I cannot remember the cover names we used. And what a surprise for me: Panzer 224 set off at once. My own driver followed as fast as the terrain allowed and we reached the position on the ridge. To my great relief we did not come under fire: the Russians had run for it, leaving behind all their guns and some American jeeps which were now becoming an increasingly common sight here in the East. The attack had been a success, my first as commander! For me all my doubts were dispersed and now gradually I became an experienced platoon leader while a relationship of trust developed between my panzer men and myself: we could rely on each other. It lasted until the end of the war. Nothing now prevented the relief of 16 InfDiv. We had carried out our mission and the three Tigers were to make their way back to the company at Proletarskaya. I don't remember what the distance was. Maybe 30km?

It was reported that Tiger 224 had engine damage. It could not be started up and would have to be towed, a difficult job over so long a distance. Scherf told me that he would go on ahead to Company with his Tiger to inform the retrieval platoon and send them out towards me. With our radio equipment it was not possible to contact the company over such a distance. I was given the order to tow 224 as far as

I could, in an emergency I would have to blow it up. We needed to get a move on. After the division's troops had pulled out we were now alone in wide-open country and our route passed for the main part through No Man's Land. Scherf bustled: we attached the towing hawser and my platoon set off at a very reduced speed, as one can imagine. We could not make out the road, everything lay under a blanket of snow and the tracks in the snow could equally well have been made by Russian as German troops. While daylight remained I could see Scherf's Tiger tracks in front of us quite well but soon darkness fell and standing in the open turret hatch it was damned cold. Careful – if one's ungloved hand touched the armour, it stuck. From his seat the driver could see even less than I from the commander's position in the turret and so I had to talk him through it.

'Herr Leutnant, the engine is boiling, I have to stop,' he called up to me after a while. Damn, right in the middle of the steppe. There was damage to the fan, and our limited tools aboard did not extend to this kind of repair. The cooling water thermometer read over 100° while 80° was normal. We had to wait for the temperature to drop. After a quarter of an hour the driver reported that we could proceed. Now we had to go slower than before so as not to overtax the engine, then again: 'Engine too hot.' How were we going to cross the steppe like this? The moon rose. It became a little brighter and easier to see the tracks in the snow. The engine noise could probably be heard for miles in the stillness of the night, all the worse for the rhythm of turning off, waiting to cool, starting up again. These noises proclaimed that here was a lame duck, ripe for the taking. When the engine was switched off, we too listened out for noises, but all we heard was the howling of wolves. When we stopped, the loader lit the blowlamp which every panzer carried for pre-heating the engine. It was our only source of warmth. It sooted up and the sticky lamp-black got everywhere, especially on the skin. Freezing to death was, however, worse.

It began to get light. Where we were and how far we had to go to the nearest German positions we had no idea. I had no map. In any case our trail was not a road which might have appeared on a map. To my left on the horizon some black dots suddenly appeared, moving towards us – Russians? I watched them through binoculars: Russian horsemen (there were no Germans on horses here), twenty to thirty of them, who now halted and watched us. We had just made a stop to cool the engine: 'Gunner: turret three o'clock, riders, range 2,500m, HE shells, fire at will.' That was how it was ordered by the book: in this situation it was done a little less formally, but quicker. Three rounds into their midst and I saw them turn about and disappear into the countryside. We moved on and came to a small wooden bridge over a ditch. Because of drifting snow it was hardly noticeable. The panzer under tow went too far left, the driver failed to recognize the situation and slipped off the bridge into the ditch. On that smooth surface I could not pull him free with my panzer. Only recovery vehicles could help, with their winches they could retrieve even heavy vehicles such as this. So what now? I could not leave their crew here in No Man's Land. I did not trust myself to blow it up. Scherf had gone off to alert the retrieval platoon, but where was it? Thirteen hours had passed since we had separated. Depending on how the decision to destroy the panzer by explosives was viewed, as justified or premature, I would have one foot in a court martial. I took the five men of the crew into my panzer and we drove on. I was in luck. In the distance I saw vehicles and a white flare rose up, meaning these were our own troops. I responded with the same. Another ten minutes and we had met up. They were elements of 17 PzDiv, they knew about us, had expected us, contacted Division by radio and told me that our recovery vehicle was on its way to us. We drove back to the casualty in order to be on the spot for all eventualities, in case Russians surprised us, which in this vast territory was possible at any moment. Three tractors turned up in all, the job was not difficult and we went back to Proletarskaya in convoy, which took hours. Since Oberleutnant Scherf had left us, we had been on the move or at a standstill for exactly thirty hours. Hauptmann Lange greeted me, 'Well, that was a nice little trip across the boating lake.' It was clear to me from his reaction what an event it had actually been.

Meanwhile the hour had long passed when the men in the pocket at Stalingrad could have been rescued by means of a counter-offensive. The pressure on the pocket was already such that the units of the surrounded army no longer had the strength to break out (which Hitler in any case had expressly forbidden), and the available forces for a breakthrough to Stalingrad from the Kalmuck steppe were much too weak. Our company received orders to transfer in its entirety to Rostov. This city had to be held until all German troops falling back from the Caucasus had passed through.

Another, newly formed, Tiger Abteilung had also arrived in our sector in January, Heavy PzAbt 503, which had been formed in Austria and had two complete Tiger companies. After the end of the fighting on the Kalmuck steppe we were initially subordinated to this Abteilung and then, as its 3 Company, absorbed into it completely. So we lost our independence, the surplus supply units had to be given away and we were once again a normal company of about 150 men. All the same, behind the official designation 3 Company/Heavy PzAbt 503 we always added in parentheses (./502) and we kept our symbol, the mammoth, and never put the 503 symbol on our panzers. That was the case until the end of the war, although by then it was no longer 503 but '*Feldherrnhalle*', of which more later.

We had fixed quarters in Rostov until the beginning of February 1943 though without water, light and heating. These had to be improvised. The repair teams worked flat out and gradually got every panzer operational. From a radio panzer we got ourselves a medium-wave radio and now could receive the official German station. Its transmissions were continually jammed by the Russians. Suddenly we

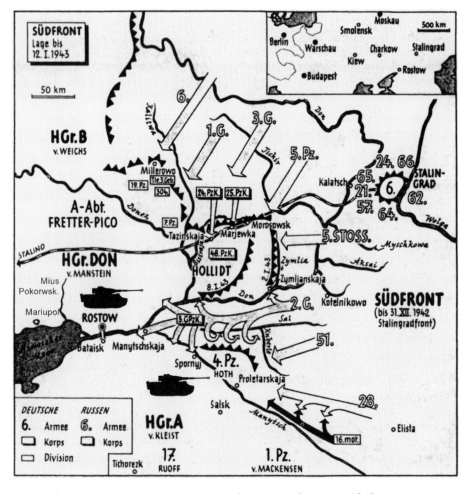

A view of the overall situation on the southern front up to 12 January 1943.

Shortly before Christmas 1942 several rail transports went to Gomel via Cracow and Minsk. There the battle tracks were changed in temperatures of -30°C. The railway journey continued via Kharkov and Rostov to Proletarskaya in the Kalmuck steppe where the Tigers were unloaded and given makeshift camouflage on 1 and 2 January 1943.

The flat, greyish-white Kalmuck steppe formed the battlefield for the company's first engagements. Counter-attacks stopped the Russians in various places.

Company commander
Hauptmann Lange of
2 Company/Heavy PzAbt
502 with his platoon
commander Walter
Scherf. From 14 January
1943, 2 Company/
Heavy PzAbt 502
was incorporated into
Heavy PzAbt 503 as
3 Company.

(above) Bearing
makeshift camouflage of
steppe grass, Panzer IIIs
and Tigers stand ready
near a Russian farmhouse.

(right) Hauptmann
Eberhard Lange and
Walter Scherf during a
halt on the icy Kalmuck
steppe in the winter of
1942. In the background
on the left is a Panzer III.

Our hosts: Kalmucks are very similar in appearance to Mongolians.

Hauptmann Lange orienting himself from his commander's hatch. The viewing slits already bear evidence of anti-tank rifle fire.

Platoon leader Scherf's driver, Gotthold Wunderlich, on a meal break. A good view here of the adjustable thick shutter mechanism of the driver's viewing slit. Above it can be seen the two emergency spyholes for use if the shutter has to be closed completely because of heavy enemy fire.

Platoon commander Walter Scherf, having exchanged his 700hp Tiger for a 1hp steppe pony.

Tiger 211, with Feldwebel Fritz Müller in the turret, has a hit on its 'mammoth' symbol. On the left is a Panzer III of the Light Platoon. The chalky colour has almost completely disappeared from the bodywork of this panzer.

(left) The old turret number of 2 Company/ Heavy PzAbt 502 was initially retained after the company was absorbed into Heavy PzAbt 503. Gotthold Wunderlich is sitting on the smoke projectors.

(below) I Platoon leader Oberleutnant Scherf with his crew during a halt. This Tiger has already lost a section of track cover.

Gotthold Wunderlich
(right) with comrades
by his Tiger. The semi-
circular hole in the track
cover was presumably a
step-up for boarding the
panzer.

A gutted factory at Proletarskaya served as the panzer workshop. In the foreground the
retrieved Tiger 224. Behind it an 18-tonne tractor and a Panzer III.

Tiger 213 being refuelled from 200-litre barrels. Peter Miederer and Günter Kuhnert are seated on the gun barrel. Taken near Rostov, early February 1943.

Tiger 211 with track damage. Individual track segments are laid up on the hull.

A column of Tigers of Heavy PzAbt 503 in a Russian village near Taganrog, spring 1943.

Tigers of 3 Company at a security stop. The forward Tiger still bears the turret number 224 and the mammoth symbol on the front plating.

Hauptmann Eberhard Lange being given a hearty send-off. Meanwhile 3 Company/Heavy PzAbt 503 has been created from 2 Company/Heavy PzAbt 502. Oberleutnant Scherf, Hauptmann Lange and the author Leutnant Freiherr von Rosen at Pokrovskoye, March 1943.

Carefree days in Pokrovskoye: Walter Scherf with the author.

Moving out, spring 1943, Ukraine. Behind the two Tigers are two Panzer IIIs. At the bridge is an Abteilung vehicle to monitor smooth passage.

After the award ceremony at Pokrovskoye for the Iron Cross First Class: from the left, Gotthold Wunderlich, Karl Heinz Jammerath, Peter Miederer, Heinz Gärtner, Rot and Fritz Müller. Hauptmann Lange is seated.

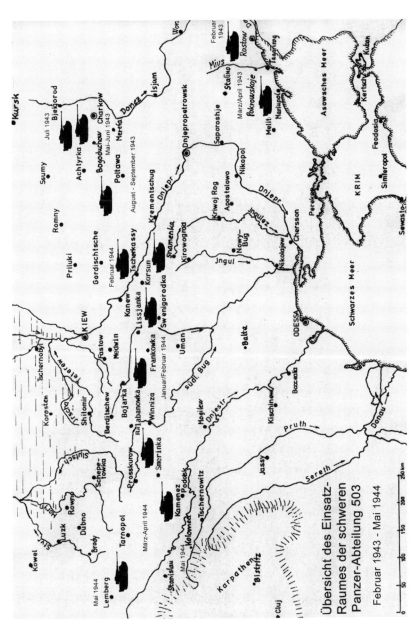

Operational area of Heavy PzAbt 503 from February 1943 to May 1944 (reading from far right, Rostov/Don, February 1943 to far left, Lemberg, May 1944).

heard in sonorous tones: 'Stalingrad – mass grave, Stalingrad – mass grave.' Every day the Wehrmacht High Command transmitted its bulletins. Especially in times of crisis this tended to be ambiguous, but if you read between the lines you saw that the situation in the south of the Eastern Front and especially around Stalingrad was catastrophic.

How did we get news in those days? Before transistors, a radio set was equipped with valves and was relatively large. Front-line units would therefore not have one. Listening to radio news broadcasts – except for the official one – was therefore not possible. This meant that we were practically cut off from all sources of information beyond our immediate vicinity. We really did live in the 'Valley of the Ignorant'. This made it all the easier for rumours to blossom. One could pick up a lot in field post letters from home, but these were a long time in coming and had to first pass through the censor. We learned a lot from official channels, and through contact with the higher command authorities. We had contact with the Luftwaffe on Rostov airfield. It was from here that the supply aircraft took off for Stalingrad, but now there was little activity of that kind. The airmen told us that they couldn't land in Stalingrad any more, only parachute-drop their cargoes. The Russians had broken through and split up the pocket. The wounded couldn't be flown out. It must have been ghastly, what was happening there. On 2 February 1943 the last German resistance was extinguished. Several hundred thousand soldiers went into captivity. We knew that from the Luftwaffe. The events there affected us to the very core and our faith in the leadership suffered a heavy blow. Until then we had been certain that they would always find a way to get us out if we were cut off, surrounded or got ourselves into some other hopeless situation. This confidence had now been shattered. Sixth Army had been quite consciously and senselessly sacrificed. We often spoke about it and blamed the highest political leadership but also the military commanders, who had allowed the moment to slip away when the chance still existed to break out from Stalingrad and save thousands of our men. Stalingrad was a turning point in not only the military sense, but also the psychological one. Nothing would ever be as it was before.

On 8 February the whole Abteilung pulled out of Rostov. Parts of the city were already in Russian hands. For three whole days we warded off strong attacks and destroyed many of their tanks, including some American types. Then my own panzer had radiator damage and needed attention at the workshop, which had no fixed location during the retreat. I received the order to get all damaged Tigers to the workshop and arrived at Taganrog on the Sea of Azov two days later with a convoy of five Tigers and ten tractors. The journey was very difficult because the Rollbahn crossed many sections of iced-over gulches. At Taganrog I requested special railway wagons which appeared as if by a miracle and I loaded up my fighting force. We left Taganrog station on the last train out, destination unknown. The transport commander had no idea what to do with us in the confusion of the retreat. The Russians had pushed very far forward and broken into the Donetz Basin, the great industrial conurbation of the Soviet Union. The permanent way was broken in many places, so I could not transport my panzers back. I succeeded in contacting the Abteilung through Corps at Stalino. The workshop was being moved to Mariupol, and I headed there. Left to our own devices, we helped ourselves to food from poorly guarded provisions trains and compounds and so did not live badly on the way there.

At Mariupol the panzers were dealt with in descending order, depending on the seriousness of the damage, and so I got my panzer back after ten days' stay at the workshop. I finally left with this vehicle at the beginning of March 1943 and set off for my company which was occupying a collective farm behind the Mius front. A few days before, the Abteilung had wiped out a Russian tank corps which had broken through the Mius position.

After a few days the company was transferred to Pokrovskoye on the Mius, about 20km east of Taganrog. Here we stayed six weeks expecting a Russian attack. Besides vehicle care we had the usual duties but also reconnoitred the entire area which included regular visits to the infantry in the front-line trenches. Frequently very senior officers came to look over our Tigers. In the evening I often sat with the commander and played skat, which usually involved me in heavy losses. Meanwhile the period of mud had arrived and the Mius thawed. The company got wonderful pike, perch and carp from a fisherman. We watched a film, *Wir machen Musik* with Ilse Werner, and the whole time we indulged ourselves with alcohol.

At that time Hauptmann Lange was transferred back to Germany with heart and liver complaints and Oberleutnant Scherf, who had commanded I Platoon until then, was made company commander. Leutnant Weinert received I Platoon, I got II Platoon and Oberfeldwebel an der Heiden got III Platoon with the Panzer IIIs. Also at Pokrovskoye we received Russian volunteers ('Hiwis') who stayed with us loyally until the end of the war. According to an edict from Army High Command, 'Hiwis' were to replace as many German soldiers as possible in the supply services. 'Hiwis' wore German uniform without insignia, received pay appropriate to their grade and carried out duties not requiring a weapon. Scherf gave me instructions to recruit as many of them as I could. I placed my requirements before the local mayor, who was not very taken with the idea, but within an hour a young man reported to me. He spoke good German and wanted to accompany us. Alex hated the Soviets. He was given a uniform, the same issue of clothing as ourselves, a week's pay, evening rations with cigarettes and was happy. In his new gear he strutted up and down the village street, admired by the local beauties, of which there were quite a few. Alex could be very useful to us as an interpreter. He rode in the sidecar of one of our dispatch riders, Gefreiter Reichmann, the pair of them becoming an inseparable team. Later Alex got himself a Russian sub-machine gun because he did not like being unarmed. Next day, encouraged by Alex, another ten young men came forward for their uniform, pay and cigarettes. I chose six of them, a tailor, a cobbler and four men for the fuel detail. When we withdrew from the Mius region in April 1943 and the Russians occupied it later on, there was no going home for these 'Hiwis'. When leave was given out, all our Russians were taken by men of our company to stay with their families in Germany. We did what we could to lessen the burden of their fate and for us they became members of our company.

On Easter Sunday we received orders to move out. The entire Abteilung was transferred to the Belgorod area, about 60km north of Kharkov. This came with rumours of a new German offensive for the spring of 1943. I was advance-party leader for the Abteilung and had to arrange parking for all the companies who would be arriving the next day. No 3 Company was given a very beautiful wood just coming into leaf. Each crew put up a tent and settled in as best they could. The days were filled with technical work. After the long journey there was plenty to do, the panzer tracks in particular needing attention, and furthermore things had to be readied for the imminent operation. The territory and roads to the front, which ran about 30km along the Donetz, had to be scouted and all commanders given a most exact picture. I reconnoitred personally the possibilities of crossing the Donetz at the Belgorod bridgehead. Day and night huge convoys drove along the nearby Kharkov–Belgorod Rollbahn. Almost all SS divisions were represented. Grass airstrips had been laid out all around for the Luftwaffe, heavy Flak in emplacements everywhere to cover the massive advance. The Russians made a few bombing raids by day and often at night but were not very successful.

Meanwhile new Tigers had arrived for my Abteilung from Germany which now had to be unloaded and transferred to the companies. A great amount of work was required to get these panzers operational, some being already damaged, and this took several days. Each company now had fourteen Tigers, the Abteilung as

An impressive photograph of an advance in the spring of 1943. In the background are several Panzer III Ns, a 1-tonne tractor, VW Kübelwagen and motorcycles. The Tiger is climbing a steep slope in order to detour around a doubtful bridge. The tracks left by its predecessor can be clearly seen. The Panzer IIIs want to try the bridge anyway and are turning back to the Rollbahn.

Tiger 324 with engine trouble under repair in a village street at Mariupol.

(left) Oberleutnant Scherf sharing experiences with the author during a meal at Bogoduchov. Taken at Easter 1943, the sun is shining but the trees are bare.

(below) The special Reichsbahn low-loaders for Tiger transport known as 'Ssyms' required extra-narrow tracks for transport within the Reich. In Russia they were not needed because the railway line had sufficient space for trains to pass.

The author's Tiger 313 at Pokrovskoye camouflaged with straw. From left to right: (seated) Edgar Eisner and Günther Kuhnert, (standing) Leutnant von Rosen, Rothemann and Rolf Matthes.

Leutnant Jammerath, 1 Company Light Platoon commander, abandoned the Panzer III Ns at Bogoduchov on account of their having too many breakdowns on operations with Tigers. From the end of April 1943, the three companies were equipped exclusively with Tigers.

In the woods at Tolokonoye at the beginning of May 1943: Oberleutnant Scherf, Leutnant von Rosen and Hauptfeldwebel Haase stand ready for a celebratory swig from the bottle in the hand of Kisseberth, the newly appointed Hauptfeldwebel of 3 Company.

The crew of the author's Tiger 321 at Tolokonoye, spring 1943. Left to right: Gefreiter Spiekermann and Gefreiter Werkmeister, Leutnant von Rosen, Unteroffizier Fuhrmeister and Unteroffizier Ziegler.

At their stations on Tiger 321: radio operator Hans Spiekermann, loader Ludwig Werkmeister, commander Leutnant von Rosen, driver Adolf Ziegler and gunner Franz Fuhrmeister.

The woods at Tolokonoye east of Kharkov in daylight, Oberleutnant Scherf giving his orders. To the left is a BMW-R75 motorcycle combination, to the right a long overdue shampoo.

Oberleutnant Scherf distributing orders in the woods at Tolokonoye to Leutnant von Rosen, Hauptfeldwebel Rondorf, Oberschirrmeister Krex and Oberfeldwebel an der Heiden.

Hauptmann Clemens Graf von Kageneck, Abteilung commander from June 1943 to January 1944. Knight's Cross 7 August 1944, Oak Leaves 26 June 1944.

In April 1943 the author visited his cousin Oberst von Rosen, 1 General Staff Officer of an Army Corps.

May 1943, and although it is springtime a cold wind blows across the fields where guns are being calibrated.

a whole forty-five. We had given away the remainder of our Panzer IIIs. Besides the work we spent some very pleasant hours. Quite close by was a beautiful lake for bathing though the water was very cold. Reasons for festivities were sought and found. We had several promotions to celebrate, for which the commander always released plenty of alcohol. Those who over-celebrated could sleep it off in the open. At this time there occurred a change of 'Spiess'. The former CSM had volunteered to command a Tiger, and Stabsfeldwebel Kisseberth took over from him. This was all properly celebrated. Every evening I arranged for the company band, consisting of two accordions, a violin and a drum, to give a concert which the whole company would attend. It was a very pleasant camp life. To enhance our living conditions I held a competition for my platoon. The crew which set up the best tent and surroundings would receive a bottle of cognac. All crews worked at it for two days until I awarded the prize to Panzer 323. My platoon had rigged up tables, benches, washing facilities, lighting and much more in the short time allowed. Every day we awaited the order to commence the operation, the fire fuelled by the craziest rumours. But nobody knew anything definite. At the beginning of May I discovered that the planned offensive had been postponed for several weeks and the Abteilung would be returning to Kharkov.

The company was kept in the dark about it all. I went as the advance-party leader to Kharkov to set up quarters. The lodgings were very nice, each panzer crew having its own little house. In my house were three adjoining rooms, one for me, the second for the Unteroffiziers Fuhrmeister and Ziegler, and the third for Obergefreiters Spiekermann and Werkmeister. I had a beautiful room with a writing desk, sofa and white bed. The billeting people were very attentive towards me; after the primitive experiences of the past I could ask for nothing more. The commander had the best quarters, a living room with piano and a bedroom. This was the venue for our larger festivities to which the officers of the other companies were invited and which generally ended in the early hours. The longer these parties went on, however, the more important it was that the next day should start punctually.

The company often had the opportunity to visit the theatre or cinema. I saw an excellent performance of the *Gypsy Baron* by Ukrainian actors, though never understanding a word of it. I spent a lot of time in my VW searching out additional sources of food for the company and so got to know Kharkov and its surrounding districts with all its collective farms and stores intimately. Of all the Russian cities of over a million inhabitants that I saw, this was the one I liked best. The city centre today is just as it was before the war. Small, single-storey houses mostly brick-built and embellished with carved work. Only a few districts had suffered badly from the earlier fighting. The city centre was fully European, some parts positively American! The buildings were very impressive. The city streets were broad and clean, trams and trolleybus routes went everywhere. Large department stores were to be found alongside concert cafés in which anything could be ordered, from pure coffee to whipped cream, but at what a price! My gunner came back one evening having spent 40 Reichsmarks. What was really surprising was how quickly the citizens of Kharkov had adjusted to the new situation. Everywhere, German advertisements were to be found alongside Russian posters. Commerce flourished and exceeded that of a German city in peacetime.

We had a change of commander: Hauptmann Graf Kageneck brought dash and refinement to the Abteilung. We would go through fire for him. We knew meanwhile that Operation *Zitadelle* was planned, but not the date. We were also advised that in the coming operation the Abteilung would not work as an integrated unit. No 1 Company would be subordinated to 6 PzDiv, 2 Company to 19 PzDiv and our 3 Company to 7 PzDiv.

The pace of everything was stepped up. Once the panzers were in shape we had panzer battle instruction, lessons in tactics and exercises. Twice a week in the afternoon we had officers' training with map exercises or conferences about the terrain. The platoons went daily to the environs of the city in order to complete their own training. Great activity prevailed in the Tiger driving schools from where the greatest possible numbers of panzer drivers had to be obtained. In places the terrain around the city was very difficult and made great demands on the drivers. I had to take charge of driver training, Oberleutnant Scherf convinced himself now and again of the progress being made. At that time the Tiger and its capabilities were fairly unfamiliar to the men in the field.

To illustrate this and other new weapons 7 PzDiv, to which 3 Company belonged, held a demonstration before an audience of illustrious spectators. All commanders from the divisions, regiments and Abteilungen of the corps were ordered to attend. With my platoon I had to pass through a swampy area which had been made passable by a log road made by pioneers of the grenadier regiment. Would it withstand our 58-tonners? I led my platoon safely over this log road with its tree trunks but by the fourth Tiger things got very problematic. Next I had to lead our platoon down a woodland track. Seeing a large group of spectators standing either side, I suspected that this was where the next event was to happen, and I was right: suddenly smoke bombs with tear gas were hurled by grenadiers at my panzer from both sides. Turret hatch shut. 'Gas masks on!' An unpleasant acrid dense smoke filled the interior, enshrouding the driver. I ordered him to go full ahead and directed our vehicle out of the woods. It hadn't affected us much and we were still operational but the poor grenadiers caught some of the smoke.

The remainder of the exercise went off smoothly and we left behind a very good impression. We had practical gunnery training on the nearby front at Chugyev on the Donetz. I and my platoon were subordinated to one of the infantry divisions there for three days. We fired from three different spots as ordered by the sector commanders at the easy-to-hit Russian positions on the forward slope. The infantry was extremely grateful to us: now they would have some peace for a while. As confirmed by the infantrymen, my platoon destroyed around sixty bunkers, anti-tank gun and mortar emplacements. My platoon had one man slightly wounded. We considered the whole thing as light entertainment.

Towards the end of our time in Kharkov I got to know a German farm manager who was in charge of a collective farm nearby. I had come across this collective farm in my search for fresh vegetables and potatoes for our field kitchen – we received only the dried type, which we had had up to here. When he heard my surname he told me that there was a Russian family called Rosen in Kharkov which came from an old line of nobility. He said he would look up the address so that I could research further. I knew that there was a branch of the Rosen line which my family had lost contact with since the Russian Revolution. I knew from the family history that a certain Andreas had lived in the Kharkov area, but the sudden order to move out prevented me from making further enquiries.

(right) Driver Gotthold Wunderlich (right) has run his Tiger up a slope. The photo shows the broad tracks clearly. The floor of the Tiger hull was only very lightly armoured and in action such a manoeuvre would have been highly inadvisable.

(below) An interesting collection of signs at a Kharkov crossroads. To the right of 'Entlausung' (delousing) are pointers to important places through where Atb 503 passed, such as Bogoduchov, Merefa and Poltava. The pointer above Merefa indicates where to find the quarters of 3 Company/Heavy PzAtb 503.

(above) The famous Red Square in Kharkov, Ukraine. This photo was taken in the 1930s. The very modern concrete high-rise buildings impressed even the many German infantrymen who passed through the city.

(left) From about 10 March 1943 the Abteilung returned to Kharkov city from the woods at Tolokonoye. The column crossed the broad plains of the Ukraine.

(right) A Tiger of the Abteilung under inspection by the repair group at Kharkov.

(below) A Russian T-34-76 tank wrecked and minus tracks during the fighting in the spring of 1943 when Tiger Abteilung 503 was at the Mius.

In preparation for Operation *Zitadelle*, Peter Miederer's Tiger 323 had to ford a tributary of the Donetz. The three officers (left to right) are Oberleutnant Scherf, Oberschirrmeister (senior motor pool intendant) Krex and Leutnant von Rosen.

Oberleutnant Scherf (left) and Leutnant von Rosen look on as the exercise begins.

The water level is low and the Tiger crosses the river safely.

The massive Tiger climbing the slope from the river bed.

During the exercise while attached to 7 PzDiv in June 1943, Leutnant von Rosen can be seen in the commander's turret of Tiger 321 as it rolls out of woodland and down an incline towards a swamp where pioneers have laid a log road.

7 PzDiv pioneers straightening up the log road for the next panzer already approaching from the woods. The author is seen here with his hands on his hips.

The second Tiger completing its negotiation of the log road. Pioneers stand clear just in case while the author watches the Tiger roll towards him.

On 5 June 1943 south of Kharkov a major exercise was held by 7 PzDiv in which 3 Company/ Heavy PzAbt 503 was involved. Generalleutnant Werner Kempf and many other officers including Luftwaffe observers were present.

The author's Tiger 321 served as a target for infantry training in close combat against tanks. Grenadiers have just hurled new-type smoke and tear-gas grenades at the rear of the panzer.

Dense, acrid smoke got into the panzer through every crack. Leutnant von Rosen's arm can be seen just prior to closing the turret hatch.

Summer 1943. During a transfer journey Tiger 332 has bogged down in swampy ground.

Tiger 332 being towed from the swamp by 321 and 331. The Tigers' tracks have meanwhile churned up the entire area.

Pioneers have erected a bridge from freshly sawn logs. Tiger 331 is now testing its weight-bearing capacity. In the left of the picture is 332, still stuck fast.

A Tiger being resupplied by an Abteilung lorry. Two 18-tonne FAMO tractors of the recovery platoon can be seen approaching along the street: on the left is a light ammunition carrier of an SP assault gun unit.

Oberleutnant Scherf's Tiger 300 during a halt. Sitting on the panzer, left to right: unknown comrade, Gotthold Wunderlich, Fritz Müller and Josef Weiland. On the motorcycle combinations, left to right: dispatch rider Bechtel, 'Hiwi' Alex and Reichmann.

Oberleutnant Scherf now in 323. The track cover shows damage.

On 27 June 1943 a Turkish delegation visited and were shown the new Tigers. Generalfeldmarschall von Manstein (foreground) was not satisfied with the gunnery performance. Left of him is General von Funck commanding 7 PzDiv. The Turkish generals are the officers in the lighter-coloured uniforms.

Oberleutnant Scherf displaying Tiger 300, which has just fired a round, hence the smoke.

Tiger 333 with crew on the turret. To the left is 332. The 'Turkish Exercise' took place on 27 June 1943 in the area between Kharkov and Chuguyev. The Battle of Kursk began a few days later.

Tiger 313 demonstrating the crossing of an anti-tank ditch for the Turkish delegation. Manstein (with sunglasses) stands beside the Turkish officers. The gun is at 6 o'clock, all hatches are being shut. The stowage box can be clearly seen. Oberleutnant Scherf is on the far right in the photo.

5

Operation *Zitadelle* (June–July 1943)

At the beginning of June I received my orders for the coming operation. From the beginning of the attack my II Platoon would be attached to Panzer-Grenadier Rgt 7/7 PzDiv. This regiment was to cross the Donetz using inflatable boats and establish a bridgehead on the enemy bank. For lack of a bridge, my platoon of Tigers would have to ford the river and support the regiment's attack.

For this purpose I was to make immediate contact with the foremost elements right on the Donetz in the sector they occupied south of Belgorod, and we were to reconnoitre together for a suitable place for my Tigers to cross. It was a beautiful summer's day when I arrived. From an observation post well forward I had a view over the downward slope to the Donetz, the two river banks, both bushy and overgrown, and the gentle rise of the land on the far bank where the Russians had their front-line positions and were dug in. At the river itself there were only a few German outposts and so we assumed the same for the Russian side but naturally nothing was known for sure. Towards evening the commander of XXV Panzer-Pioneer Platoon, Oberfeldwebel Baumann and two corporals, reported to me; they would be leading the necessary pioneer part of the operation.

When it was dark and the moon hidden by cloud, we went with a panzer-grenadier scouting party down the kilometre or so to the river's edge. No sound could be heard but the murmur of the waters: the Russian side was as silent as the grave. The high undergrowth was favourable for an approach to the river bank. I took a good look at it: it stood vertical about a metre and a half above the water. If the far bank was the same, mounting it from out of the water would be difficult. Now we had to measure the depth of the water and the suitability of the river bed for a 58-tonne Tiger. In the opinion of the grenadiers, who had been here a week, this was the shallowest part in the entire sector. I got undressed and the grenadiers took up positions along the river bank. I listened out for any activity on the Russian side and then slipped into the water, only 1.5m deep. The waters flowed past calmly and I waded, only my head above water, to the other bank. The river bed was firm and not muddy but the bank on the other side was as steep as our own. Furthermore, the bank fell almost vertically for about 2.5m. The Tigers could not manage that.

I regained our side of the Donetz, was pulled out and helped up and then we held a conference in the cover of the bushes. Oberfeldwebel Baumann, the pioneer, saw no great difficulty in flattening the river banks with explosives to make it negotiable for the Tigers. The bed of the river itself and the depth of water did not present us with a problem. Back at the panzer-grenadiers' command post we were served hot tea and then the plan for crossing the Donetz was agreed upon. I returned to Kharkov that night in good humour. Our task was now clear, but what remained unknown was the date when it would all start.

28 June 1943 was my 21st birthday and I had come of age. Oberleutnant Scherf handed me a certificate confirming this fact. In the evening we had something of a banquet with much alcohol flowing, attended even by our new Abteilung commander, Major Graf Kageneck. My parents told me in a letter that they had sent me two blackcurrant cakes and two cheesecakes: I cannot remember what else there was to eat but it would certainly not have been just soldiers' rations.

A few days later we were informed that the attack would begin on 5 July. The Russians in Kharkov had already told us that three weeks earlier. On 1 July the Abteilung moved back to a readiness area 30km south of Belgorod which we had occupied before we got to Kharkov. The arrival of the newest German panzer, the Panther, was awaited. None of this would come as a surprise to the enemy: since the beginning of March he would naturally have been well informed of the forward progress of the German forces, from which he would not have found it difficult to predict their intentions.

The projection of his front line either side of Kursk offered the chance of a pincer attack which would not only shorten the German front line by 150km, but also isolate a large part of his operational forces at the border between the central and southern front. It was clear to us that the Russians had used the time to expand their defensive positions. They had also brought up reserves and so we knew that the operation was not going to be easy. Moreover, we had not anticipated the extent of the expansion of the defences. They had made great strides in the training of their officers and men, and we would discover that the Russian soldier we would face was no longer the man of 1941–2, but a soldier our equal in fighting efficiency and morale.

On the day before the attack the company moved out at around 1800hrs and headed towards Belgorod where a readiness area was occupied behind the companies of Panzer-Grenadier Rgt 7. The four panzers of my II Platoon drove further on to join the advanced elements of Rgt 7. As some weeks previously, I stood at the edge of the woods above the gentle downward slope to the Donetz. Oberfeldwebel Baumann arrived with his panzer-pioneer platoon and now we waited. My men slept in the panzer, which I would like to have done as well, but the responsibility of being the 'can opener' for the panzer units following up put a heavy burden on my shoulders.

The next morning, at 0415hrs on 5 July, a forty-minute period of softening-up by artillery and Luftwaffe heralded the attack in our sector. The men of Panzer-Grenadier Rgts 6 and 7, and Oberfeldwebel Baumann's pioneers, went down quickly to the Donetz. While the first inflatable boats were crossing, the pioneers prepared the explosive charges to reduce the height of the fording points on the river banks. Our engines were warm, the crews in their positions, the radio plugged in: we awaited the signal to go. From beyond the far bank we heard the first sounds of fighting: the rattle of MGs, the rumble of Russian mortars and artillery – in the pale light of dawn the mushroom-clouds of smoke from impacting shells were visible. Finally the signal came: two green flares from Oberfeldwebel Baumann told us that the demolition charges had been laid.

Panzer Marsch! Flat out we crossed the open terrain and in full view of the enemy headed for the fording point. The order in which my four panzers would cross the river and where the others would wait had been set down precisely. Baumann confirmed 'all clear' with a movement of his hand. We manoeuvred down the reduced slope at slow speed, went into the water, motored across to the other bank and began the climb out. The explosion had loosened the earth considerably and the surge of water forced back towards the bank by the bow of the panzer clogged the bankside with mud. As my panzer began to climb up out of the river, the tracks had no firm ground to grip and slipped round. A second attempt was equally unsuccessful, and now we began to receive mortar fire uncomfortably close. This was not good. I reported by radio the failure of the fording attempt and received the order to remain where I was with my platoon.

Soon the commander of the pioneer battalion appeared. He had orders to erect a bridge with a capacity of 60 tonnes near my fording points. My job was to protect the pioneers, for a Russian counter-attack was possible. First I had to get my panzer ashore again on our side of the river. Feldwebel Weigel's Tiger 324 had to tow my vehicle up the bank. His gunner, Unteroffizier Jäckel, carried out the very arduous task of attaching the towing hawser to the rear of my panzer, for the coupling hooks were under water and difficult to release. We were obliged to stand chest-high in water for this work while subjected to Russian harassing fire. It succeeded, the panzer was towed out and now we positioned ourselves at the bridge-building point where meanwhile the first pioneer vehicles had arrived. It was calculated that it would take five hours to build the bridge, during which time the panzer-grenadiers would have no tank support.

Soon the first wounded came back in the inflatable boats. They were not friendly greetings they shouted at us. The Russian resistance was strong and well organized, the two attacking panzer-grenadier regiments has sustained many casualties and were making only slow progress. For us the waiting at the river was almost insufferable. Constant mortar fire – we felt sorry for the pioneers working without cover. Additionally it was getting hotter, and the air in the panzer, where we were condemned to inactivity, ever stuffier. I don't know exactly when they finished the bridge, it must have been around 1400hrs. Start up and drive across the bridge and through the territory which the grenadiers had overcome during the morning. I reached the railway line, crossed it near Razumnoe station and found the command post of Panzer-Grenadier Rgt 7. The foremost Russian defensive position, which had held up our grenadiers for so long, was right here at the railway line. Short situation report using a map, brief instructions to my panzer commanders and we set off.

We reached the leading grenadier companies and were involved in bitter fighting the whole afternoon. The Russians had built a deep-layered defensive system with earth bunkers and anti-tank guns, superbly camouflaged and therefore difficult to spot. The grenadiers heaved a sigh of relief that they had us to get this enemy off their backs, as they already had enough to do dealing with Red infantry in countless foxholes and MG nests which had to be winkled out in hand-to-hand fighting. Here we could be of little assistance, for the Russians allowed our panzers to trundle over their holes and then they appeared in front of the grenadiers coming up behind us with all the more determination.

We fired only HE shells: I cannot remember seeing an enemy tank on this first day. When darkness fell we came away from the road and received from Company Tross fuel, ammunition and rations. During the night I received my orders for the next day.

Oberleutnant Scherf had crossed the Donetz bridge immediately behind my platoon, leading Platoons I and III. He had fought in the Panzer-Grenadier Rgt 6 area which lay on the left flank of Rgt 7 and therefore had had the strongly fortified and very bitterly defended village of Razumnoe on his left flank to contend with. I have the impression that the Russian defence on the outskirts of this village was more determined than I have just described for my own area with Panzer-Grenadier Rgt 7. The entire attack on this first day took place after crossing the Donetz in the valley of the Razumnoe river. This area was very difficult to survey: many bushes and much shrubbery reduced vision, while stagnant waters and numerous swamps canalized the action.

The battle area of Panzer-Grenadier Rgt 7 was bordered to the right by a steep rugged range of hills. The strongly defended town of Krutoi Log lay on the plateau of the latter. The 7 PzDiv attack was to have been continued against it. The difference in height was about 50m and there were only a few tracks rising steeply upwards from out of the valley. During the night the grenadiers captured a track by use of which VII Reconnaissance Abteilung secured a small bridgehead on the plateau as a starting point for future attacks.

On 6 July I was subordinated directly with my II Platoon to PzRgt 25 and was given their radio codes, which changed daily. My orders were to reach the plateau in the early morning using the track cleared by the grenadiers and there expand the bridgehead to the north and east so that PzRgt 25 following up could take it over for their jumping-off point to attack. Then, upon receiving the order, we would return and together with the spearhead company of PzRgt 25 break through the defensive position thought to be there and carry forward the attack into the hinterland, passing Batratskala Dacha.

The climb to the plateau was difficult but passed off without breakdowns. We assumed battle formation and, initially without coming across the enemy, headed in the direction ordered. On the horizon about 3km away I made out a broad area of woodland across my line of advance. I felt uneasy about it and we approached slowly, then I had my platoon halt to wait for PzReg 25 behind me to catch up. I opened my turret hatch and saw that I was directly alongside a foxhole from where a Red Army soldier looked up at me in fear. I beckoned him to come up and then make his way to the rear. He made no move. I drew my pistol and repeated my hand movements, making clear to him what he had to do. No reaction. I fired a round near the foxhole to reinforce my order. No reaction. Then I took a hand grenade, pulled out the pin and threw it down. The Russian picked it up and threw it back at the panzer. In the face of such courage I drove forward 50m. He would have been captured by the grenadiers following later. I have no idea how long we remained stationary there. The ascent from the Razumnoe valley to the plateau took the panzer regiment some time, for the access route was not without its problems.

When I Abteilung had arrived and taken up its attack positions, I received the radio message to advance. About thirty to forty Panzer IIIs and IVs were behind my platoon. What was behind them I do not know, but I assume it was Panzer-Grenadier Rgt 7. Everything before all this had been a mere prelude. The opposition we were about to encounter was something we had never experienced before. Our panzers set off again and approached the wood. There was no way through it except through a glade to the right which forced us to close up but there was no alternative. Therefore we drove towards the glade, to the left it was about 500m to the wood, to the right a bit more, but it was also thick woodland there too. Suddenly we saw muzzle flashes, at first from the right, but not from standard anti-tank guns, whose flashes were different. Afterwards I established that they came from SU-152 self-propelled assault guns armed with a 152mm flat-trajectory howitzer which we had not previously come up against. They had a low profile and were therefore easy to camouflage but slow in reloading. My two Tigers of the right-hand group were in good form, engaged the enemy and shot better than the Russians. Black smoke rose up from the vehicles hit, but at the same moment the Russians opened up from the edge of the wood to the left – four, five, six muzzle flashes like a necklace of pearls. They seemed to be T-34s. We knocked out some of them and then felt our way cautiously forward. When we had the wood closer on both sides we received fire from the left again, but the right side was silent. My Tiger was hit, but the front armour was thick and thank heavens the tracks and wheels escaped damage.

I don't know for certain how many of them we finished off. It was unpleasant driving through the woodland glade, apparently the Russians had either not defended the wood in depth or we were going into a trap. We discovered later that their hidden anti-tank guns let us pass by without firing in order to get at the lighter-armoured Panzer IIIs and IVs behind us. Thus PzRgt 25 had some losses here. Our initially rapid advance now developed into a tough struggle through this deep-layered Russian defensive front. We were continually raked by fire from right and left. It was of some comfort for me that the tanks of PzRgt 25 were close behind. From the map I saw that we were coming to a ridge, or better still an extended rise, around which we had to detour in order to maintain the direction of advance. We kept going, the glade broadened out and I saw the rise before me about 2km ahead. I was just thinking that we were through the defensive positions when more than twenty barrels flashed from countless anti-tank guns dug in on the forward slope of the rise. It was not possible to determine at first whether they had heavy-calibre guns and dug-in tanks there also. We stopped and then turned about for cover. Never before had we come across such a concentration of firepower.

I reported this by radio and the panzer regiment answered swiftly: 'Hold your position, Luftwaffe requested.' Shortly afterwards, 'Luftwaffe attack in thirty minutes.' It was a summer's day and boiling hot inside the panzer. We were sweating, thirsty, hands and faces black with powder smoke, but now at least it was possible to open the hatches a little and let in some air. During an attack the hatches had to remain shut. On these first Tiger models the commander had a cupola about 20cm high with observation slits of glass blocks. The hatch lid remained upright when open and was the aiming point for all manner of enemy projectiles. Head injuries were common amongst tank commanders. So we proceeded with the hatch closed but vision severely hampered. Later Tiger models had a recessed commander's cupola and corner periscopes for vision, and so the head was much better protected. When opened, the turret lid remained horizontal so that even in an attack the cupola could be kept open.

Now began a fantastic show: wave upon wave of Stukas with sirens wailing dived down on the Russian positions to give them hell. It was a brief but effective spectacle. Everything must have been totally churned over. The last Stukas had not yet left when the order came by radio to move out. We drove through the narrows between the woodland and the rise and past the totally wiped-out positions. The worst seemed behind us, but it was a hard nut we had had to crack.

My panzer drove the furthest left, near the edge of the wood, the other three panzers to my right and with a good distance between them. Suddenly there was a powerful jerk almost as if the panzer had made a small jump. Unteroffizier Ziegler, my driver, pulled up at once, I opened the cupola and saw the right track lying behind us. We had run over a mine. I warned my platoon and the regiment by radio. At first there was a general halt, the spearhead company of the panzer regiment swung wide and passed us, taking over the lead. Two Tigers of my platoon attached themselves to the spearhead, my third panzer, Oberfeldwebel Burgis', I retained for close protection. I sat with the gunner behind the panzer in the rut we had left so as not to step on a mine. The damage was not too bad. The panzer was standing on the torn track, unrolled to its full length. First we had to inspect the ground around the panzer for mines to ensure that nobody got blown up during the repair. The radio operator stayed by his equipment, the rest of the crew searched. Apparently just a few mines had been strewn very quickly near the edge of the wood. We found eight to ten mines in wooden boxes not dug in but left loose and covered over with grass for camouflage. The fuse could be unscrewed without any danger: all commanders had practised doing this in preparation for *Zitadelle*, and so now it paid off.

The panzers of the regiment had gone on ahead. Oberstleutnant Schulz, its commanding officer, stopped briefly to exchange a few words; I told him, 'I will try to catch up once we move off.' The important thing now was to replace the track and change its three damaged segments. This was gruelling work, everything was heavy. To my surprise and joy the main body of the regiment was followed by supply vehicles and a 1-tonne tractor of our 3 Company repair group. A half-track, fully mobile cross-country, it followed at the rear of the regiment, ready to provide help quickly in the event of a breakdown. It was naturally very helpful to us. The experienced mechanics got to work and, much quicker than we could have done it alone, had us mobile again. The damage to the track was insignificant and could be attended to later. Thanks, handshakes and mount up – to chase after the regiment. We found it north-west of Batratskaya Dacha. The leading elements had come across another Russian defensive line, the right flank on the heavily defended village side was vacant and exposed. This was secured by other forces.

We adopted an all-round defence or 'hedgehog' and posted sentries all around: we, who had spent all day as the battering ram, could now rest. In the course of the night we replenished fuel and ammunition, and changed the oil and radiator water. 'First the horse, and then the rider' – this cavalry motto also applied to us. First tend to and make ready the panzer, then the man. We slept behind the panzer. Hard and short.

I can only attempt to reconstruct Oberleutnant Scherf's operation with our 3 Company (less my II Platoon). The company was deployed first on 6 July at Krutoi Log on the plateau, I assume together with II Abt/PzRgt 25. As I recall, it was plain to me that PzRgt 25 operated in two separate groups. At Krutoi Log, 3 Company had two killed: Feldwebel Heinz Wunderlich of the repair group and Obergefreiter Adalbert Essler, radio operator in a I Platoon panzer. After 106 InfDiv became involved in the battle for Krutoi Log and the situation improved, II Abt/PzRgt 25 and 3 Company/Heavy PzAbt 503 followed the advancing I Abt/PzRgt 25. This attack group also tangled with the second Russian defensive line in the wooded area and Red Army troops left lying in wait, but then followed I Abteilung's line of advance until ordered to protect the right flank against the village at Batratskaya Dacha. In the fighting there on the evening of 6 July, 3 Company/Heavy PzAbt 503 had four dead: Unteroffizier Ernst Angerer of the repair group, Unteroffizier Herbert Petzka (gunner), Wilhelm Stühler and Robert Steininger (loaders).

On the third day of the attack, 7 July, I took up my former position as 'can-opener' with my four Tigers leading. I thought it was unlikely to be any more difficult than the previous day. Soon after setting out in the early morning we came across another Russian defensive line, much weaker than expected and without any depth, and broke through it relatively quickly. On that day I don't remember that we had any stronger resistance than that to break down. We advanced, now and again we came across groups of Russian stragglers, but no cohesive or organized resistance. Towards evening we were near Miasoedovo, a heavily defended crossroads. Our panzer-grenadiers forced their way into the town, while we ourselves remained outside.

During the course of the next day we moved up to protect the right flank of 7 PzDiv on high ground about 4km south-east of Miasoedovo. PzRgt 6 had previously captured it. We positioned ourselves on a reverse slope, far away from the panzers of I Abt/PzRgt 25. I had orders to protect the main body to the east. I positioned myself with two panzers behind the crest so that I could observe and fire over it without offering myself as a target. Before me lay a moderate slope with the occasional bush. In the valley bottom, in a large semi-circle, was sparse deciduous woodland with thick bushy undergrowth at its edges. If I looked left from my high point I had a good view over the terrain. The air shimmered with heat. We stood four-hour watches, turn and turn about, with two panzers each. At last we could wash. There was little water, but each of the five crew received a bowlful. It felt good. Usually we washed our hands with petrol. The night passed quietly and I slept well again: I had a lot of sleep to catch up on.

PzRgt 25 continued to protect the division's left flank. No great change was expected for the following day. I was summoned to the regimental commander. He gave me the task of reconnoitring the wood in the valley bottom: tank noises had been heard there during the night. Two of my panzers stood watch on the ridge, giving me covering fire at the same time. I led, accompanied by Feldwebel Weigel's Tiger. Hatches shut, battle readiness, *Panzer Marsch!* We rolled slowly down the long slope through open country towards the wood. Four hundred metres short of it we stopped to observe. Nothing was to be seen. We continued forward and then suddenly there was a flash. For a fraction of a second I could see the shell

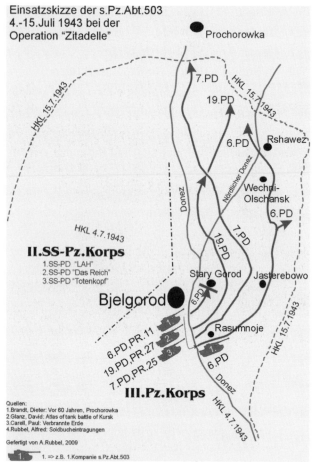

Operational area map of the three Tiger companies of Tiger Abt 503 as spearheads of the three panzer divisions.
Title: 'Sketch of Operation, s.PzAbt 503 4–15 July 1943 as part of Operation *Zitadelle*'.
Key:
HKL = Main Front Line
PD = Panzer Division
PR = Panzer Regiment
Quellen = Sources
'Gefertigt von ...' = Prepared by A. Rubbel, 2009.
Tank symbol numbered 1= (e.g.) 1 Company/ Heavy PzAbt 503.

Artillery explosions on the horizon, Tiger main gun searching for fresh targets. The Battle of Kursk began on 5 July 1943 and became one of the hardest-fought battles of the war.

For the first time at Kursk, the Russians deployed the SU-152 assault gun armed with a
152mm howitzer. It was a dangerous opponent even for a Tiger. This SU-152 blew up after
being hit and parts of its superstructure are missing.

A view through an observation slit over a harvested field with a Tiger advancing.

The Russian villages and their inhabitants in the combat zone suffered greatly.

Tigers 331 and 321 roll past peasants' burning cottages.

(**above**) Tiger 311 being run in for repair. In the foreground the twin roller wheels which had their place at the centre of the inner box. The drive wheel has also been removed.

(**right**) The commander's cupola of a Tiger after a hit. The closing mechanism of the hatch is damaged and needs to be replaced. Oberleutnant Scherf on the right.

(left) Traces of hits on Leutnant Weinert's Tiger 311. The hit on the front armour tore off the corner edge of the hull.

(below) Repair work to the tracks of Tiger 334. Between the men is the rear drive wheel.

Under the cover of a long hedgerow, armoured personnel carriers wait to push forward with the Tigers.

The battlefield near Byelgorod: a Tiger passing a wrecked T-34.

(above) The issuing of orders to Tiger 334, a Zündapp motorcycle combination of the company with field-post licence in the foreground. From left to right: Gebling, Oberleutnant Scherf (back to camera), Rondorf, an der Heiden, Weinert, Kisseberth, Fritz Müller. The others are not known by name.

(right) Unteroffizier Jäckel observing an air battle. His Tiger 331 is camouflaged with bundles of straw: the Soviet air force had many fighter-bombers on the way. Numerous hits from shell splinters and small-arms fire can be seen on the exhaust covers.

Oberleutnant Scherf in relaxed mood discussing future movements. In the back seat of the Kfz 15 is a Sonderführer (a civilian with specialist skills drafted into the Wehrmacht for the duration).

'And we have to go along here.' Oberleutnant Scherf showing Oberfeldwebel Rondorf and Burgis the route of the advance.

A Panzer IV of 7 PzDiv and Tiger 321 crossing a harvested field. The Panzer IV is fitted with so-called 'schürzen' ('aprons') at the sides and turret, the purpose of which was to detonate hollow-charge shells prematurely.

Oberleutnant Scherf wearing headphones in the turret of his Tiger, his gunner beside him. There are no photos of the author from the Battle of Kursk.

Near Byelgorod around 20 July 1943. Oberleutnant Scherf's Tiger 300 was left unattended with engine damage while waiting for the recovery unit but a Russian counterattack intervened and Tiger 300 became a Russian prize.

The horrors of war. The dead driver is hanging out from the leading T-34, other burnt bodies lie beside it. Wrecked T-34s of various types remain on the battlefield.

heading directly for me. It hit the bow of the panzer, and so did the second one. The air was shimmering: I couldn't make out anything and fired an explosive shell towards where I suspected the source to be. We received another hit, this time from the right. I pulled back and drove in reverse to our starting point. Both Tigers had some fresh scars each, but nothing had penetrated. There was less concern about a shell entering than a hit to the lateral gearing which would have put the drive wheel out of action. It was our weak point and the Russians knew it. The two panzers I had left behind on watch had seen everything and also opened fire. They saw two SP assault guns appear at the edge of the wood, fired at them and then withdrew behind cover. I reported the incident to the commander orally. Now we had to be doubly cautious so as to avoid any nasty surprises.

In the evening Feldwebel Grohmann, our 3 Company orderly room sergeant, came by with mail and a box of Shoka-Cola for everyone. He told me that Oberleutnant Scherf was in action with the company at Miasoedovo. Gefreiter Albrecht Schmidt had fallen there on 8 July: on the first day of the attack Leutnant Jammerath of our 1 Company had been killed. He had been my classmate on the officers' course at the Panzer Training School at Wünsdorf. News like that came as a blow to remind me how many guardian angels I had had until then. Mail from home: everything was all right there, the family was going to Oberbärenburg again. Yes, it was always so beautiful there.

Next morning while on watch I could not believe my eyes. The Russians were pulling out of the wood. I had a brief glimpse of three tanks before they disappeared at great speed behind natural cover. By the time my gunner had got them in his sights two more had appeared for a short time and then also gone into cover. We fired but scored no hits, corrected for deflection and this time got a hit, white smoke enveloping everything. We fired one more for luck and all fell silent again. At least ten enemy tanks had escaped us, but we had hit one for certain and another fell by the wayside afterwards.

At PzRgt 25, meanwhile, a real military camp had been set up, people were tinkering with panzers, cleaning weapons, enjoying the sun, taking it easy, playing cards. How long would this Eldorado last? We also benefitted from it. Our crews not on watch did the same. A break in order to generate energy. I went to the Regimental HQ several times: there was nothing new to report regarding the situation. I had a schnapps with the commander. I was slowly becoming a person again.

On the morning of 11 July 1943 I received orders to drive back to 3 Company with my platoon. I was shown the meeting point a few kilometres away marked on the map. This ended my attachment to PzRegt 25. I reported with my platoon to the regimental commander.

'Well done,' he said, 'it was a good cooperation.' The way to 3 Company led past Miasoedovo through an area not yet securely in German hands. To avoid this uncertain region would require a long detour, and therefore I decided for the shorter route. When we got to No Man's Land I ordered battle readiness: seal hatches and prepare for action. Everything went well, however, and I thought we had come through. Suddenly at a bend in the road with much undergrowth there came a flash from close range. We were hit! Inside the panzer it fell dark, the interior lighting failed: I hung jammed by my arm between the gun deflector plate and the turret roof. Ziegler reversed, everything happened automatically and in seconds. The Tiger half right behind me fired an HE shell and destroyed an artillery piece which had taken up position on the concealed section of road only 30m ahead of us.

An HE shell had hit the cylindrical shield of our gun. HE shells, even of large calibre, could not penetrate us though they still had considerable effect. The force of the shell had knocked the 8.8cm gun of the Tiger from the toothed wheel of the elevation machinery, and the long barrel with muzzle brake, now no longer retained by the wheel, fell down, causing the breech of the gun with its apparatus to rise up and hit the turret roof. The panzer commander's seat was to the left of the deflector plate. Because with every round fired the gun recoiled about 30cm, the deflector protected both the commander and the loader on the other side. If the hatch was shut and the commander's seat was at its lowest position, the deflector offered a ledge upon which to rest one's right elbow. This is what I had done, and now my arm was jammed between the deflector and the turret roof. Fortunately the elevating machinery was still functioning and the gun could be brought horizontal again. This allowed me to be freed, but there was a lot of bleeding. The gunner, Unteroffizer Fuhrmeister, applied a temporary dressing and I sat back in my commander's seat in a state of shock, and the panzer got going again, though with another panzer leading. Once again my guardian angel had saved me. If the hatch had been open I would have been killed.

No more incidents occurred. Finally a white flare rose skywards ahead of us. This meant our own troops. We replied with a white light and approached a vehicle of VII Reconnaissance Abt: we had made it. Just another fifteen minutes' drive with open hatches and we arrived at the meeting point ordered. I reported my return to Oberleutnant Scherf.

The Abteilung surgeon, Stabsarzt Dr Schramm, attended to my wound. The sleeve of my jacket was cut away: I had a flesh wound the size of the palm of my hand down to the bone of the right elbow, and a fractured radius. Next day I was admitted to the military hospital at Kharkov. For me, Operation *Zitadelle* was over. It was especially important for me that I had no one killed in my platoon.

A company car took me to Kharkov. I spent one night in my old quarters where I had left my valise for I had gone off into battle with a soldier's pack only. I kept everything I needed for my stay in hospital, the rest I sent home via the company. I did not know how long I would be away, nor whether I would be returning to the company. Next day I had them take me to hospital, and not before time: the wound on my right elbow was the size of a hand, the bone was fully exposed and everything was inflamed. I was deemed unfit to travel and stayed in Kharkov for fourteen days.

To my roommate, an infantry colonel, I dictated letters to my family, brother and sisters to inform them that I was *hors de combat* but that there was no reason to worry.

In the summer of 1943 the Wehrmacht was once again able to throw a large number of vehicles and weapons into the struggle. Here a Steyr infantry carrier is followed by a 12-tonne tractor towing an 8.8cm Flak gun.

Im Namen des führers und Obersten Befehlshabers der Wehrmacht

verleihe ich

dem

Leutnant von R o s e n ,

3./Pz.Abt. 503,

das

Eiserne Kreuz 1. Klasse

.Div.Gef.Stand..., den ...23. Juli....19.43

1.

Generalmajor u. Div.-Kommandeur

(Dienstgrad und Dienststellung)

The official certificate for the award of the Iron Cross First Class to Leutnant von Rosen, 3 Company/ Heavy PzAbt 503, signed at the Divisional Command Post on 23 July 1943 by the divisional commander 7 PzDiv, Generalmajor Hasso von Manteuffel.

Panzer—Regiment 25

Kommandeur

Rgt.Gef.Std. , den 23. 7. 194 3

L i e b e r   R o s e n !

Mit großer Freude kann ich Ihnen im Namen des
Führers heute das Eiserne Kreuz 1. Klasse verleihen.

Tragen Sie das E.K. lange bei bester Gesundheit;
es möge Ihnen gleichzeitig eine Erinnerung an die Zeit sein,
die Sie in schweren Kämpfen zusammen mit dem Regiment verlebt
haben.

Für Ihre militärische Zukunft wünsche ich Ihnen
weiterhin Soldatenglück und viel Erfolg.

Heil H i t l e r !

Dieses Schreiben gilt als vorläufiges Besitzzeugnis, da dasselbe von oben-
stehendem Truppenteil wohl angefordert, aber bis heute noch nicht einge-
troffen ist.

i.A.

Oberarzt

The high regard for the author held by Adalbert Schulz is clear from this letter.
'3/PzAbt 503 fought shoulder to shoulder with 7 PzAbt at the Kursk Bend.' The text reads:
'Dear Rosen! It gives me great pleasure in the name of the Führer to award you today
the Iron Cross First Class. Wear the Iron Cross long in the best of health: at the same time
may it remind you of the time you spent with the Regiment in heavy fighting. I wish you a
soldier's good luck and much success for your military future. Heil Hitler! Yours.'

The legendary Oberstleutnant Adalbert
Schulz, commanding officer PzRgt 25/7
PzDiv. He was one of the few soldiers to
be awarded the Diamonds to go with his
Knight's Cross with Oak Leaves and Swords.
He fell on 28 January 1944 at Shepetovka.

This photo taken in 1944 shows the author
wearing both Iron Crosses.

Hans von Hagemeister also had to be admitted to the military hospital at Kharkov on
15 July 1943.

BESITZZEUGNIS

DEM

Ltn. Richard Frh.v.Rosen
....
(NAME, DIENSTGRAD)

3./schw.Pz.Abtlg. 503
....
(TRUPPENTEIL, DIENSTSTELLE)

IST AUF GRUND

SEINER AM 14.7.43 **ERLITTENEN**

1 **MALIGEN VERWUNDUNG – BESCHÄDIGUNG**

DAS

VERWUNDETENABZEICHEN

IN Schwarz

VERLIEHEN WORDEN.

Zwickau **. DEN** 9.11.43 **19** 43

Reservelazarett I Zwickau/Sa.
Der Chefarzt:
i.A.
(UNTERSCHRIFT)

(DIENSTGRAD UND DIENSTSTELLE) Oberarzt

The author was not awarded the Wound Badge in Black until November 1943. The text merely confirms that the named recipient 'is awarded the Wound Badge in Black on the grounds of his single wound suffered on 14 July 1943'.

Tiger Abt 500 at Paderborn trained Tiger crews for the Abteilungen in the field.

The Inspector-General of Panzer Troops, Generaloberst Guderian, on an inspection at Paderborn in 1943.

I had a visit from Frau von Hühnersdorf, the head of the soldier's hostel at Kharkov. Her husband, the commanding officer of 6 PzDiv, General von Hühnersdorf, fell a few days later in Operation *Zitadelle*. The Red Cross nurses did everything they could to feed me up. I could have anything I liked and ordered an omelette soufflé. It was gigantic and made me feel ill. My right arm was fixed stretched out. Every day the discharge of matter got worse. Nevertheless I was quite content to have nothing to do, nothing to decide and nobody to order around, having left all the horror behind me and being able to allow my thoughts to roam back to my comrades in arms and the company, forward to more rest, my parents, Germany.

Finally I was declared fit to travel. I was flown to Dnyepropetrovsk, where I spent the next ten days and then boarded an ambulance train for Germany. I believe it took six days, just like a holiday trip. I had an upper bunk by a window, but couldn't get up. Food and treatment were first class: twice a day a doctor visited.

At the end of 1943 the author was recovered enough for Christmas leave ('Festtagsurlaub 43/44' – '2nd Class Military Hospital case') with his family. Here is one of the coveted War Leave Passes for the railway journey from Zwickau to Rastatt/Baden and return. He signed the certificate at the bottom left to the effect that the conditions had been brought to his attention: he could only use the normal route for such a journey; long detours, zig-zags and round-trips were forbidden, as was the use of Wehrmacht tickets or ordinary tickets for the stretch covered by the leave pass.

It was made clear to me how lucky I'd been. Immediately below me lay a young lieutenant, completely paralysed. Every day a doctor came to empty his intestines with rubber gloves. Dreadful, to be without any hope of a future, only able to continue vegetating with the help of others. Our train made slow progress. The rails were held together by simple bolts and no great speed was possible. Again and again there were long halts.

Every ambulance train had a travelling security squad: armed soldiers distributed to individual coaches and on the locomotive. The whole rear area through which we travelled was infested with partisans. They made daily attacks on the railway line, and trains also were attacked, including hospital trains, although these were always identified with the Red Cross symbol. Between 7 July and 3 August 1943 alone in the Army Group Centre area, partisans derailed fifty-six trains. In the course of August they destroyed the tracks in over 12,000 places. Right and left along the stretch of railway line we saw overturned and burnt-out wagons. We came through unscathed, however. Our destination was Lublin in Poland. Here I was hospitalized again after a thorough delousing.

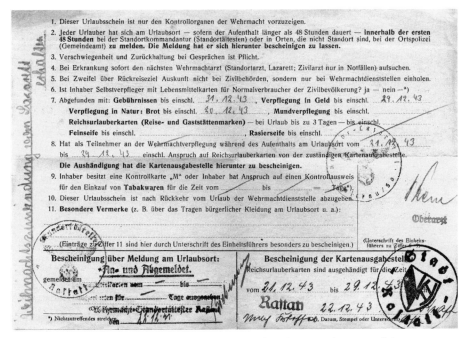

The rear of the War Leave Pass had to be produced to the control organs of the Wehrmacht as specified for rubber-stamping.

Now came the selection process. A patient would be sent to one or other German hospital depending on the nature and seriousness of his wound. In Lublin one had the sensation of being almost home. I discovered with great pleasure that my room nurse was a young Red Cross assistant from Rastatt and a former schoolfriend of my elder sister.

They would not let you know where you were going to end up. The new hospital train headed for Saxony. I would have found Dresden to be just right for my stay in hospital, but my carriage kept going. We were unloaded at Zwickau. A wing of the great provincial hospital there had been set aside as a reserve military hospital. I arrived on 21 August 1943 and remained there until 12 February 1944. My parents and sister Elisabeth visited me on their return from Oberbärenburg and I spent eight days' Christmas leave at home with them.

At the Zwickau military hospital I received a small packet and a letter from the commander of PzRgt 25, Oberstleutnant Schulz. Enclosed was the Iron Cross First Class. 'Wear the Iron Cross long in the best of health: at the same time may it be a reminder of the time you spent with the Regiment in heavy fighting.' A few months later, as Generalmajor and commander of 7 PzDiv, he fell in the East. He was the sixth soldier of the Wehrmacht to be awarded the Knight's Cross with Oak Leaves, Swords and Diamonds.

My wound healed very slowly and lasted until the suppuration stopped. Having to dictate all my letters got on my nerves and so I learned to write with my left hand. I even did some sketches, but none has survived. My right arm was completely stiff. Every couple of days under anaesthetic the doctors moved it forcibly and then put it in a plaster cast at the desired angle. I would stay in bed for a day after that: when the anaesthetic wore off the pain was hellish. Between these appointments I had a chance to visit the theatre, concerts and the cinema: I was determined to make the best of the time. I had contact with my company, mainly with Leutnant Weinert, who fell that November. I also received news of the death of von Cossel.

My stay in hospital was rounded off with a course in Bonn for convalescing officers. I gave this short shrift and went to Paderborn where our Tiger Reserve Abteilung was stationed, hoping as always to be sent for by Scherf. Instead of that I caught diphtheria, was admitted into the Leokonvikts isolation hospital at Paderborn and not discharged until the end of April 1944. I received another period of convalescent leave which passed very pleasantly, and then finally came orders from 503.

(**above**) The author at the head of 3 Company, parading before Hauptmann Scherf and Unteroffizier Gärtner.

(**left**) Unteroffizier Heinz Gärtner (left) of 3 Company/Heavy PzAbt 503 was presented with the German Cross in Gold by Hauptmann Scherf in a ceremony on 10 June 1944 at Ohrdruf. Scherf is seen wearing the Knight's Cross in this photo.

The new King Tigers arriving at Eisenach (unfortunately no photos exist of the delivery of the new Tigers to 2 and 3 Company).

A period of rest and recuperation for the Abteilung following the heavy rearguard actions fought by Tiger Atb 503 at the end of 1943 and beginning of 1944 after the Battle of Kursk.

The Inspector-General of the Panzer Troops, Generaloberst Guderian, came on 22 June 1944 to inspect the new King Tigers with Porsche turrets supplied to 1 Company.

The senior officers of the Inspectorate stand watching as the main gun of the new King Tiger is cleaned.

Unteroffizier Heinz Gärtner,
a very successful Tiger
commander, seen here in
new King Tiger 314.

Knight's Cross holder
Hauptmann Fromme
took over as Abteilung
commander at Ohrdruf.

A document signed
by the new Abteilung
commander to accompany
the author's driving permit
authorizing Leutnant
von Rosen to drive all
company vehicles in his
capacity as company
leader.

6

The Invasion Front, 1944

1944

6 Jun	Allied landing in Normandy.
14 Jun	US breakthrough on the Cotentin Peninsula.
26 Jun	Capture of town and port of Cherbourg.
9 Jul	Capture of Caen by the British.
18–20 Jul	Operation *Goodwood*.
24 Jul–4 Aug	Operation *Cobra*: US breakthrough at Avranches.
by 29 Jul	1.5 million Allied troops put ashore in France.
9 Aug	Capture of Le Mans.
12–21 Aug	Falaise Pocket.
25 Aug	German forces surrender Paris.
11 Sep	Allies cross the frontier of the Reich north of Trier.
21 Oct	Capture of Aachen by the Americans.

On 6 June 1944 the Allies landed in Normandy. After Operation *Zitadelle*, from the summer of 1943 until the spring of 1944, Heavy PzAbt 503, as part of Army Group South, was involved in constant rearguard fighting through the Ukraine and Romania to the Hungarian border. Graf Kageneck, our CO, was awarded the Knight's Cross with Oak Leaves. The Abteilung had now arrived at Ohrdruf troop training depot in the Harz mountains for rest and recuperation. I rejoined the unit at the beginning of June 1944. Hauptmann Fromme had been appointed its new commander while Scherf, now also with the rank of Hauptmann and the wearer of the Knight's Cross, remained in command of 3 Company. I found that many old faces were no longer around. No 3 Company was the last of the Abteilung to arrive at Ohrdruf from the Eastern Front, and most of its men were now on leave.

Hauptmann Fromme employed me at first as officer for special duties at Abteilung HQ. I had to prepare for the visit of the Inspector-General of Panzer Troops, Generaloberst Guderian, and as his liaison officer ensure the smooth running of his programme. On 15 June he was a guest at our officers' party. During the course of the evening he came to our lieutenants' table and spoke gravely about the situation on the Western and Eastern Fronts. He made it clear to us how difficult the task was going to be for us personally in our probable area of defence at the invasion front in France: 'If we do not succeed in destroying the enemy bridgehead in the next fourteen days, the war is lost for us.'

I could not get the Generaloberst's words out of my head. On 14 June the V-weapons offensive on London had begun. Our Propaganda Ministry went to town, boasting of immense damage inflicted on England. This would bring the turn of the tide in the West! And more V-weapons would be coming! After the V-1, the V-2 with an even more devastating effect . . . in the fifth year of war people were more sceptical and no longer took such things at face value. The media put rumours into circulation, and people said, no smoke without fire, they wouldn't have just made it all up. People liked to talk themselves into believing it but now the fact that the Allies had been able to gain such a firm foothold in Normandy in such a short time had given them food for thought. And the Allies' air supremacy! Where was the Luftwaffe? Had Göring dried up? At the same time, on 22 June, the Soviets launched their major offensive against Army Group Centre. It was appalling how the German front crumbled. We tried not to think about it. The imminent readiness of the Abteilung for the coming battle made the fullest demands of us.

One Sunday in nearby Erfurt we watched the final game of the 1944 German football championship. It was played on a park pitch, not in a stadium as it would be nowadays. I wasn't interested in football, but it was good to get away from the troop training ground for a day. It seems almost unbelievable that football was not then what it is today. The favourite sport was field handball, which was a great festive occasion for all companies in the hours set aside for sport.

On 26/27 June 1944 the Abteilung was listed for transfer to the invasion front in eight trains. I commanded one of these. On the evening of 27 June my train was first for loading at Ohrdruf and was due to pull out at 0600hrs next morning, my 22nd birthday. After we finished loading I drove to Erfurt in the VW-Kübelwagen. I had a chance meeting with an old acquaintance a few days previously and he wanted to wish me well and celebrate my birthday with a few drinks. I set my alarm for 0400hrs and it failed to go off. I awoke at 0530hrs, thirty minutes before the scheduled departure of my train from Ohrdruf! It was a crazy drive. From far away looking towards the goods yard I saw a great cloud of smoke rising from the locomotive, which was frequently letting off steam. I could see the transport still standing there. Ten minutes later we took the last bend at top speed, roared up to the loading ramp and came to a stop with a squeal of brakes. I jumped out of the car, told the impatient railway official that he could show the driver the green flag and leapt onto a wagon. The train was set in motion at once. Everything had turned out well again.

Once more we were the leading transport with priority over all the others. Systematic Allied air attacks had disrupted the railway network repeatedly in the initial stages of the invasion. Often we waited for hours in a tunnel if the aerial situation came to a head: again and again there were long detours whenever wrecked bridges or railway installations made it necessary. All the transports finally reached their destinations undamaged, but not until 2 and 3 July. We were unloaded at Dreux, about 70km west of Paris, then moved by night via Verneuil–L'Aigle–Argentan–Falaise to our future operational area east of Caen. It was not possible to move by day because of enemy fighter-bomber activity, and so every night, depending on the weather, we took to the road from 2300hrs until 0300hrs, then sought shelter in a wood until the following night. We were always happy to see the sky overcast because this prevented enemy aircraft from flying. On one of our nocturnal runs we passed a V-1 launch site: the flying bombs rose into the skies trailing fiery tails and disappeared westwards. It was very impressive, but would this bring about the turn of the tide in our favour or be decisive in the outcome of the war, or was this just the Propaganda Ministry merely buoying up our hopes? I had my doubts, for until then the V-1 had not changed anything. When would the V-2 be coming? This was allegedly a much more powerful and accurate weapon. Was this all fantasy or was there really a miracle weapon? If this was only propaganda in order to keep us fighting to the last, then it would be the greatest crime imaginable that had ever been committed against the German soldier. But I preferred not to believe it yet.

Heavy PzAbt 503 joined LXXXV Armeekorps on 7 July 1944. Next day we were attached to PzRgt 22 of 21 PzDiv which until then had only had a Panzer IV Abteilung. In association with the latter we now formed the armoured reserve which would be held in readiness for any eventuality immediately behind the front line. While the regiment lay at Troarn, we were assigned to the Emiéville area.

Up to the time of our arrival at Emiéville the situation on the invasion front had developed as follows:

- Twenty-one divisions of the Wehrmacht and Waffen-SS were defending a front 140km long between the Orne estuary and the western coast of the Cotentin Peninsula. Our losses were increasing.
- The British had occupied a 25km² bridgehead east of the Orne since the first day of the invasion. A fixed front line with trenches had not developed and the front was in constant flux as a result of limited attacks, defensive successes and pinning-down operations by both sides. The Allied forces had not yet been able to achieve a decisive breakthrough, but it was obvious to everybody that they would have to try it eventually.
- On 8 July the battle for Caen began, German troops abandoning the town as ordered on 10 July. The front line was pulled back to the eastern bank of the Orne. The suburbs to the south-east of Caen therefore remained in German hands and blocked the Allied advance into the Falaise plain.
- Our 3 Company lay in the park of the Maneville stud farm, 2.5km from the Abteilung command post at Emiéville. The rearward Tross was some distance away at Troarn.

In the second week of July our commander Hauptmann Fromme was admitted to a military hospital in Paris for several days to have an inflamed eye wound treated. In his absence Hauptmann Scherf took command of the Abteilung and I, as the senior Leutnant in the company, took over the fighting Staffel of 3 Company. I informed all panzer commanders of our future operational area and the various approach roads to the front line so that we would know the local circumstances well. I pored over the map, trying to imagine every possibility the enemy might use for an attack and imprinted the map as accurately as possible in my mind, for in action very much depends on it. Every fighting company of the Abteilung was scheduled for a twenty-four-hour spell as Alarm Company and had to be at immediate full readiness during this period. Initially the front line remained quiet.

We had made ourselves at home under the cover of ancient trees in the Maneville Park. A trench had been dug under each panzer: some of the crew slept in the vehicle, the others below it. I always slept in the trench, for I could stretch out there: in the panzer I would have to spend the night sitting in my commander's seat. Below the main building of the stud farm were cellars where a dressing station had been set up by the Luftwaffe field division which had been stationed here before us. My favourite place was the field kitchen, for food sets the mood of the company. The stud farm also had a market garden: the old gardener had decided to stay on and I paid him a decent price in francs for large quantities of vegetables and salads, and from other sources more delicious ingredients of value in the kitchen. Our meals at this time were really excellent and the 3 Company kitchen was highly regarded – with envy – by the whole Abteilung. Now and again a large barrel was filled with cider and everybody could help himself from it (provided that he was not from that day's Alarm Company). In the evening the crews would frequently prepare extra dishes, especially fried potatoes and pudding. I would often be invited to join them and one evening I had three invitations. There was no shortage of alcohol and soon a stag-party atmosphere would develop. Near the park was a field with wonderful new potatoes where Leutnant Fürlinger set up our Flak protection. He was always a welcome guest at our parties (unfortunately he fell in Hungary in 1945). Those evenings in the open air were glorious, and we enjoyed the unexpectedly peaceful mood. Only rarely did one hear firing from the front only a few kilometres away. It reminded us that this idyll would not last for ever.

Duty took me to Caen on 8 July or thereabouts: the city was a sorry sight. The destruction inflicted by Allied bombing before the invasion was enormous. Only a few civilians had remained behind. By midday I was back with the company. When one looked west from high points in the countryside towards the sea, countless barrage balloons could be seen on the distant horizon. They served to defend the unprecedented assembly of warships of the Allied invasion fleet against the Luftwaffe, but what Luftwaffe? It was depressing to accept that our Luftwaffe was no longer capable of effective action. In the West it had disappeared from the skies. That night there followed a renewed air attack on Caen. We could see the glow of the fires above the city: a terrible conflagration must be raging there. Here a different war was being fought from what we had known in the East: the enemy's air supremacy was undisputed. Next morning the battle for the city flared up: our troops pulled out two days later. Now the front had edged closer to us.

Towards 0500hrs on the morning of 11 July 1944 an Abteilung dispatch rider awoke me. Immediate alarm readiness: I was ordered to the Abteilung command post in person. In haste I distributed my orders and rode there pillion. Hauptmann Scherf explained the situation to me: after a brief, heavy artillery bombardment, enemy forces, that was to say British armour and Canadian infantry, had broken through our main front line between Cuverville and Colombelles and occupied the high ground north of the factory complex at Colombelles. Luftwaffe Jäger-Rgt 32 had avoided contact with the enemy at Cuverville, and the roads to Giberville and the region east of Caen now lay open to the enemy. A large number of tanks had been observed. My orders: '3 Company is to destroy the enemy force which has broken through by attacking it immediately, restore the main front line and hold it awaiting further orders.' The dispatch rider returned me to the company. The engines were warmed up, the crews in their panzers and the commanders were awaiting me at the command panzer. My instructions were soon passed on: mount up, go to battle readiness, pull out. Thirty minutes after the alarm the company rolled at top speed for Giberville. Actually 3 Company had not been the Alarm Company that night: the other two companies of the Abteilung had also been roused but I had reached the command post first and therefore 3 Company received the assignment. The rest of the Abteilung remained at alarm readiness to see how things developed.

We reached Giberville a quarter of an hour later. Here we were halted when the vibrations of the passing panzers caused a badly damaged house to collapse on top of the second vehicle. Nobody was hurt but it had to be dug out first because the company could not pass, the road being too narrow for more than one panzer at that point. It always happens when one is in a rush! I used the time to go by motorcycle to the northern end of Giberville village to make contact with our units there. In the last house, a baker's shop, an artillery observation post of Sturmgeschütz Abt 200 was located below the roof. I went up and through the scissors telescope was shown a cluster of houses below St Honorine where a number of British Sherman tanks had taken up position. It must have been these which had forced out the grenadiers of the Luftwaffe field division. These were therefore our target.

I returned to the company, assembled the commanders and gave my orders for the attack: 'Commanders sitting up, clear for battle.' Scarcely had the first panzer (Leutnant Koppe) reached the northern exit from the village than he came under heavy fire. We came to a standstill for a moment and then everything turned out wonderfully. I Platoon under Oberfeldwebel Sachs bore left, II Platoon (Leutnant Koppe) bore right, leaving me in the centre between both platoons at the level. I had left III Platoon (Leutnant Rambow) a little behind me in reserve. This spreading of the company was a major moment of weakness from the enemy point of view and soon my panzer was receiving the first hits. No sooner were the other two platoons in position than they returned fire. By radio I gave the order '*Überschlagender Einsatz*' in which one platoon advances at high speed under covering fire of the other platoon, the manoeuvre continuing alternately until something else is ordered. There was no reaction to my radio order and I repeated it in a sharper tone of voice. Nothing changed, my panzers continued to engage the enemy from where they were. Thick black clouds of smoke were rising from the British tanks: now and again I saw a stab of flame from an internal explosion. When the other panzers continued to ignore my order I blew my top: 'If you don't attack at once, I shall turn my turret to six o'clock and fire behind me!' Incredible. No reaction. All the time shells from the enemy tanks were hitting my panzer or whistling close above it. I could imagine more pleasant places to be. Just then I noticed through the viewing slit of my cupola that the wireless aerial had been shot away. I realized at once why my company was not responding. What to do now? I couldn't change panzers for one with an intact radio, and in any case my panzer was receiving too many hits. Therefore I was left with no choice but to attack.

I went ahead at full speed for 300m and received no hits. When I looked around I saw to my satisfaction that I Platoon was following me while II and III Platoons were stationary, giving covering fire. My platoon commanders had therefore grasped the situation and knew what to do without further orders. We now made the attack without radio communications, all movements were done automatically as if on the exercise ground. One platoon gave covering fire, the other moved forward at top speed. There was nothing more to be seen of the enemy tanks, for the farmstead around which they had formed now lay behind a cloud of black smoke. The enemy infantry also retired behind a smoke screen, and when this had lifted somewhat I saw the enemy tanks. Every round we fired hit a Sherman which then burst into flames. Our panzers, on the other hand, had ceased to receive fire and with one last 200m advance to the farmstead I reached the old main front line. What I have just described lasted perhaps thirty minutes.

The terrain offered little natural cover and I arranged the company as best I could. Scarcely had we finished these movements than a British artillery spotter aircraft appeared high above us. This did not bode well, and soon we found ourselves at the centre of an artillery bombardment that robbed us of our senses of sight and hearing. It was as though gigantic peas were raining down upon us – ten impacts simultaneously – the ground shook and trembled as if in a great earthquake, and at once with so much dust and filth whirling around in the air it became as dark as night. This lasted five minutes. We recovered quickly from the horror even though we had never experienced anything like it before. I had never believed such a massive barrage possible. It fell quiet for an hour, I pulled us back 500m and then it started all over again. There was nothing we could do but keep our heads down in our panzers and sit it out. My Tiger received a direct hit, we all felt the hefty blow, the lights failed and we were dazed for a few moments, then surprised to find we were still alive. The British were firing with sensitive fuses but luckily, shortly before leaving Germany, the turret had been given an additional layer of armour. Some of the welded seams had torn, which would require repairs once we got back. We were marooned there for over eight hours waiting for the relief to arrive, during which time the same bombardment was repeated several times. The British naval gunnery was so accurate that though we kept changing location every salvo straddled us while most of the shells exploded amongst us. Because we put a good distance between our panzers we had no further losses. The artillery spotter aircraft, a slow propeller machine, kept contact with us until finally he ran short of fuel and after that we had some peace.

This gave me the opportunity to leave my panzer and have a closer look at the enemy tanks: eleven Shermans strewn around and burnt out. Most were armed with 75mm guns, but a few were 'Fireflies' with the heavier 17-pounder which posed a greater threat to us. We had also destroyed five anti-tank guns. I noticed between the houses of the farmstead two totally undamaged Shermans which had collided and got locked together while trying to turn, these had then been abandoned by their crews. In one of the tanks I found a whole handful of material with plotted information, radio codes, orders and suchlike. I got these back by the quickest route to our Abteilung, which had set up an advanced command post on the railway line near Demouville. In the course of the morning Hauptmann Fromme returned there from the Paris hospital, and upon hearing my report he gave me the task of towing in both Shermans if it were possible. I drove forward and arrived just as the grenadiers of the Luftwaffe field division returned to reoccupy their old positions and relieve us. Leutnant Koppe led the company back to the Maneville stud farm. With my panzer and two drivers from the repair group I remained forward to protect the Shermans. After a while we got them running again. Under the eyes of the British, who were able to watch all this from nearby St Honorine, we drove off proudly with the two Shermans. We considered this to be a triumph. The company had no casualties and the damage to the panzers from hits was repairable. On the drive back my column passed a troop of British tankmen made PoWs that day. Wide-eyed, the poor fellows recognized their Shermans. Under interrogation later, they expressed their appreciation of our rules of engagement, for I had forbidden anybody to fire at tank crews abandoning their vehicles.

We did not have long to enjoy our triumph. The next few days were not so tranquil, for in the park and around it artillery and rocket-launcher batteries had driven up and practised briefly now and again. The enemy's reply was never long in coming, and when they supported this with the ships' gunnery from offshore it became more unpleasant for us and we had to spend many hours in the 'heroes' refuge' below our panzers. There were many indications of a British offensive in the offing. After our success of 11 July we believed we could handle it, but we really had no inkling of what we would be up against. The commanding officer had promised me the reward of a few days' leave in Paris, but unfortunately nothing came of it.

Many years later I discovered from British sources what the purpose of their attack of 11 July 1944 had been. On 9 July the CO of 51st Highland Division, Major-General Bullen-Smith, had received orders to occupy the village of Colombelles with its factory complex and so enlarge the British bridgehead east of the Orne in preparation for Operation *Goodwood*. 153 Brigade under Brigadier Murray, reinforced by one squadron of Sherman tanks of 148th RAC (Royal Armoured Corps) and two platoons of 17-pounders of the 61st Anti-tank Battalion, was detailed to carry out the attack.

At 0600hrs on 11 July, Major Wright of the brigade reported the appearance of my Tigers in front of his company. At 0745hrs he reported that ten of the eleven Shermans had been destroyed in less than forty-five minutes. At 0800hrs the CO, 153rd Brigade, broke off the attack and ordered a general retreat to St Honorine. The divisional artillery of the Highlanders protected the withdrawal with a smokescreen. The British plan had failed. The panzers of PzRgt 22 and two companies of PzGrenRgt 192, which had been put on alarm status in the early morning, were no longer required. Our first engagement on the Normandy Front was successful, but was only of local significance and could not influence the overall situation.

Overview of the Allied
attacks in Normandy,
June/July 1944.

Generalfeldmarschall
Rommel inspecting the
Normandy coastal
sectors shortly before
the invasion. General
Feuchtinger (right)
explains the defensive
measures. Later Rommel
inspected the Sherman
tanks captured by the
author. On the left Major
Becker, commanding
officer Sturmgeschütz
Abt 200.

The huge Allied invasion fleet approaching the Normandy beaches at daybreak on 6 June 1944 as seen from behind the German beach obstacles.

A US landing craft with ramp lowered and GIs wading through waist-high water towards the shore in order to establish a beachhead for units following behind.

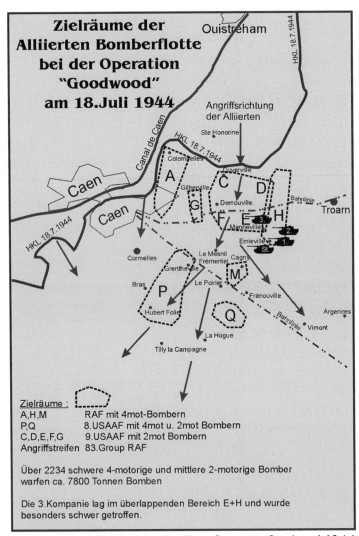

'Target Areas of the Allied Bomber Fleet, Operation Goodwood, 18 July 1944.'

HKL = Main front line

Angriffsrichtung = Direction of Allied attack

Bahnlinie = Railway line

Zielräume = Target areas

A, H, M = RAF with four-engined bombers

P, Q = 8 USAAF with four-engined and twin-engined bombers

C, D, E, F, G = 9 USAAF with twin-engined bombers

Angriffstreifen = 83 Group RAF

Over 2,234 heavy four-engined and medium twin-engined bombers dropped about 7,800 tonnes of bombs. The author's 3 Company was in the E/H overlap on the map and was particularly hard hit.

A Panzer V Panther and grenadiers of 12-SS PzDiv *Hitlerjugend* prepare for a counter-attack. In the opening weeks of the invasion, German troops offered the Allies strong resistance.

In June and July 1944 in a massive bombing effort, the Allied bomber fleets destroyed all important railway junctions in France used by the Germans for supply. In the photo are Abteilung members Rhode, Fürlinger and Wiegand at the totally wrecked railway station at Versailles.

(above) Hauptmann Scherf at the wheel of a tracked motorcycle (Kettenkrad) in the Dreux woods, a trusting tawny owl perched on his wrist.

(left) Gotthold Wunderlich and Hannes Schneider with the tawny owl perched on the barrel of the anti-aircraft MG. Notice the home-made wooden-soled sandals worn by Wunderlich.

Hannes Schneider in the
commander's cupola of
a Tiger I in the Dreux
woods, July 1944. There
is a good view here of
the angled mirrors all
installed at 45° to provide
an all-round view.

The well-camouflaged Tiger 323 passing through Canon on 6 July 1944 . . .

. . . before the accident. The bridge over the railway gave way under the weight of the Tiger, collapsed and it ended up on the railway line.

(above) Over a glass of claret at the command post of Heavy PzAbt 503: adjutant Oberleutnant Barkhausen, Hauptmann Scherf, Commander 3 Company, Hauptmann Wiegand, Chief of the HQ Company and Hauptmann von Eichel-Streber, Commander 2 Company.

(left) The Abteilung command post was set up in this mansion, Schloss Emiéville. Hauptmann Scherf saluting in the magnificent rose garden. The building was very seriously damaged by Allied bombing on 18 July 1944.

The 2cm quadruple Flak was an effective weapon against low-level aircraft but the gun had no protective shield, which exposed the gunners to high risk during an exchange of fire.

Some successes were obtained against the invasion troops. With 3 Company, the author destroyed a number of Sherman tanks and captured two undamaged. The photo shows a captured tank with German national markings being looked over by General Feuchtinger. This Sherman was later thoroughly evaluated.

7

Operation Goodwood

The overall position on the invasion front in mid-July was quite favourable for us. The British were intent on changing this at all costs, to break through the static front lines and gain territory beyond. To achieve that they needed to extract their armour from amongst the great hedgerows and sunken roads, favourable to the defenders, and reach the plains near Falaise suitable for the deployment of their tanks. The crux of these wide-ranging British plans was the Bourgebus Heights, the key position for launching their operation which lay 8km east of the British bridgehead on the Orne. From there the British would bring the German panzers and reserves to battle and wipe them out and so clear the way to Paris.

On 18 July 1944 British VIII Corps with three armoured divisions, including the Guards Armoured Division (a total of 877 tanks) left the Orne bridgehead. The right and left flanks of the attack divisions were protected by one British and one Canadian corps. The attack was prepared by 2,077 bombers, which dropped 7,870 tonnes of bombs, and 270 medium and heavy guns with 250,000 shells at their disposal.

From 0545hrs until 0630hrs 1,056 RAF heavy bombers attacked, then from 0700hrs until 0730hrs 539 USAAF bombers and from 0800hrs to 0830hrs another 482 USAAF bombers. Especially hard hit by this bombing preparation were the villages of Emiéville, Cagny and Maneville, where our 3 Company lay. Never before had such an armada of bombers been used to soften up an enemy prior to an attack. By comparison, in February 1945 Dresden was attacked by 'only' 1,054 RAF and USAAF bombers which dropped 3,425 tonnes of bombs.

At 0800hrs British 11th Armoured Division with 29th Armoured Brigade and 159th Infantry Brigade crossed the start line, encountering no resistance because the advanced battalions of 16 Luftwaffe Field Division had been wiped out by the carpet bombing. At 0830hrs the British spearheads crossed the Caen-Troarn railway line; here too they met no resistance in front of the readiness area of Heavy PzAbt 503.

In the 3 Company readiness area I was the 'Premier', namely the I Platoon leader who was also the representative of the company commander, and what I said went. Hauptmann Scherf was 'lodging' at the Abteilung command post in Emiéville. The mansion house there was quieter than our camp in the open. He was rarely to be seen at that time with the company's fighting Staffel, but on the days between operations he had much to catch up on, going back and forth between the orderly room and the Tross, including catering, the repair group and the workshop, all a fair stretch from each other.

But back to the evening of 17 July. Leutnant Heerlein, Abteilung ordnance officer, had invited all available officers to a party at the Abteilung command post. Soon after it started it was interrupted by a fairly heavy artillery bombardment which led to two dispatch riders being killed. Everything was broken off at once. I had been informed previously that a civilian had been shot dead on the front line trying to cross over to the British side. On his body the troops had found precise sketches of the company positions and the Abteilung command post. The commanding officer had immediately issued instructions for the Abteilung to move to another readiness area, for possibly other agents had managed to reach the British with similar sketches. But the High Command, probably Army Group, had not approved the change of position. After the artillery bombardment, I drove back to the company as fast as possible to find all quiet. Therefore I did not know how to interpret the artillery bombardment. It had been heavier than usual. Was it merely a nuisance barrage or several batteries zero-ing in before a major operation? There was no way of telling. I inspected the sentries, warned them to wake me if anything strange happened, crawled under my panzer, wrapped myself in my blanket and was soon asleep.

My companion in the slit trench beneath Tiger 311 was Unteroffizier Werkmeister, my gunner; the other three crewmen slept inside the panzer. I was awoken at 0600hrs by the sound of many aircraft engines, crept out of the trench and through the foliage saw 'Christmas trees' in various colours slowly sinking to the ground. Target-marker flares for bombers, I thought at once, but I had no more time to reflect. Two hundred metres from our wood a series of great fountains of earth and smoke reared up and I was struck by a violent pressure wave which almost hurled me to the ground. Seconds later I was back beneath the panzer, and not a moment too soon, for a second stick of bombs fell much nearer, the panzer shook and my eardrums hurt with the pressure. I realized at once that this attack was aimed at us personally. From now on I could not think, I was as helpless as a drowning man tossed into raging seas. The air was filled with the whistle of falling bombs and instinctively I pressed myself closer to the ground. Then followed the deafening explosions and attendant air pressure, increasingly louder as the chain of explosions ran its course towards us. Each aircraft dropped not a single bomb, but a batch of fifteen or twenty. The bombers came in staggered formations of ten to fifteen aircraft, all dropping their bombloads simultaneously, wave after wave. The ground trembled. It surprised me that I could have survived it.

I had a feeling of total helplessness in the presence of these explosive forces. There was no running away from them. I had no idea how long the bombing would go on: all idea of time was lost, it seemed an eternity since I had lain peacefully asleep under my panzer. Suddenly Werkmeister and I were catapulted by the blast into a corner of the trench, covered over with earth and were probably unconscious for some time until we came to. The blast had swept away the excavated earth which we had lined alongside the tracks and wheels, and so I could now see out through the wheels. My neighbouring panzer was ablaze. Tiger 312, Unteroffizier Westerhausen's panzer, had received a direct hit. That was all I could see from my slit trench although I realized that the blast had shifted my own panzer slightly to one side: probably the near-miss which knocked us out had caused it.

Then it all started again. Down came the next shower of bombs. As I seem to remember, the whole performance lasted two and a half hours with short pauses. It would be superfluous to repeat the same event occurring over and over. I lay under my panzer with my fingers in my ears and bit my blanket so as not to cry out.

Finally the attack seemed to come to an end. What a sight met my eyes as I crawled out from under my panzer. Of the once so beautiful parkland nothing remained but shredded trees, churned meadows and giant bomb craters so numerous that they overlapped – a grey, repulsive moonscape and a mist of dust which made breathing difficult. Through the thick fog it was possible to see the red glow of trees and cornfields burning. That was my first impression as I stood behind my panzer and had a look around. It was incomprehensible how the surroundings had changed. Then life returned, the crews crept out of their slit trenches under the panzers, or from within them, pale and bewildered, more suspecting than knowing how close to death they had been. I went to the panzer on our right. It had received a direct hit and looked like a giant opened sardine tin. Flames licked the wreckage. Of Unteroffizier Westerhausen and his crew there was no trace. I worked my way through a veritable primeval woodland and now came to the gigantic crater in front of Oberfeldwebel Sachs' Tiger 313. The panzer itself had been flipped over by the blast and now lay on its turret, wheels in the air. We found two crewmen dead under it, and of the other three there was no trace. Where my front-line repair group had been was only a crater. There would have been five or six men who had sought shelter beneath their two panzers, but now they could not be found.

The platoon leaders arrived, still confused. We had no time to discuss what we had just lived through, however: now we had to act. We had to restore our panzers to operational status, but most of them first had to be shovelled free from the earth piled up to the turret. Some had fallen trees across them, and their tracks broken. With our few tools aboard, two shovels and a pickaxe per panzer, how were we to get the company operational again? Additionally the work had to be broken off frequently when salvoes from heavy artillery, probably naval guns, targeted our area. The men made a superhuman effort, for we knew now that it was life or death. I also noticed that 10m behind my panzer was a crater 6–8m deep which would have swallowed it up comfortably: if the bomb had landed a fraction of a second later it would have been a direct hit and these memoirs would never have been written. The thick armour plate over the engine at the rear of the panzer had been deformed as though hit by a bomb that had failed to explode: upon examination we established that the cooling unit had been damaged by blast. My panzer was therefore not combat-worthy and I had to change vehicles again.

Our situation was now fairly difficult. We could hear tank guns and MGs firing not too far off. Had the British broken through and were they already close? I had not been able to restore radio contact with Abteilung, and had no idea how they might have got on. I also had no idea who on our defensive front would still be in a position to repulse a British attack after the murderous bombardment. In order to clarify the situation I set off on foot for Abteilung. The whole time, enemy artillery fire was incessant, much louder than before, and the shelling reaching much closer to us. I jumped from crater to crater, always with an eye for cover whenever I heard a fresh salvo whistling over. Thus my progress was laborious, what with the tree trunks and great craters I had to surmount. Finally I reached the path which led along the boundary of the parkland to Emiéville. There were fewer bomb-pitted areas here and the going was easier. From behind a bend in the road the Tiger I of Hauptmann Fromme came towards me. I reported the status of the company and he ordered me to get it out of the readiness area as soon as possible and set up a defensive front on the left flank of the suspected British attack corridor between Maneville and Cagny. This would prevent a breakthrough in the direction of Emiéville.

At first it remained uncertain how long the company would need before it could move out. The noise of fighting from the west had grown so loud meanwhile that I could not be sure that the British would allow me the time to restore operational readiness. I could hear a great droning sound as if a large number of vehicles were moving from north to south but nothing could be seen; a delicate veil of smoke lay over the land.

I hurried back to the company, taking cover whenever the heavy-calibre naval shells howled over, whirling splinters and clumps of earth everywhere when they exploded. At Company it still looked unpromising. The least damaged was Leutnant Rambow's III Platoon. Three Tigers of my I Platoon were write-offs, and work was going all-out on the fourth. II Platoon reported the hope of having three panzers operational soon. My main concern was whether we could beat the British to it. If their tanks arrived right now in this readiness area, we would have to attempt to evade capture using close-combat weapons.

The operational panzers went to the park entrance gate. It was difficult to steer these mighty and to some extent cumbersome Tigers between the giant craters. Anybody who has seen woodland after a hurricane, with giant trees lying everywhere, can perhaps imagine how the once well-cared for park now looked. We still kept hearing the noise of vehicles nearby, between it the reports of tank guns and the clatter of MG fire, though these noises of battle seemed to be coming from much further afield. Had the British already passed us by? Where were German troops? Had the carpet bombing wiped them all out? We had no contact with any of them, either by radio or messenger.

It might have been about 1000hrs, perhaps later, when we had six panzers roadworthy. They were still listed for the workshop but at least running and, so I believed, could fire their guns. I have no idea which number panzer I boarded. The main thing was, we were rolling. After 1.5km along the park wall we were held up south-west of Maneville. Two of my panzers had engine fires and could only follow at a slow speed.

Around 1100hrs we saw two Shermans advancing through a depression, carrying out reconnaissance against us. It was only then that we discovered more damage to our panzers from the carpet bombing than had been detected earlier. We opened fire with our guns but fired wide: the blast had decalibrated them. Where one round had been sufficient before, now we needed three. Where we had parked was also not ideal. Our view was obstructed by hedges and bushes so that although we were to some extent under cover we could only use our firepower with difficulty. In order to have a better field of fire we shifted our position, for to judge by the noises, the British corridor through which they were making inroads had to run immediately in front of us. My aim was to attack them in the flank. Going around a small wood, the company drove at first to the south-west in the direction of Cagny, from where it would then turn west to the Le Prieuré farmstead. That at any rate was the plan. During the manoeuvre there were two sharp explosions one after the other. Feldwebel Schönrock's panzer burst into flames. It had been penetrated by a hit from ahead, as had the panzer of Feldwebel Müller. We retrieved the wounded and took them on the rear of a panzer to the nearby dressing station at Maneville. The worst case was Unteroffizier Matthes, with severe burns. The other Tigers pulled back 200m on my orders and took up fresh positions. We did not know exactly from where the fire had come. As both panzers had received frontal hits, the shells must have been fired from Cagny, 1,200m ahead of us. But at this time Cagny was in German hands. It was one puzzle after another, for until then we knew of no British weapon which could penetrate the frontal armour of a Tiger.

At last I had finally managed to restore radio contact with Fromme, the Abteilung commander. He was with the panzers of the Abteilung HQ very near the Maneville 'Château'. Hauptmann Scherf was also there with his Tiger 300. Since it had fallen quiet in my vicinity, I walked there and reported the status of my company: two Tigers total write-offs after frontal penetration, guns decalibrated, engine fires due to failure of cooling systems. We also had sixteen dead. All our panzers ought to have been at the repairers, but in this situation in the face of the enemy we had to act for as long as possible as though we were capable of a really serious resistance. From there I went to the main dressing station again. Unteroffizier Matthes looked dreadfully mutilated, he had been given injections but I doubt if he recognized me. He died a short time later. I went back to our previous readiness area. The crews of the panzers abandoned there had meanwhile been brought out by our Tross. I looked over the panzers. My 311 could really have been towed out. The damage to the other panzers was too serious. Oberfeldwebel Sachs' 313 lay upside down. This 58-tonne panzer had been simply blown over. What forces this bombardment had unleashed! I still could not believe what had swept over us there. Where my front-line repair group had been earlier I found a 20-litre canister of cold tea. I shouldered it and returned to my company. They had nothing to report.

We were grateful for the tea in the midday heat. Towards 1600hrs Hauptmann Fromme ordered 3 Company to decamp, recovering those panzers still capable of repair with the available tools. I put together a towing platoon. The roadworthy panzers, mostly those with external bomb damage, towed the ones immobilized by engine or running-gear damage. While the towing platoon went off to our rearward services at Rupiere, I returned with my Tiger to our readiness area to try to tow out my 311. While my crew set to work with a will under great pressure of time, I looked over the other stranded panzers, which included Sachs' 313.

The upside-down monster was quite impressive. Some of the wheels had been dislodged and the tracks ripped off. As I stood behind it staring, it struck me that the emergency exit hatch on the turret, which could only be opened from inside, was a few centimetres ajar. This hatch was so constructed that if opened from inside, the weight of the lid would cause it to open fully. Because the panzer lay on its turret, the hatch could not be opened and a great lifting force would be necessary to raise the panzer first. Anybody still inside the fighting compartment was therefore trapped. I climbed up to the small gap of the partly open hatch and called inside. As if by some miracle I got an answer. I found that my attempts to open the hatch any wider were fruitless, and summoned three men to help. With our combined force we got the hatch open and shored it up with a thick wooden beam. Oberfeldwebel Sachs was the first to emerge, then the gunner and finally the driver. All had bruises and contusions, and burns from contamination with battery acid. They had been unconscious for some hours, then awoke to find themselves in an overturned panzer hopelessly trapped and wedged in and we brought them out more dead than alive. Now it was high time for us all to get out of there.

The Abteilung had gone to clear up a breach in the line near Cagny, and a new defensive front had been set up about 5km further back. I was not aware of this and scouted first of all a route wide enough for a tow and when darkness fell I got my Tiger 311 towed away with the greatest difficulty. Obergefreiter Siehl distinguished himself especially, steering the panzer despite his serious burns. Shortly after we had vacated the park the British arrived to occupy it. Once again I had come through unscathed.

A British report attributes the failure of their forces to capture Cagny until the late afternoon of 18 July – much later than their planning had allowed – to the attack on the left flank of their advance by six Tigers of Heavy PzAbt 503, which had miraculously survived the carpet bombing. The Wehrmacht report for 24 July 1944 states:

Since midday Tuesday, German forces have put out of action 420 British and North American tanks on the invasion front. Most of the enemy tanks were destroyed or

The blast from the Operation *Goodwood* bombs even overturned a 60-tonne Tiger. The explosion tore off the forward pair of running wheels with their axle and the pair of drive wheels (far right).

Feldwebel Sachs of Tiger 313 was one of three survivors from this incident, but two crew lost their lives.

The woods at Manneville as seen in a US aerial reconnaissance photo taken on 18 July 1944. The area was churned up by carpet bombing, many Tigers being destroyed.

The grave of Unteroffizier Rolf Matthes of 3 Company/Heavy PzAbt 503 who fell at Manneville/Emiéville on 18 July 1944.

Tiger 323 half buried, the armoured turret torn off its mounting.

captured in the fighting eastwards of the Orne. From the numbers in a single day the bitterness of the fighting and the course of the operations can be inferred. Heavy Panzer Abteilung 503 under Hauptmann Fromme and Artilleriepanzerabwehr [anti-tank artillery] Abteilung 1039 under Hauptmann Witzel, caused the enemy especially heavy losses. Hauptmann Witzel's Abteilung put thirty-five British tanks out of action before he died a hero in the bitter struggle.

Having joined the Tross at Rupiere I rolled myself in my blanket under a large tree and slept and slept. On 19 July I saw to it that my panzers went into the workshop, then I received the commanding officer's order that I was to take three days' convalescent leave in Paris. I shook hands with him and anybody else I saw in delight at this well-deserved pause in the fighting. Oberleutnant Dr Barkhausen, the Abteilung adjutant, came along too. He knew Paris well from his student years and was an excellent tour guide. Our departure on the morning of 20 July was delayed for having celebrated too much the previous evening with the workshop company and upon awaking we found ourselves not yet fit to travel. At midday we set off for Paris in the Volkswagen full of expectations, a wonderful journey completed in three hours. How did we get there? The co-driver sat on the right-hand mudguard looking backwards to keep an eye on the sky for enemy aircraft, the driver and passengers kept watch ahead. On this run we were not molested by aircraft, although apparently the enemy fighter-bombers were all over Normandy.

We lodged at the Hotel Commodore on Boulevard Haussman, a Wehrmacht hotel. Barkhausen went with me that first evening to the 'Lapin Agile' on Montmartre. It was a really highbrow literary cabaret. I had been expecting to see a bit more flesh, but such cheap pleasure was not on Dr Barkhausen's agenda. When we got back to Boulevard Haussman towards 2200hrs we were approached by some ladies of the night and from them we learned of the attempt to assassinate Hitler. They also told us that at that moment in Paris, the SS was being arrested by the Wehrmacht. It was amazing that the news could have got round so fast. What were my feelings at hearing this news? It had less effect on me than its far-reaching consequences might have led one to expect. Nobody knew anything for certain, it was all just rumours. Finally we learned, without further details, that the attempt had failed. I have to confess that the entire event, the fact of the attempt and its failure, excited my interest very little at first although I did feel a certain satisfaction at the arresting of the SS. Not at the Front, but in the 'Etappe', the occupied areas between the front lines and the Reich, as here, there were substantial reservations about the presence and preferential treatment shown to the SS. In the Etappe, however, there were also substantial reservations about service centres of all kinds for us '*Frontschwein*'. Despite what one may imagine about how it was then, in Paris for the first time we were captivated by the flair of the city. After the fighting in Normandy only two days previously, it was marvellous and beautiful in an unreal way with its easy living, its pleasures, its elegance, its peaceful appearance, life and work. All we wanted to do at that moment was experience it and enjoy it. In those first few hours I was like a peasant farmer visiting a great city for the first time, and once it had begun to sink in I acclimatized very quickly to the environment both inwardly and outwardly.

We visited all the must-see tourist attractions: Les Invalides, the Louvre, Jeu de Paume, Notre-Dame, Sacré-Coeur de Montmartre, Palais de Trocadéro and the Eiffel Tower. In the flea market at the Porte de Clignancourt I spent all the cash I had on things to send home, finally even buying a bolt of cloth which I exchanged when the money ran out. The first two days passed very quickly, and on the morning of the third day we were supposed to set off back. To my great surprise Hauptmann Scherf appeared at the hotel to inform me that 3 Company was to pass all its available panzers to 2 Company before transferring to the troop-training depot at Mailly-le-Camp near Châlons, where it would receive an issue of new Tigers. Leutnant Koppe was handling the transfer of the company and was expected with the company in Paris in a few days on the way to Mailly. During the period of rest and recuperation we would be attached to PzBrig X at Rheims, and Hauptmann Scherf drove me there at once to make contact. On the drive he revealed that he was being transferred and would probably be taking over another Tiger Abteilung and, what was more important for me, that I would become company leader of 3 Company.

An advance party from the company went to Mailly, myself following two days later. I found that the best possible preparations had been made there. A day later I was ordered back to Paris in order to organize the delivery of our new panzers with HQ West, Transport Command and all other imaginable useful or superfluous administrative offices. The paper war had blossomed and especially in Paris a great number of offices needed to justify their existence. Our expected panzers had not yet left Germany and therefore we had a few days free. So as to give the soldiers of our company something of Paris, Hauptmann Scherf allowed the transport from Normandy to Mailly to pause for two days in the French capital. The men could

(left) A German soldier salutes the Unknown Warrior at the memorial below the Arc de Triomphe in Paris.

(below) King Tigers of Heavy PzAbt 503 rolling through the magnificent deserted boulevards of Paris en route for the Front not far west of it. In the background the Arc de Triomphe. Soon after, Paris would be back in Allied hands.

stroll the streets in small groups and see the sights. They were accommodated in the château at Vincennes.

At the training depot we were given space to bivouac near the village of Sompuis. At the beginning of August, 3 Company's panzers arrived. They were the newest version of the Tiger, SdKfz 182, the Tiger II (King Tiger). A large amount of their equipment was missing, and a squad was dispatched at once to Germany to fetch it. I sent one of the lorries to pass through Rastatt to drop off my purchases from the flea market. Meanwhile we worked all-out to get the new panzers operational. The days were filled with painting on the camouflage scheme and turret numbers, running them in and calibrating the weapons. Meanwhile a group of photographers from the Propaganda Company came by to snap 'the daily routine of an operational panzer company'. While doing so, the panzers of Feldwebel Seidel and Unteroffizier Jäckel suffered damage to the engine and gears respectively.

I went forward again to the Abteilung command post in order to report to the commanding officer in person on the status and difficulties of our refresher period. On this journey I came into contact for the first time with the French resistance movement, the Maquis. There was some danger, but I came out of it unscathed. Nevertheless my impression after this journey was that the situation looked anything but rosy. At the command post I heard the broadcast of the speech by Dr Robert Ley, who as head of the German Arbeitsfront was one of the most unpleasant firebrands. This was his notorious speech following 20 July in which he characterized the nobility as 'blue-blooded Schweinehunde' and made some frightening threats – I was disturbed and shocked. We discussed it. Fromme said in his dry way, 'Young man, don't let it get to you, we shall protect you.' Meanwhile the names of some of the group of assassins of 20 July had been made known. The greater part of them came from old noble families, which irritated me. I could not beleive that these men would have acted from pure self-interest or whatever other reason had been put forward by officialdom: much more likely the most serious reasons lay behind it. Whatever it was, it had nothing to do with me. It was a pity that Rommel was out of action after his severe wound of 17 July. We had great faith in him. A word from him now would have helped us greatly.

I discussed my fears with Hauptmann Wiegand, head of the supply company, Oberleutnant Dr Barkhausen, our adjutant and also with Hauptmann von Eichel-Streiber, commanding officer of 2 Company. We were in shreds inwardly, but we could see no way out of the hopeless situation, neither for the German *Volk* nor for ourselves personally. Nevertheless, at the centre of all considerations was the urgent need to get the company operational as quickly as possible, for it was needed at the Front. We knew that no turn of the military tide was going to come and that the leaders could no longer deceive us with their all-too-transparent pleas to hold out until it did so. What we did hope, however, was that by fighting on we might be able to force an honourable armistice. This became the new catchphrase. For that reason we were prepared to keep all our forces active. We also spoke frequently of the idea that after the war, first of all, there would have to be a good clear-out of the Interior. After 20 July the Wehrmacht had found itself on the defensive, everything was moving towards an SS state. Himmler had been appointed Commander of the Reserve Army, so that the Personnel Office, training and the officers' schools were all under his direction. The Wehrmacht was ordered henceforth to use the Hitler salute, the military salute was abolished. This affected us deeply, for the latter was what distinguished us outwardly from the Waffen-SS. We held them in high esteem as outstanding troops, but for us they were the Nazi Party's army, and we did not want to be that under any circumstances.

On 11 August 1944 I was able to load the first transport train with five King Tigers. I took charge of it myself. The unloading yard was Paris since Normandy was out of the question: the Front was approaching the French capital at alarming rate. We received another three wagons with ammunition for our panzers and two wagons of spare parts and workshop equipment. Because a 72-tonne King Tiger was a great burden for the bedding of the railway tracks, the Tiger transporters could not be coupled to each other but had to have a so-called protective wagon between them. In our case these were not empty wagons, but the previously mentioned five with ammunition and spare parts. Because of enemy air supremacy this was an unpleasant situation, but there was nothing I could do about it.

It was a wonderful summer's day when the rail journey began. We had just passed Sézanne and were happy to have the station behind us because it offered rewarding targets for enemy airmen. We lay in the sun behind the panzer on the Ssymswagen enjoying life. Ssymswagen were special Reichsbahn railway transporters for Tigers. Suddenly, from a clear sky, machine-gun fire. The locomotive blew off steam, whistled plaintively and the train came to an abrupt halt. My first thought was the Maquis, who were very numerous in this area. Then I saw a line of Thunderbolts flying towards us, one behind the other. I jumped up and took cover below the Ssymswagen and between the rails, but splinters from the explosive shells sprayed all around me, forcing me to shift my position. I waited for the attack to finish and then jumped up to the panzer in which my crew were seated. By a stroke of bad luck the commander's hatch jammed and in my excitement I failed to open it. The aircraft banked for a fresh attack. I lay on the turret without any cover and watched them dive down towards me, saw the muzzle flashes, and the shells whizzed 10m above my head. While I was trying to get the hatch open another attack came in, this aircraft so close that I could see the pilot. I escaped unhurt this time too and the panzer crew finally got the hatch open from inside. I was still sliding into my commander's cupola when the next attack arrived, the shells exploding in front of me on the turret. Because I had pulled my arms across my chest to get through the narrow hatch opening, I caught a quantity of small splinters in my lower right arm and a few larger ones in the chest. I was extremely lucky not to receive injury to my face or eyes. At the same time my radio operator Obergefreiter Tannhäuser, who had opened his entry hatch a few centimetres, received a severe wound to the neck through this small gap, and my gunner, Unteroffizier Werkmeister, was wounded in the hip. We applied emergency dressings to each other while one attack after another ensued. When I looked out through the viewing slit of my cupola I was horrified to see the rear of our panzer burning brightly while the two ammunition wagons either side of the Ssymswagen were also on fire.

The shells nearest us exploded with a great roar. The fire radiated enormous heat. It was difficult to see if the flames were coming from the engine compartment of the panzer or from the surface. Meanwhile the fighter-bombers had withdrawn, having done their worst. I stood with the fire-extinguisher in the turret fighting every flame which licked at me. In the panzer, soon we could hardly tolerate being half-drowned by the foam any longer, the 8.8cm ammunition in the two burning wagons was exploding all around – it must have made quite a fireworks display. What I feared most was that the great heat would cause the panzer's petrol tanks to explode, taking us up with it. Furthermore we had eighty 8.8cm rounds inside a fully fuelled panzer. Therefore five of us sat in the panzer, three of us wounded, without being able to protect ourselves against the fire or heat. It was a frightening situation, for something worse was bound to happen, and we couldn't abandon the vehicle while the wagons were still burning and the exploding ammunition whizzed around our ears.

During our transport from Germany I had watched as a company of Panthers performed an emergency unloading during a low-level air attack. All panzers turned 90° on the platform wagon and then drove directly from the wagon onto the ground, where they dispersed widely. Later in passing I saw the tracks in a field of wheat and made a note to myself. The Panther company suffered no losses.

I recalled this procedure and it seemed to me the only possibility now. Turn 90°
on the Ssymswagen and descend. This was a double stretch of track, therefore it
was possible. I gave the driver the order. I had forgotten, however, that the extra-
broad tracks of our panzer stowed alongside the vehicle prevented a 90° turn. The
engine came to life, the panzer turned slowly, then stopped mid-turn with the track
overhanging. Suddenly the panzer inclined to the left and before we realized what
was happening it fell off and lay on its turret near the rails. Being inside as the
tank slowly overturned was ghastly. The panzer was still burning while around us
the ammunition in the open wagons continued to explode. After about an hour of
unbearable waiting the wagons finally burnt out.

I got free through the loader's hatch, then the men of my transport who had
sought cover in the panzers or in the field came running up and the fire in my
panzer was finally extinguished. As was established later, both petrol tanks had
been holed by enemy fire and the panzer would probably have blown up if it had
not overturned. Because it had done so, the fuel from the tanks had eventually run
out freely and did little damage while burning.

We retrieved our wounded. After searching the whole area we found six
severely wounded, five walking wounded and near the locomotive the dead
body of Unteroffizier Wehrheim. All the ammunition and spares wagons were
burnt out, the rails were torn up and so the last railway line into Paris still
functioning had been disrupted. We brought the wounded to a nearby railway
worker's house. I borrowed a bicycle and went along the railway line with a
local to the nearest station at Esternay in order to telephone the German rail
authorities and request that a military hospital be informed. I did not succeed in
the latter but when I got back to the wrecked train the French Red Cross was
in attendance with an ambulance and German doctor. The French had watched
the attack from Esternay and had set out at once with their ambulance. Shortly
before the air attack began a German ambulance train had passed us on the
neighbouring tracks heading for Germany. On seeing the attack the train had
stopped and came back. Therefore my wounded were in good hands straight
away though Oberfeldwebel Bormann died during the journey. I couldn't leave
my transport without a commander and so merely had my wounds dressed and
accepted a tetanus shot. I sent a dispatch rider with my report to the remainder
of the company at Mailly and another to Paris where I expected Hauptmann
Scherf would be at the Hotel Commodore. I was not aware of it at the time but
Hauptmann Fromme was also there after gathering the wheeled vehicles of the

Abteilung together at Pontoise as they came back from the Falaise Pocket and the Seine.

After a few hours a Reichsbahn railway-construction train with an 80-tonne crane arrived but did not start work until the surrounding area had been searched for unexploded bombs and shells. After the body of Unteroffizier Wehrheim had been buried on the edge of the woods, a locomotive came and took the remnants of my transport to the nearest small station to be disembarked. We stayed there for four days because the line ahead of it and behind was under continual air attack. The time I spent there was not pleasant because of the heat, we had no food, I heard nothing from Company and my wounds caused me a lot of discomfort. It surprised me greatly that I did not hear from Company. Both dispatch riders had returned without a reply. Therefore I could only wait until the transport was able to continue. On the fourth day a Hauptmann arrived from the HQ of the General of Panzer Troops West, who had been at Mailly. He was accompanied by Leutnant Rambow who now relieved me. The Hauptmann brought me to his HQ in Paris where I was interrogated closely respecting the events of 12 August and had to submit a full written report. I did not feel uncomfortable about any action I had taken, however, and ultimately the matter was forgotten.

After the process ended, it was late evening. The General's command post was at St Cloud. When I was stationed in Paris after the war, I often passed this building, which always reminded me of my interrogation. At my request I was taken to Hotel Commodore on Boulevard Haussman, where I met Hauptmann Scherf. We sat talking for hours in the hotel bar but if I asked what steps he had taken regarding my transport I cannot remember the answers. Next morning I went to the assembly hall for the wounded at the École Militaire on the Champs de Mars. As it was getting decidedly unpleasant in Paris at that time and the military hospitals there were being evacuated, I was taken to the military hospital for the SS-Leibstandarte *Adolf Hitler* at Meaux where I received the best of treatment.

After two days this hospital was also pulled back and I came to Château-Thierry, really primitive and the town a miserable place. Next day I took the first opportunity available to go to Rheims. Here the hospital was that kind of huge operation in which I would not have dreamed of being interned, and I landed up in the wounded-assembly area. I skilfully avoided being put on the transport for the Reich, which was the last place I wished to go, and reported back instead to PzBrig X responsible for re-equipping the company at Mailly. Here I was given a very friendly welcome. I was told where to find a hotel room, I got a new uniform, my pay, money for my food and ration coupons. Now I was in the right place and received my walking-wounded discharge at the wounded-assembly point though I had to report back there for a check-up every other day. At first those days I spent in Rheims were pleasant. I ate in a restaurant and took coffee in a coffee-house complete with dance-orchestra where for the first time I heard American jazz. I remember well the 'Tiger Rag'. In the Reich this kind of music had been prohibited for years and so I had never heard it before: I found that it struck a chord with me. Whenever I hear 'In the Mood' or the 'Tiger Rag' nowadays, it reminds me of my time in Rheims.

By chance I came across a number of Abteilung men who had all lost contact with their companies through their stay in military hospital. I myself had no idea where the Abteilung was to be found either and so found them quarters in Rheims and gave them orders to report to me at noon every day at the hotel. Paris had already been lost to us by this time.

At Rheims I met Oberschirrmeister (Senior Motor Pool NCO) Haslbeck who had come from the company at Mailly and told me that it still had two driveable Tigers which had to be got out before the Americans arrived. Also, my Panzer 311 lay beside the railway embankment with a burnt-out engine. Haslbeck had not had contact with the company for several days but I felt that I really had to make the effort to re-establish contact, so I left my people at Rheims and went with Haslbeck in his Volkswagen to Mailly.

The situation regarding the two panzers at Mailly was very unfavourable. One could manage a few hundred metres under its own power, the other needed to be towed. Next morning I had both of them brought to the loading ramp and changed their tracks for the train journey. This was very difficult because half of the narrower tracks required were missing from the Ssymswagen. After much puzzling it over, my clever people found a solution even here. I went to the Transport Kommandantur at Châlons, requested wagons and a departure number, and arranged at Épernay station for a locomotive to be available for my train at the hour indicated. It could only be a few more days before the Allies arrived, and none of the foregoing was as easy as has been described, because it had to be argued out with both the Wehrmacht and Reichsbahn departments. They were all afraid of giving out any orders which were not routine. Some bureaucrats showed complete indifference.

This was all about two Tigers. I still had several long journeys to make and since I needed to be independent, the most important thing was to obtain wheels from somewhere. On the drive through Châlons I made a stop at the motor pool and

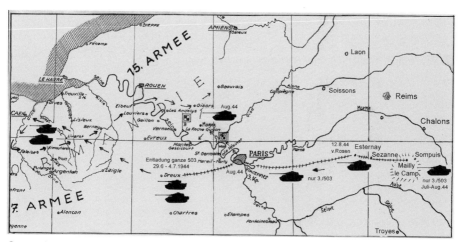

General map showing locations of Heavy PzAbt 503 in France, July and August 1944. 'Entladung ganze 503' = Entire Abteilung 503 unloaded.

Joachim Jäckel and Gotthold Wunderlich in front of the Arc de Triomphe. The author spent a brief leave in Paris in July 1944.

Hauptmann Scherf at a briefing, behind him Leutnant Koppe while Orderly Room Feldwebel Grohmann works at his list.

Feldwebel Heinrich Skoda posing before a new King Tiger at Mailly-le-Camp in August 1944. The 80cm width of the tracks is particularly in evidence in this photo.

(above) King Tiger 300 with Hauptmann Scherf in the turret on driver familiarization training. The running number already has the white surround. This is the Henschel turret: the first fifty King Tigers completed had the Porsche turret with the rounded front.

(left) Troop-training depot Mailly-le-Camp at the beginning of August 1944. Here Hauptmann Scherf is wearing captured British goggles, Hannes Schneider stands behind him.

King Tiger 332 rolling out for calibration work on the long 8.8cm 43 L/71 gun. The other Tiger in the protection of the woods is having maintenance work carried out with the aid of a Bilstein crane.

After the bombing raids of 18 July 1944, 3 Comp/Heavy PzAbt 503 relinquished its remaining Tigers to 2 Company and the personnel relocated to Mailly-le-Camp to re-equip. 3 Company then received twelve Tiger II with Porsche turrets and two with Henschel turrets. In this photo a new Tiger II is being sprayed in camouflage livery. In the background can be seen a company lorry with 'general issue' wooden driver housing.

Group photo aboard King Tiger 300. Hannes Schneider occupies the radio-operator's position, in the driver's hatch in shirtsleeves is Otto Kroneisen.

Calibration exercises. Here King Tiger 334 with Unteroffizier Gärtner is seen at the large troop training depot at Mailly-le-Camp south of Châlons-sur-Marne.

King Tiger 300 being camouflaged with branches and brushwood from the nearby
woodlands. 3 Company/Heavy PzAbt 503 spent some quiet weeks behind the lines at
Mailly-le-Camp.

During a pause in an exercise, Leutnant Koppe (left in picture) exchanges photos with the
author (centre). Leutnant Rambow is on the right.

The author was in charge of the first Tiger transport from Mailly-le-Camp to Paris on 12 August 1944. The train was attacked by Allied fighter-bombers west of Esternay/Sézanne. Ammunition wagons exploded and camouflage materials caught fire. The photo shows the train after the attack. The leading wagons were undamaged

After it caught fire, the author attempted to make an emergency unloading of his King Tiger 311 by turning it through 90° while fitted with the temporary narrower loading tracks. The normal 80cm wide tracks stowed alongside the vehicle hindered this manoeuvre, causing the vehicle to tip over and land on its turret.

The author was wounded by fighter-bomber fire. His King Tiger was hauled upright by a railway crane and towed to the road a few days later. On 14 August 1944 it was captured by advancing US troops.

The rear section of the train transport was totally destroyed when the ammunition wagons exploded. The King Tigers remaining on the low-loader were still operational, however.

The author with arm wound at the grave of Unteroffizier Wehrheim.

The cross marking the grave of Unteroffizier Ernst Wehrheim who fell on 12 August 1944.

The comrades-in-arms of Unteroffizier Wehrheim pay their last respects at the graveside. He died as a result of wounds received during the fighter-bomber attack on the train transport, 12 August 1944.

Another comrade, Oberfeldwebel Bormann, died in the hospital train on 13 August 1944 of wounds received during the same attack the previous day.

Not until several days later was the stretch of track cleared and the remnants of the Abteilung transported to the park at Paris-Vincennes. At this time the author was already at a military hospital in Rheims.

after much talk I managed to convince the Etappe jackass of the importance of my mission. The last available motor car belonged to the Châlons gendarmerie. I got a requisition docket for this vehicle and finally took possession of the black Citroën. In this vehicle over the next few days I covered over a thousand kilometres, including the stretch between Rheims and Mailly three times. The Tigers were loaded and as everything seemed to be going smoothly, I returned to my Tiger 311 near Sézanne. The panzer had been got back on its tracks and my next problem was to have it towed out of the danger area, for the 18-tonne tractors needed for the purpose were probably the rarest vehicles in the German Wehrmacht. I wanted at least three of them to tow my Tiger. First I went back to Mailly. The transport with my Tigers had already left the station. The enemy armoured spearhead had already been sighted at Arcis-sur-Aube, about 15km away. They could arrive at Mailly at any moment. After I had helped to clear out the soldiers' hostel I went back to Rheims. It was my last night there; the next day I set out on the hunt for the tractors. I tried my luck at PzBrig X and all the workshop units of the Luftwaffe without success – none was to be found anywhere. Slowly my hopes of getting the panzers out began to evaporate. The vehicle returned at midday and reported having seen no sign of the advancing enemy. Therefore I sent the Volkswagen to Sézanne to get the rest of the crew to safety: they were there to destroy the panzer once the enemy turned up. In the Épernay area, however, the Volkswagen was held up for two hours by fighter-bomber attacks and when they finally arrived at Sézanne they ran into the American spearhead. I was told all this the next day when I returned to Rheims. (The workshop supervisor and driver, who had remained behind in the panzer, were taken prisoner by the Americans but arrived home safe and well a couple of years later.)

Meanwhile I had discovered a panzer recovery platoon in the area around Laon, but my journey there bore no fruit, for all their tractors were out on jobs although I did at least discover the location of the HQ of the General Commanding Panzer Troops West. A Führer-HQ had been set up near Laon-Soissons consisting of three large compounds with all the usual trimmings. The HQ was now housed in the so-called Führer-compound after having been forced to flee from Paris. They were unable to help, but referred me to the so-called 'Göring Compound', where I ran into my former PzRgt 35 regimental commander, General Eberbach. He was taken prisoner a few days later with his staff. The C-in-C West told me that a panzer recovery platoon was in the woods at Compiègne. Therefore I drove there through the night. The description 'the woods at Compiègne' was fairly imprecise and more by luck than anything else I found the unit. Finally I had run to earth the long-sought three tractors and would have set off with them straight away for my Panzer 311 via Château-Thierry and Sézanne had they had any fuel. Where could this be conjured from? After two hours of searching I contacted some Corps Staff or other who granted me 1,000 litres from a compound in Compiègne. The tractors tanked up before daybreak but taking to the road with these three towing machines by day would have been pure suicide. The slow and cumbersome vehicles would have been certain victims of the fighter-bombers, and so there was nothing for it but to wait for nightfall.

By chance I met an Abteilung vehicle and learned that the Abteilung was operational with its remaining panzers near Beauvais. I gave the driver a report for the commanding officer advising him of my impending return to the Abteilung, then went back to the HQ of the General of Panzer Troops West at Laon. From a glance at the map I saw that since the position of my panzer was now behind enemy lines my objective was frustrated and so I released the tractors and took the most direct route back to Rheims. These drives were very tiring for we rarely had a night's rest, the distances to be covered were getting longer and we always had to keep a lookout for enemy aircraft. On several occasions we were very lucky and got our car under cover just in time.

Back at Rheims the whole city was in the throes of great excitement – the enemy was at the gates. Oberschirrmeister Haslbeck was waiting for me. He told me about the efforts involving my 311 and also that through the negligence of the driver his Volkswagen had been stolen. Also that the train transport with the two panzers and crews had arrived at Rheims and had been re-routed onwards immediately by the Reichsbahn because of the proximity of the enemy. He had also put aboard the train all the personnel of the Abteilung I had gathered together in Rheims. So at least those two Tigers were safe.

Now I had to go to Charleville, where I arrived that evening with Haslbeck. Whereas in Rheims chaotic, undisciplined disorder had reigned, and ugly scenes had been played out, at Charleville all was still calm. At the station command post they knew nothing of my train transport. The friendly station commander took us both into his home and I finally had a wonderful sleep. The command post was set up in the station house in which the Kaiser had stayed during the First World War. Next morning I saw my transport train in a goods yard near Charleville. I took charge of it and, after making many telephone calls to arrange a locomotive for the later stage of the journey, set off for Liège where there was a large panzer workshop.

Meanwhile panic had also broken out in Charleville, rumours were rife and everybody was simply fleeing aimlessly. The soldiers' hostel had been abandoned in great haste by the Red Cross nurses: infantrymen plundered it, the field gendarmes were powerless. I brandished my pistol to prevent some sly foxes making off with the cigarette stocks and arranged for a fairly reasonable distribution. Haslbeck had meanwhile found a garage containing three cars in pristine condition abandoned by the field kommandantur. Quickly and skilfully these were changed – tactical insignia etc. painted over – while I forged some documents (I felt justified in doing this) proving our right to the vehicles. Providing the rightful owners did not recognize them, there was practically nothing to stop us.

I made a gift of my rather tired Citroën to an infantryman returning from military hospital to help him in his search for his unit. All thirteen men not needed for the panzer transport now piled into my three cars. Fuel was still a problem but we solved that at Bethel railway station where we found a rail tanker wagon. Despite every imaginable objection we got our petrol. Because the road via Laon was already in enemy hands we had to retrace our steps to Charleville and from there head for Beauvais via Hirson–St Quentin–Ham–Montdidier. The journey was very tiring because at night column after column was flooding back eastwards along this road. We reached our destination; the Abteilung had put up clear road signs and thus I reported back to my commanding officer with three vehicles and thirteen men.

The Abteilung command post had been established in a château in the middle of a small wood. My surprise reappearance from military hospital and the recovery from Mailly of the two panzers, already written off by Abteilung, gave rise to great joy and raised our spirits. Benjamin (the Ordnance Officer) put me in the picture regarding the situation.

The Abteilung, hard pressed in fighting east of the Orne, had been surrounded in the great Falaise Pocket. Although it had managed to fight its way out almost at once, it must have experienced a great drama in doing so, followed by crossing the Seine under constant enemy air attack. North of the Seine, only the freshly delivered panzers of 3 Company were available to oppose the American bridgehead at Mantes, and here they had suffered heavily. The enemy's material superiority and air supremacy were simply too great. Only one of the Abteilung's panzers was still operational, that of Leutnant Rambow. The situation around the command post was uncertain and higher command had no clear view as a result of the rapidly changing situation. Therefore we had ourselves sent out scouting parties from our reconnaissance platoon. I learned that Hauptmann Scherf would very soon be sent on the Abteilung command course and that I would be taking over 3 Company as company leader. We were still in good spirits when the information came that the Americans were nearby. We left the château in a long column of cars, led by the open car of the commanding officer. A bottle of cognac was passed from car to car. Then my vehicle went on strike and I fell behind the column. Because I had no map and did not know the area, Leutnant Brodhagen's car stayed behind with me.

The commanding officer wanted to go to the Tross. Since night was now falling and we could not begin anything in our condition, we pushed the car into cover and slept until daybreak. We awoke to find the roads remarkably empty, only the odd lone vehicle. We were told that the Americans had reached Amiens, which was where we were headed, therefore our rear services would probably have pulled out long before. Our purpose now was to skirt around the enemy, by-pass Amiens and cross the Somme. We were led to believe that all bridges over the Somme had been blown up during the night and so assumed that our Abteilung would already have crossed.

We got the car going again but the unlikelihood of reaching the Somme before the Americans got there worried us. Approaching a small village, we heard MG fire close at hand. Standing on the bonnet I could see American tanks moving in from the other end of the village. We turned around and fled at full speed. Using country lanes and tracks across fields we reached the Somme and by a stroke of luck found a small bridge still intact. At Péronne we met up again with German troops but could find no trace of the Abteilung. We pressed on through Arras and Lens to Lille, pursuing unsuccessful enquiries at every kommandantur along the way for news of our Abteilung. The many military cemeteries, some German, reminded us of the heavy fighting which had raged in this region during the First World War. Finally in Lille we spotted an Abteilung signpost, made contact and reported to the command post in the nearby village of Seclin.

The previous evening the commanding officer had ordered a complete withdrawal, in the process saving the Tross from capture by the Americans at Amiens. At Seclin I also found 3 Company. It had lost the last of its panzers at Amiens although the bulk of the company Tigers had been lost to enemy action at Vexin (Mantes), or for lack of the possibility of repair.

At Seclin I stayed two days in fine private quarters with bath. High Command had provisionally ordered the Abteilung to Liège but it had no fuel, this being something which each company had to organize for itself. While the other companies went from one fuel compound to another and found nothing, I discovered the whereabouts of a petrol dump, drove there and with much cunning and deception got a chit for 5m³. I had gained experience in how to deal with such departments and the word 'Tiger' still had its allure, even here. Thus not only 3 Company but the whole Abteilung was able to move out. In normal times, of course, my methods would have been impossible, but amidst all this hopeless confusion and the total collapse of the Front it was every man for himself.

Over the next three nights the Abteilung travelled about 300km to the north-west. The companies made a motley impression. Having no panzers but most of the crews it was a problem to transport these men. Almost every panzer crew found a parked car somewhere and got it going, and so the company had more than fourteen additional vehicles. Scherf had a fantastic American Packard, a sports car able to achieve a speed in excess of 100kmph, phenomenal for the time. To see it and then be invited to drive such a vehicle was a real joy. Our course took us through Tournay–Leuze–Waterloo–Leuven. A company Muli (a fully tracked lorry) was set on fire in a low-level fighter attack: one man was killed. After parking in a wood near Tienen I was given a special assignment by the commanding officer. The Abteilung was to proceed to Sennelager camp near Paderborn to rest and reorganize. I had to fetch the written orders from an outpost of the General, Panzer Troops West at Liège. In order that the Abteilung should have their contents as soon as possible after receipt, I was assigned a radio car. The Liège outpost did not have the documents, and so I had to continue to the HQ of the General, Panzer Troops West. This was located in a small wood in the Ardennes which I reached after a long drive. Here I was informed by the 1a General Staff Officer that I would have to call at the HQ of Generalfeldmarschall Model at Spa near Liège for the document. Model himself was in Namur, and so that was my next port of call. The town was not a very inviting-looking place with hardly any German troops but many suspicious figures lurking in the shadows. Of course, Model was not in Namur, but I could find him at a conference with SS-Obergruppenführer Sepp Dietrich at Gembloux. I simply had to get these written orders: Model had already left Dietrich's HQ and there was nothing more I could do except return to Spa. I got there at 2300hrs and towards 0200hrs our movement order was in my hands. I passed it on to Abteilung by radio and completed my assignment.

I arrived back in Liège in the early morning. One could sense everywhere the eleventh-hour mood: apparently the enemy was not far off. In the street I met Major Skultetus, whom I knew from Fallingbostel. In conversation he remarked casually that there was a fuel train in the goods yard at Liège. I saw my chance, excused myself as quickly as possible and drove to the station. There the train stood with about 500m³ of fuel. A junior lieutenant was responsible for sharing it out. I requested one wagon for my Abteilung and because the word 'Tiger' worked its magic again my request was fulfilled. By radio I informed Abteilung, which had got to Maastricht, and asked for the entire fuel detachment to get here in order to take it over. At that distance they needed four hours to arrive. During that time I would have to protect my fuel. From all sides vehicles now appeared like moths to the flame to bag some. At first I did a patrol around the wagon, believing that my mere presence would keep all undesired visitors away. Not so. Scarcely had I put a few steps between myself and the wagon than it was opened at the rear and the first barrel started walking. I spotted it in time and from now on sat on my barrels, pistol in hand, and only left my perch when Leutnant Koppe arrived with the fuel detachment. The journey back through Liège was anything but pleasant, the first shoot-outs had begun, always a sign that the Americans would soon be arriving.

Towards evening I reported back to the Abteilung. The company was in the small town of Meersen where I was given a very nice room by a pro-German family. During the two days we spent here, this little Dutch place seemed like a small paradise. In Maastricht a German provisions warehouse was being thrown open in order to prevent the contents falling into enemy hands. With Leutnants Rambow and Wagner, who had meanwhile been transferred to 3 Company, I happened to be passing just at that moment. I got my driver to fetch an empty lorry from our company and we packed it full with tinned food of all kinds, chocolate, wine, liqueurs, cigarettes: we towed out case upon case of foodstuffs for our field kitchen. For whom had all this been originally intended? We *Frontschweine* would never have got to see it. In the weeks following we in the company gorged ourselves. Peas with carrots or asparagus were now to be found on the menu more often. A change from dried vegetables and dried potatoes! Later at Paderborn every man going on leave received a packet to take home.

On 5 September 1944 we left Meersen. We knew the road from here perfectly and the individual company vehicles were sent out at five-minute intervals because of the danger of air attack. I took a German family with me in my car since they had no other way to get back to the Reich. After a few incidents with enemy aircraft, that afternoon we crossed the German border. It was a strange feeling to be back in Germany under these circumstances, and not wonderful. Our destination was Düren, and 3 Company was lodged in the village of Elsen. It was an odd coincidence that my old 1 Company/PzRgt 35 had also stopped here before the beginning of the French campaign. Thus I soon renewed contacts, for the inhabitants of the village remembered us well. The company was given the best of everything, the villagers competing to outdo each other.

Next day our vehicles were loaded at Düren station, and on the afternoon of 7 September I travelled with the commanding officer, Hauptmann Scherf, Hauptman Wiegand, Stabsarzt Dr Schramm and Benjamin in one of two saloon cars for the drive to Sennelager camp at Paderborn.

Many members of Tiger Abteilung 503 struggled back to Germany in August/September 1944 in requisitioned motor vehicles.

8

At Sennelager Camp
(September–October 1944)

The Abteilung HQ settled in at Schloss Neuhaus near Paderborn, and 3 Company was given outstanding private quarters at Hövelhof. Exercises were held for an hour every morning and soon the company was a picture of tight discipline even in appearance. Then most men went on leave, the married men first and also Hauptmann Scherf, commander of 3 Company.

There now began a very busy period for me. A new KStN (War Strength Instruction) for the Tiger Abteilung had been issued by Oberkommando des Heeres (OKH – Supreme High Command), compelling us to reorganize in such a manner as to require fewer men. This would be known today as a time-and-motion study. The repair group had suffered heavy losses in France which now had to be made good. I often went to the Panzer Reserve Abteilung at Paderborn to select the people I wanted in my company. This was mostly achieved by bribing the adjutant of the Reserve Abteilung. I also rid the company of 'undesirables'. The chemistry between myself and the 'Spiess' was not good. He had built up a clique with the field kitchen staff and others for extra rations. I did not want to work with this man. With the help of the commanding officer I transferred him out to 1 Company where the equivalent post had fallen vacant. I appointed my Oberfeldwebel Müller as his replacement, where he proved of invaluable service to myself and the company. In this way I rebuilt the company into something close to the design I had for it. I never regretted the reshuffle although it did strain my relationship with Scherf somewhat since he considered my treatment of his protégé to be unfair. There were other difficulties. For his transfer, Scherf wanted to take with him his entire panzer crew. This was not normal practice but I agreed to it. When he started picking and choosing other good men for himself I had to refuse, which did not go down well.

The commanding officer gave me an assignment near Strasbourg where a few things had to be sorted out with a higher echelon in the Vosges. I visited home for thirty-six hours, driving my French motor car. It was wonderful to see my parents, who were very concerned that the Front had moved so close to the Rhine: even Rastatt was now being attacked by enemy aircraft more frequently. Their favourite target was the railway station with the railway bridge over the Murg, not too far from our house. We discussed the 20 July assassination attempt which in my father's opinion had been the chance to end the war: nobody would sign a peace treaty with Hitler. This had been clear to me for quite some time. I received good news of my sister Aja from Sweden and my brother Wuller in Dresden. My other sister Elisabeth had been at the Spetzgard boarding school on Lake Constance for some time. As soon as the situation in Rastatt got more critical, my parents wanted to evacuate to Rotenfels at the von Blanquet property. One was less exposed there. They went eventually in December 1944.

When we continued to Strasbourg we were surprised in broad daylight by an air-raid alarm and spent over an hour in the cellar of a brewery before going on. On the return journey I went home for a few hours where a longer air raid prevented me leaving on time. The journey after that was a strain on the nerves for the tyres of my car were in such poor condition that I had a puncture ten times. Since we had no spare tyre my poor driver, Obergefreiter Glasl, had to patch them up. The journey having taken fourteen hours, I arrived back at Company at Hövelhof very late.

Scherf returned from leave and at the end of September a company parade was held to mark his departure, and the transfer of the company to me. A company march-past concluded the transfer ceremony. Now I was also officially company commander after having held the position *de facto* for weeks. The Army Personnel Office had originally wanted to transfer in a Hauptmann but Fromme had declined, insisting on my appointment. At that time it was an absolute exception for a Tiger company to be commanded by a junior lieutenant.

Meanwhile our King Tigers had arrived and the usual work on them took up all our time. One weekend we had to show off the amphibious qualities of the panzers in the River Senne for the film boys from the Propaganda Company. Eight weeks later the pictures were released on the *Wochenschau* newsreel. We would have preferred an off-duty Sunday instead.

Then finally something surprising came – orders to move out. Wondering where our next battlefield would be therefore came to an end. The loading went off well and many tears flowed as our transport train steamed out of Paderborn station. The transport ran without incident via Halberstadt–Halle–Eger–Pilsen– Prague–

Brünn–Pressburg, and in the early morning of 14 October 1944 we reached our destination, Budapest.

Hauptfeldwebel Fritz Müller, 3 Company/Heavy PzAbt 503, appointed by the author as 'Spiess' of 3 Company in September 1944.

(left) From left to right on new King Tiger 300, Obergefreiter Urbanski, Unteroffizier Schneider, Feldwebel Georg Heider (with pipe).

(below) A fine group photo at Sennelager taken in September 1944 posing in front of a King Tiger. Back row, left to right: Justus Bornschier, Ernst Weigl, Eckhardt Rambow, Günther Kuhnert, Hannes Schneider. Bottom row, left to right: Hermann Seidel, Kurt Schmidt, Leutnant Wagner, Georg Heider, Toni Urbanski and, lying, Gotthold Wunderlich.

(**above**) From right to
left, Oberfeldwebel
Sachs, Obergefreiter
Bräutigam and Feldwebel
Heinrich Skoda before
a 3 Company King
Tiger with rail transport
tracks at Sennelager,
Paderborn, September
1944.

(**right**) Unteroffizier
Jäckel reading a label.
On his forage cap is the
Abteilung insignia, a
King Tiger in profile. His
family still has it today.
The leather jackets were
taken as booty in France.

(above) An Abteilung VW-Kübelwagen was used by the cameraman of the Propaganda Company to film scenes of the panzer parade. Next to the cameraman is Feldwebel Skoda and a comrade whose name is not known.

(left) The Abteilung was up to strength in men and King Tigers and this was the reason for filming the panzer parade commanded by the author for the *Wochenschau* weekly cinema newsreel. All of 3 Company and parts of 1 Company took part in the parade.

The author at the inauguration of the new panzers. In the background is a 2 Company King Tiger. Only the rail loading tracks were carried by the panzers at the parade in order to spare the crews the heavy labour of changing them.

The King Tigers of the Abteilung after receiving their camouflage paint. Most vehicles had by now been given turret numbers.

An impressive picture of the parade for the *Wochenschau* as the author in Tiger 300 drives slowly past the assembled King Tigers of the Abteilung.

The King Tigers coated with anti-magnetic Zimmerit paste to protect the panzer against enemy limpet mines being affixed during close combat. The new camouflage design was state of the art at the time.

These King Tigers still lack the turret numbers which indicate their company and platoon.

The massive turret of the King Tiger overlapped a section of the engine compartment at the rear. The large exit hatch at the rear of the turret can be seen clearly.

The author gives the command '*Panzer Marsch!*' and the colossi begin rolling behind his Tiger 300.

In this picture the narrower loading tracks for rail transport can be seen. The operational tracks were 80cm wide.

The mighty 8.8cm gun of the King Tiger. Facing the camera from the turret the gunloader (left) and commander.

The author in the autumn of 1944 as company commander, 3 Company/ Heavy PzAbt 503.

Returning from the parade, King Tigers of the Abteilung passed a column of Panthers belonging to a newly formed unit.

Unteroffizier Kurt Knispel also took part in this unusual parade at Sennelager on 25 September 1944 as a King Tiger commander. Credited with over 160 enemy tanks destroyed, at the end of the war he was one of the most successful panzer gunners and commanders of the Second World War. He fell on 28 April 1945.

The new Tigers' guns had to be tested, broken in and adjusted. This was also filmed for the *Wochenschau*, and shown in all cinemas. As a preliminary to the main film it was very important propaganda for the Nazi regime.

9 October 1944: King Tigers of 3 Company/Heavy PzAbt 503 fitted with the narrower loading tracks and heading for the rail loading yard at Paderborn. The men still did not know at this time where they would be heading. A crisis had developed for Germany's Hungarian ally and it was hoped that the mere presence of the Tigers would be sufficient to deter a possible coup.

9

The Collapse, 1944–1945

1944

30 Aug	Major Soviet offensive against Army Group South Ukraine. Romanian troops collapse.
31 Aug	The Red Army enters Bucharest.
12 Sep	Armistice between Romania and the Soviet Union: Romania declares war on Germany.
19 Sep	Armistice between Finland and the Soviet Union.
Oct	Soviet troops enter East Prussia, Czechoslovakia and Hungary.
28 Oct	Armistice between Bulgaria and the Soviet Union.
23 Nov	The French reoccupy Strasbourg.
3 Dec	US forces break through the Westwall at Saarlautern.
16 Dec	Beginning of the German Ardennes offensive (until 27 Dec).

1945

7 Jan	German push from Lake Balaton to relieve encircled Budapest.
12 Jan	Beginning of the Russian winter offensive from the Baranov bridgehead.
20 Jan	Armistice between Hungary and the Soviet Union: Hungary declares war on Germany.
13 Feb	The last German troops in Budapest surrender.
13–15 Feb	Bombing of Dresden.
13 Apr	The Russians capture Vienna.
25 Apr	Total encirclement of Berlin.
30 Apr	Hitler commits suicide in Berlin.
7 May	Unconditional surrender of the German Wehrmacht at Rheims.

The Operation in Hungary (October 1944–February 1945)

Immediately after arriving at Budapest East station I had my VW unloaded and set off to make contact with the Abteilung. I got lost driving through Budapest but finally met up with the unloading officer, Leutnant Bayer, who had been sent out to find me. My company was to camp at Taksony, a small village south of the city. I convinced myself that the unloading was bound to have gone smoothly, gave my orders and then drove my Packard, which had become my command car along with the VW, to Taksony together with an advance party. On the way I made the acquaintance of the Honved (Hungarian military) who stopped me on account of an air-raid warning. When I tried to move off they even aimed their rifles at me, but I convinced them in the nicest possible way that a German officer was not to be intimidated by such shenanigans, and then they let me through.

In Hungary at that time there was as good as no German military presence, only a few divisions having been pushed up to the front line. Budapest was still behind the lines. I noticed along the streets everywhere that anti-tank guns and Flak had been installed with the guns pointing in the direction where the enemy was presumed, and in Taksony there were also road blocks. This puzzled me, but by the following day we understood what was being played out here.

I reported to the local mayor, who was in conference with Hungarian officers, and I cannot say that I received a warm welcome. Having foreign troops billeted on your village is never good news. Apart from that, however, the local people took us in with great cordiality and treated us royally. The old Austro-Hungarian veterans of the Great War wore their German decorations with pride and spoke of the old brotherhood in arms which we were now renewing.

I drove back to the railway station, where the unloading of the company had been achieved in record time. The panzers were now standing camouflaged in an alley and were due to move out at 1300hrs. Two-thirds of the men were absent, having been invited for lunch by the enthusiastic inhabitants of Budapest, but none returned late. We were mobbed by Hungarian men and women who wanted to know everything possible from us. Here I was also made aware of the possibility that a putsch was in the offing. For the first time I heard the name Szálasi, who was leader of the right-wing Hungarian Arrow Cross party. We wanted to show German discipline: as if on the parade ground I had the men fall in before their panzers, climb aboard at a hand signal and then we pulled out in perfect order through Budapest to Taksony. On the way the citizens threw apples, cigarettes and chocolate on the hulls of our panzers. From all corners came encouraging shouts from many beaming faces.

Our quarters at Taksony were good. The Abteilung command post was in the next village and that evening I reported to the commanding officer that all the men

were present and the company operational. My men sat up until late in the night
with the villagers in the bars. At 0200hrs on 15 October I was brought instructions
by dispatch rider to report to the Abteilung command post. Here I received orders
thus: 'At daybreak transfer the company and all elements to Budakeszi.' It was
suspected that the Hungarian government, and also the Hungarian military, might
be about to stage a putsch. The few German troops available were to proceed to the
left bank of the Danube in order to keep a close watch on the situation. Budakeszi,
a minor suburb on the Danube, had been chosen for the purpose. We were warned
to be prepared for possible counter-measures against us by the Hungarian military,
but nothing actually happened.

In the afternoon the situation became clearer. Admiral Horthy, the Hungarian
vice-regent, had sent the Soviets a request for an immediate armistice. Hungarian
radio had broadcast a speech by Horthy in which he made his decision publicly
known. The attitude amongst the Hungarian troops towards us deteriorated fast
and even took on a hostile character. It was now inadvisable to show ourselves in
the city, because the Honved had put up barricades everywhere. The population, on
the other hand, appeared to be rather downcast. We were often stopped and told
that we should not allow this disgrace to be perpetrated. It seemed to me that the
honour of the people had been deeply wounded.

The Abteilung went to combat-readiness. Meanwhile previously prepared
measures and action by the Hungarian right-wing opposition came into play. The
Arrow Cross, who saw the radio proclamation as the signal for their long-awaited
'seizure of power', occupied the radio stations and broadcast a counter-order. As a
result, Arrow Cross organizations and numerous Honved and gendarmerie units
came over to the German side. In the city there was shooting at various places.
King Tigers occupied all the Danube bridges and prevented any traffic passing
between Buda and Pest. My 3 Company was now stationed as Alarm Company
in a park right on the edge of the city. All Hungarian units not declaring for the
German side were disarmed. Everywhere small squads accompanied Tigers for
this purpose and almost everywhere encountered no resistance. I went personally
with Hauptmann von Eichel-Streiber with two Tigers to the Hungarian Military
Academy and required all the officers and men there to surrender their weapons.
As I stood in the office of the academy's commanding officer, an aged white-haired
colonel, he immediately offered me his sabre with a salute. Also with a salute I
returned the sabre – I had read of a similar scene in a book somewhere and I had
found it very impressive. Afterwards I sat in his apartment and took tea with him

and his family. He felt deeply the shame of Horthy's offer of an armistice to the Soviets.

The military action planned for the evening, for which a Waffen-SS unit and elements of our Abteilung were standing by, was called off in the early hours of 16 October. At 0535hrs Horthy bowed to the pressure of the German counter-measures and ordered his guards to offer no resistance. At 0555hrs he left Castle Hill. One battalion of the life guards in the citadel park did not receive his order so that an incident occurred in which four German soldiers were killed. The military action therefore began at 0600hrs and Castle Hill was occupied. This involved 2 Company of our Abteilung. I had detached a half-platoon of my company at the war memorial below the castle as a reserve while the bulk of the company protected the bridges over the Danube with their Tigers. There was only some sporadic shooting in the city so that German troops could be withdrawn in ready response-groups. The Hungarian military and armed Arrow Cross units now took over the national security service, and therefore our assignment in Budapest was concluded.

Against the Russians Again

As an immediate consequence of the appeal for an armistice, on the orders of General Verres, Commander-in-Chief Second Hungarian Army, 2 Hungarian Armoured Division had abandoned its positions in an especially important sector of the front and pulled back to the river Theiss. The retreat was made without regard for the troops still holding the line in the adjoining sectors of the front. Therefore on 19 October it was decided to launch an attack from the Theiss bridgehead at Szolnok with the objective of breaking through the enemy front on the eastern bank of the Theiss and pushing eastwards deep into the flank of the Soviet tank force at Debrecen.

For this purpose PzAbt 503 was attached to 24 PzDiv, and on the evening of 17 October we received the order to move to Szolnok on the Theiss. To economize on fuel the panzers were sent by rail, the wheeled units by road. 1 Company was loaded first, 3 Company next. Because not enough Ssymswagen were available, the companies went piecemeal, waiting for empty trains to return. On the evening of 18 October two transports of my company arrived at Szolnok but my third platoon had still not arrived when operational orders were received for the following

King Tigers of Heavy PzAbt 503 on the train to Hungary.

The Abteilung arrived in Budapest on 13 and 14 October 1944 and was greeted joyfully by sections of the population.

Trams come to a halt as 3 Company sets off for Taksony. Civilian bystanders gaze in wonder at the German panzers.

The first task for the Tigers was to secure the important bridges over the Danube. In the background the famous Budapest 'chain bridge'.

October 1944: King Tigers 313 and 314 at the war memorial below the government citadel in Budapest.

A view along the long barrel of 314, Tiger 313 stands beyond it. Civilians look on with mixed feelings. To the right of the picture is the Monument to the Hungarian Fallen of the Great War.

Tigers 313 and 314 parked at the foot of Castle Hill, their crews awaiting further orders.

SS-Sturmbannführer Otto
Skorzeny organized the
suppression of the putsch.
For effective propaganda
purposes he is standing in
the turret of Tiger 200 which
has just crushed a street
barricade.

Tiger 323 rolling through a Budapest street. For the most part civilian life continued as usual.

Tiger 324 seen in profile.

The commander of Admiral Horthy's Life Guard Battalion presents himself ready to serve Szálasi, the new pro-German head of government. Present are civilian officials of the new government. Hungarian and German soldiers, and Tiger 233, can be seen in the background. The façade of the house in the background has received some damage from shelling.

Hungarian Arrow Cross troops bringing up a light anti-tank gun. The steel helmets worn by the Hungarians were of similar style to those issued to the German Army in the First World War. In the background is Tiger 234. At the corner of the house on the left of the photo is a Hungarian Flak tank armed with a 4cm Bofors.

morning. We were to form the spearhead for the 24 PzDiv attack. 1 Company was present and correct, but I had only ten panzers.

Our orders were to advance at first light following a brief artillery preparation, break through the enemy positions and then turn aside to the town of Mezőtúr to the south-east and capture it. Immediately after that we were to advance north-east via Túrkeve to take the high ground at Kisújszállás. Next to nothing was known about the enemy positions, not even that a Romanian division would be facing us.

I had received the order to attack when it was dark: now the work began. Maps had to be found and pasted together, conferences with panzer commanders set up, in between I had to see the commanding officer at the Abteilung command post – I didn't know whether I was coming or going. When I arrived with the company at the readiness position in the small Theiss bridgehead south-east of Szolnok, I had the feeling that we were only half prepared and that nothing would go to plan. Yet everything went off perfectly.

Yes, I could rely on my people. The attack was scheduled for 0500hrs, spearheaded by 1 Company. The hours preceding an attack were always nerve-racking. It was still dark. I assembled the crews and went over the coming operation with them again – every man had to know what would be expected of us. The field kitchen brought us hot coffee, the panzer engines were warmed up, the radio was plugged in and the connections checked; the hour arrived and the commanding officer gave the order to move out using the codeword of the day. For frequently used orders and expressions we had codewords changed daily for security reasons. Hardly had I relayed the order to my company than the Tiger engines howled and 1 Company crossed the German front line, followed a few minutes later by 3 Company.

The attack which now unfolded was a major exception, for mostly an attack never went as expected. Shortly after we had crossed the main German front line the first Romanians came towards us. We succeeded in crossing a dam at right-angles across our direction of advance and which from the map had been our biggest worry. We reached the next village quickly, the Romanians attempting to flee in vain. We waved them aside from behind since we had no time to bother ourselves taking prisoners. There was a barrier of anti-tank guns which we crushed and with that, as we discovered, we had gone through all the defences to their entire depth. We skirted two minefields on the route of our advance and kept on going ever deeper into enemy territory. Enemy rear-echelon units were surprised, whole columns of traffic were swept off the roads, nothing could detain our forward thrust. We had appeared in this area totally unexpectedly, like phantoms.

At first my 3 Company had little to do. We kept back a suitable distance from 1 Company ahead of us and matched their speed. Towards 1000hrs, after having advanced 20km, while crossing a railway line we noticed the dark smoke of a train approaching us in the distance. Wouldn't they have been told about us? The train was coming up fast. Two of my Tigers veered off either side of the railway embankment and placed themselves in firing positions. One round: the locomotive received a direct hit and went up in flames. The train came to a stop. Now we were treated to the unbelievable sight of hundreds of Romanian soldiers pouring out of the cattle trucks and racing towards the cover of a small wood: horses running around aimlessly, some at full gallop. We had come across the transport of a Romanian division. We shot their wagons loaded with vehicles and equipment into flames, but had no time to stay, for our orders were to support 1 Company, which had now gone further ahead. Late that afternoon we reached the town of Mezőtúr, the first intermediate objective of our battle group. This put an end to our progress for a while since we had to refuel. The Abteilung formed a hedgehog in an open field, that is to say, formed a circle, guns facing outwards for a 360° defence. At the centre were placed the wheeled vehicles of the Tross from which we refuelled and took on ammunition. Mezőtúr itself was cleared by troops of 24 PzDiv. It was quite a large town and fighting erupted at several locations; during the night Russian units which had apparently been unloaded on an open stretch beyond the town also joined in. The command of 24 PzDiv was aware that the Soviets had moved strong forces from Debrecen to confront us. From now on, therefore, we had to expect to run up against the Russians, and we prepared accordingly.

The night in the hedgehog was fairly uncomfortable. In the evening whilst refuelling we were set upon by Russian ground-attack aircraft which failed to inflict any damage worth mentioning. During the night a Russian reconnaissance party got through to the commanding officer's panzer but was driven off with sub-machine guns and grenades. This was a warning for us to be on the alert. Towards 0200hrs I received orders to spearhead the advance with my company in the new direction at daybreak. Our primary objective was the small town of Túrkeve, from there continuing to Kisujszallas. This was some 50km further on again.

Shortly after setting out we came under fire, so close had the Russians come up during the night. The situation was difficult because the road here ran over a dam and on either side was impassable swamp. I would not be able to deploy my company and therefore only the leading panzers would be able to fire. I made out six anti-tank guns left and right of the road and we traded fire with these for about ten minutes until they were annihilated. The Russians fought doggedly, had the advantage of camouflage in well-chosen positions and fired accurately, while we on the other hand were being served up on a plate. For that reason we received many hits from all calibres, but none up to penetrating the frontal armour of a King Tiger. I radioed a situation report to Abteilung and we pressed on into better terrain enabling the company to spread out either side of the road. After a few kilometres we came to the next barrier of anti-tank guns. One after another we made out each gun, advised it to all and wiped it out while receiving a hail of fire ourselves. Some of the panzers were rendered immobile by hits to the tracks or gun, etc., but we pressed forward.

It was a grim feeling to be sitting in a panzer, see a muzzle flash ahead and then wait for the hit, for it did not always turn out well. We could receive a hit so powerful that it stunned us all. If you saw the anti-tank gun in the act of firing, it could be engaged. If not, which was often the case, because you cannot be looking in all directions at once, you would have to wait until they let you have a second one, hoping to spot the muzzle flash. Meanwhile you had to keep an eye out for the other panzers, ready to leap to their assistance if required. Superiority over the enemy lay in recognizing and responding to a situation quickly. This was the priority for all panzer commanders. Besides that, I had to monitor the activity of the entire company and issue tactically correct orders at the right time.

In my command panzer I had one radio transmitter and two receivers. During an attack messages were received incessantly. This panzer had recognized the position of an anti-tank gun, that one was out of action, a third had had to stop at a natural obstacle, the next was immobile after a hit and had to change radio frequency, the commanding officer had just sent some new order or other. If I had had my way I would have thrown the earphones into a corner, for apart from hearing what was going on, above all one had to observe and then make decisions.

We had now come to a Russian infantry position in a field manned by anti-tank close-combat troops. They would jump aboard our panzers with satchel charges and other fun devices. This was very unpleasant for there was little one could do to ward them off except step on the gas.

The many natural obstacles also caused problems: obstructions such as broad trenches, hedgerows, woodlands, etc. were ideal for defending troops but tended to impose long delays on the attacker. In the distance we recognized Túrkeve. I wanted to pass it on the left and then attack from the far end. That was not so easy, since the Russians had created a really masterly defensive position with anti-tank gun emplacements everywhere around the edges of the town. Here we had a very tough nut to crack. More and more of my company's panzers were falling by the wayside. My own panzer received a hit directly below the gun from a Russian gun I had failed to spot in time. The frontal armour withstood the shell but I could no longer fire. With this panzer now damaged I had only two others still fully battleworthy. The three of us covered the last few kilometres to the north-eastern end of the village and found we could enter there, for the Russians had meanwhile pulled out with their guns. Here we took a breather for a few hours. Our advance had lasted five hours and the company had put thirty-six enemy guns out of action. We had really had to fight hard for every kilometre: the Russians fought us more bitterly than I had ever experienced before. My company had some men wounded but no dead and no panzers written off.

During those few hours some of the damaged panzers were got going again by our repairs group and rejoined me so that I had six vehicles in the company. I congratulated Feldwebel Grossmann, whose repair team was always well up with the leaders of the attack and worked wonders. I remained in my own panzer although the gun was still out of action. The divisional commanding officer arrived and his praise did us good. We discussed how we should continue the advance and drank a cognac. This steadied our nerves.

Towards midday we got under way again, 3 Company in the lead. Our next objective was the town of Kisújszállás. It was now important to capitalize rapidly on our success and not allow the enemy time to establish effective defences. Apparently the King Tigers had had a substantial demoralizing effect and softened them up a bit. Thus in the afternoon we made good speed in a textbook spearhead formation as taught at panzer school. After 15km we turned off the highway and literally crept up to the town. Towards 1700hrs we reached the Kisújszállás–Dévaványa road 2km east of Kisújszállás and stopped all traffic moving along it. From there it was easy to survey the Kisújszállás–Debrecen highway. We saw an unbroken stream of Soviet tanks, lorries and above all anti-tank guns driving into the town. In a short time we counted fifty guns. Against this material superiority it would be impossible to take the town at a stroke or hold it. We formed a hedgehog and supplies came up during the night without much interference. Reconnaissance reported enemy armour reinforcements to the north-east.

On the morning of 21 October 1944 the battle group received orders to retire to Túrkeve. In the meantime the Russians had recaptured Mezötúr. Hauptmann Fromme had gone there with 1 Company and immediately become involved in heavy street fighting. At the same time I had occupied myself with the recovery of the panzers at Túrkeve which were not to be allowed to fall into enemy hands. Our Tross had been here the previous day, following our forward thrust, and had been attacked by the Russians and suffered casualties. As a result, 3 Company had its first death in Hungary, in addition to which I lost my 1-tonne tractor and a lorry, a serious loss. I was now attempting to save what I could from these vehicles. In the afternoon I was summoned by the commanding officer who was still in action with 1 Company at Mezötúr. In the short time that the Russians had been able to occupy the town they had even managed to install a 76.2mm anti-tank gun in a church steeple. Here for the first time the Abteilung experienced the American 76.2mm anti-tank gun with tapering barrel which could penetrate the frontal armour of the King Tiger.

The commanding officer told me the new plan. The whole battle group was to move out under cover of darkness to Törökszentmiklós. It had been impressed upon us that details of the enemy force had not been clarified and those panzers which had not been made driveable meanwhile were to be towed there. Because most of the operational Tigers would be needed, this time the 24 PzDiv motorcycle-borne infantry would lead the formation. The Tigers would be placed in the first third of the long column in order to be swiftly available in an emergency, swiftly, that is, after first casting off the Tigers they had in tow. Since it would only be possible to move by night, the distance to be covered would not be great and everybody hoped that the Russians would prefer to sleep.

By the early hours of 22 October 1944 we were about 15km from Törökszent-miklós when the order came suddenly: 'All stop!' I went on a further 5km without running into any opposition. Our own reconnaissance had reported strong enemy forces on the left flank, however. The hope of reaching Törökszentmiklós without having to fight now evaporated.

The Abteilung developed its attack led by the five panzers of my 3 Company, with 1 Company behind it. The weather was cold and misty. The terrain consisted of meadowlands, orchards, small scattered farmsteads and scrubland, therefore an unpleasant region for us with limited visibility with the mist reducing it further to about 100m. After 2km we saw the first Russians. Those not immediately mown down ran headlong for cover through the mist, leaving all their weapons and equipment behind. My company drove in a single file with about 50m between each panzer. Suddenly I saw before me, appearing out of the mist, a gun in an emplacement. At the same moment my panzer received a hit to the turret which knocked us senseless.

The gun was still not able to fire following the hit at Túrkeve and I had not changed panzers because I did not want to burden another commander with a panzer that was not fully battleworthy. In any case, as a company commander I preferred to lead from my own panzer and not be constantly involved in shooting. Immediately after receiving a second hit in the *Seitenvorgelege* (drive and drive sprocket for the tracks) on the right side, and then another on the left side we were immobile and defenceless and only waiting now for a hit to penetrate. Finally our neighbouring panzer grasped our plight and destroyed the Soviet gun. We saw afterwards that it was a 105mm howitzer firing over open sights. Our frontal armour had torn, and a large hole appeared in it, but the shell had not gone through. My other panzers had also come under heavy-calibre fire and we had several damaged vehicles. We broke the resistance, however, but because the ground we had won could not be occupied, my panzer, which was no longer driveable, had to be towed away by two others.

In the afternoon we linked up with the other elements of the Abteilung at Törökszentmiklós. My III Platoon, which had got lost on the rail transport before the attack began, had reappeared. It had been attached to another attack group which had headed for Kenderes. It was a heavy blow for me that Leutnant Wagner, the platoon commander, was so seriously wounded that his left arm had to be amputated.

On 23 October the advance, which had meanwhile lost its purpose through changes in the overall situation, was broken off. The three-day advance in which we had been attached to 24 PzDiv had not changed the outcome of the battle for Debrecen, which fell into Russian hands on 21 October, although it probably delayed the Russian thrust into the rear of Army Group *Wöhler*, desperately fighting its way from Eastern Hungary to the Thiess.

My non-operational panzers were towed back to the workshop, working flat-out at Jászivány. Every company was naturally keen to have as many panzers operational as possible. There was a healthy competition between the companies and especially between 1 Company and 3 Company where the constant rivalry extended as to which of the two could knock out the most enemy tanks. Those of ours still operational were divided up over the next few days into several small battle groups positioned either side of Szolnok to protect the bridges over the Theiss, and we held a bridgehead at Szolnok too. The Russians were very fast-moving and often disappeared at the sight of our King Tigers.

Meanwhile the rainy season had set in and it poured down. One might think that a panzer was watertight. On the contrary – water always found its way in.

Because movement in the panzer was very limited by how cramped it was, if it rained all day it was very unpleasant inside. Constant drips falling on your head or neck could drive you mad.

The Russians had established their first bridgeheads across the Theiss. All we could do was try to prevent their being enlarged. These operations on the Theiss were frustrating because one rarely had successes but had to always be operational, expecting an enemy attack. Apart from that it was wet, cold and one felt covered with mud.

The situation in the outer approaches to Budapest had worsened dramatically. On 1 November 1944, powerful Russian forces advanced past Kecskemét towards Budapest, encircling 24 PzDiv either side of Kecskemét, temporarily splitting it up into three groups and overwhelming the divisional command post.

Our Abteilung moved up with a panzer-grenadier regiment in order to free the encircled parts of 24 PzDiv. This time 2 Company was the spearhead, my 3 Company following, then the HQ and 1 Companies. Soon we came across Russian troops following their forces heading for Budapest and crossing our path at right-angles. They were taken by surprise, for until then their push towards Budapest had met no resistance. After dealing with the problem, our approach continued along the road to Kecskemét.

Suddenly 2 Company in front was halted by strong anti-tank units. From my position at the rear I could not intervene directly. Leutnant Brodhagen's leading vehicle went up in flames. Right and left of the road the terrain was difficult, consisting of vineyards and market gardens interspersed with patches of meadow and fields. Additionally it was now dusk and the failing light made observation increasingly difficult. The enemy emplacements could only be spotted by their muzzle flashes and aided by this point of reference alone we had to engage the enemy in the twilight. We could not attack the Russian position frontally, the spearhead was at a standstill and by radio Hauptmann Fromme gave me instructions to veer far right and attack their flank. I gave the corresponding order to my panzers.

I did not like this situation at all, and now during a short pause for observation I saw that the ground was swampy, and my panzer had begun to sink in. I could not regain firm ground and two of my other panzers had already stuck fast. An unpleasant situation in the face of the enemy. Obviously the Russians had selected their position here with foresight, knowing that on account of the difficult terrain they could only be attacked by panzers frontally and not from their flanks. The outlook for my two bogged-down panzers was extremely unfavourable, for recovery attempts under fire are very hazardous. Finally, two hours after darkness fell, we managed to get both of them free. This may be easy to describe on paper, but how many setbacks we experienced in the recovery of these weighty colossi, how often the hawsers had to be re-attached, how often they parted, how often an almost-salvaged panzer slipped back into the morass. That was truly hard work.

Now I had all my panzers on a firm road surface again. Meanwhile assault troops from the panzer-grenadier regiment had cleared out the remaining pockets of resistance. Most of the Russians had pulled out beforehand. After that we re-established contact with the encircled troops at Kecskemét and brought them out to be left behind our lines. We had completed our mission and relieved the division, but the Soviets were still heading for Budapest with no opposition. We had to disrupt them by attacks on their flanks.

I had hardly a moment's peace, for suddenly my VW arrived with my driver and Feldwebel Grohmann from the orderly room. The latter was conscientiousness personified. He had worked out where I was by reading the daily battle report to Abteilung. It often happened that he would show up at totally impossible places. At midnight I dictated my own battle report to him and whatever other company clerical work was outstanding. The paper war and the many deadlines for submitting reports were really tiresome. Were they absolutely necessary? Grohmann was relieved during the night by the 'Spiess', Hauptfeldwebel Müller, who brought up the company's mail and usually whatever special allowances he had managed to get hold of such as chocolate, smoker's requisites, wine or at least something that the other companies did not have and which gave special pleasure to men in the field. Here again there was a certain rivalry between the companies. The third man to appear was the leader of my repair group, Oberfeldwebel Grossmann. He was probably the most important amongst the company's working sergeants. He was always on the spot with his repair team, ignoring any danger and achieving little short of miracles. That particular night too he turned up suddenly to inspect the panzers for damage. He was a resourceful man and could carry out the most complicated repairs on the spot if the panzer couldn't be brought to the workshop immediately. All the credit for the company always having so many panzers operational was his. It would often be the case that he and his people had to work under fire, and often in extremely difficult situations.

The remainder of the night passed quietly. There is much I could tell about the operations, successes and losses which we had in these days. In the last few weeks we did not have a single rest day and no time for technical work. The panzers had covered between 400 and 500km and were in urgent need of maintenance. Because nearly all panzers had held up well so far, the moment finally came when almost all couldn't go on. For the massive crop of breakdowns, failures and stoppages which now occurred, the available recovery units were simply not sufficient and the still-driveable panzers had to be pooled for towing duties. The most important thing now was to restore general operational readiness.

In the following days the Soviets achieved a breakthrough, advancing almost to the outskirts of Budapest. They reached the outlying suburbs and then stopped. On 5 November the Abteilung was mentioned in the Wehrmacht Bulletin: 'In the area of Western Hungary, Tiger Abteilung 503 under Hauptmann Fromme has performed outstandingly.' We now lay at Gödöllö, a good distance from the front line. I had beautiful quarters at the home of a former captain of a Danube steamer. At last I could have a proper wash, change my underwear, write home in peace and eat more comfortably. That did me good.

On 15 November 1944 I took over leadership of the Abteilung battle group at Hatvan. Twelve Tigers from all companies were operational, and additionally I was allocated the Abteilung Flak platoon with quadruple guns on panzer chassis. In order to maintain contact with Abteilung over long distances, my battle group received Staff Panzer I, which had a medium-wave radio. Our own Tross with fuel and ammunition vehicles gave us a certain independence, for besides a field kitchen we also had a recovery and repair unit under Werkmeister Späth. I was therefore fully autonomous for the impending operations. Every two hours I had radio contact with Abteilung, every evening I made my report of successes and requested fuel and ammunition which would be brought up during the night. My battle group was now attached to PzRgt 1/1 PzDiv. The regimental commanding officer was Major D.

Up to 18 November my battle group had initially to cover a large sector which by reason of the unfavourable circumstances of the terrain was difficult to monitor, and it secured the withdrawal of elements of 1 PzDiv to a new defensive line at Gyöngyös. We had to intervene repeatedly, rather like a fire brigade, whenever enemy tanks appeared in the area. A new order took my battle group to Gyöngyöspata, a village in the Matra mountains. On the way I was stopped by an agitated Staff Officer 1a of an infantry division who informed me that 2km ahead a Russian tank had broken through into the infantry position and that our own infantry had not been able to deal with it. I sent a Tiger forward and followed in my VW in order to make contact. I worked my way forward with the infantry company commander to within 20m of the T-34. I regretted not having a Panzerfaust with me, but the infantry had had enough of such close-combat endeavours, having lost men during the first efforts to destroy the tank. I instructed my Tiger commander personally, and by the time the Russians noticed it creeping up they were already in flames. The infantry were overjoyed, but for us it was just routine. As we were about to pull out, we were surprised by ground-attack aircraft. Their bombs fell between my panzers, which were just making preparations to leave. Some of the men on the open Flak platoon vehicles were seriously wounded. How often the opportunity came to pass from this life into the next. We reached Gyöngyöspata in the late afternoon, initially as divisional reserve. The region with its wooded mountains reminded me of the Black Forest.

The Battle for Gyöngyös

On 19 November the alarm was raised at 1000hrs. In a surprise move the Russians had reached Gyöngyös. The town had been occupied by a German infantry division which had fled at first sight of the Russians, making their relatively small force a gift of the town. My Tross remained behind while I set off as quickly as possible for Gyöngyös. The first 10km were covered really fast and then we ran into the mob fleeing from Gyöngyös, blocking the road with their vehicles. It was difficult to swim against the tide, and additionally there ensued a fairly heavy attack by low-level aircraft which took the whole mess under fire. I closed the hatch of my panzer and watched through the observation slits as the Russian aircraft dived down towards us, saw the muzzle flashes from their weapons and distinctly felt the explosive shells hitting the armour of my panzer. They were shooting well but their bomb-aiming was poor and my panzers suffered little damage. Finally we reached the outskirts of Gyöngyös. The retiring German troops had blown up the road bridge over a deep gorge here, and seeing that there was no way round it we went into the churchyard and took the suspected houses on the other side under fire. Soon the lively enemy infantry fire died away. The Panzer IVs of PzRgt I gradually arrived and with them the regimental commanding officer Major D.

The following new situation now developed: the armoured elements of 1 PzDiv, amongst them my own battle group, were placed under the command of the regimental commander of the infantry division which had just streamed out of

Gyöngyös. All our elements were to join up immediately with this division, but the direct route there led through the town and was blocked. We had therefore to go about it cross-country, which would be very difficult in the mountainous terrain. We went across the vineyards. The Tigers made slow progress up the steep slopes, sinking into the soft earth in the climb and when descending the other side. A brook had to be forded, the last 50m causing us particular difficulty. In order to reach the paved road, on which we had to secure the edge of the town of Gyöngyös, we had to overcome a steep slope. The first Tiger climbed it with difficulty, but churned up the earth so badly that it had to help pull up the succeeding panzers one by one. This was not made any easier by the Russians having set up an anti-tank gun in a water tower at the edge of the town from where its gunners could observe all the goings-on from wonderfully close range and naturally keep up a hail of fire from there. We shot this gun down. The Panzer IVs of PzRgt 1 could not manage the route, and the few panzers which the regiment still had were all stationary on the slopes of the vineyards. Only the panzer of Major D. made it, being hauled over the difficult terrain by a Tiger. Some of my own Tigers had fallen by the wayside, becoming bogged down in the early morning or later, and my proud fighting force was now down to five. I had three here, while Feldwebel Bornschier had another two a couple of kilometres away on another arterial road.

When darkness fell I was summoned to Major D.'s command post and went there on the tracked motorcycle. Corps had ordered that the infantry division was to reoccupy the town with our help. It was not an attractive proposition but one could understand why they wanted it done. When I heard the details I was slightly shocked. It was ordered that we were to attack by night in two groups on two different access roads. The right group under my command consisted of my three Tigers, six or seven armoured personnel carriers armed with triple heavy machine guns and about 100 infantry. Oh my God! when I saw the infantry. They were convalescent walking-wounded cases, poorly armed and lacking any motivation. My group would be at the centre of the attack. The left attack group with Feldwebel Bornschier's two Tigers was equally 'strong' and we had contact to each other by radio.

With this force led by Major D. we were to set out at 0200hrs, fight our way through the town and link up with elements of the infantry division on the other side. This was an operation which led through houses and a confusion of streets of a not-insubstantial town occupied for twenty-four hours by the Russians, who were undoubtedly expecting an attack. What madness! Quite apart from the prospects of disaster, I had grave doubts about the fuel and ammunition situation. I would have to sort that out somehow.

I briefed my panzer commanders, Unteroffizier Gärtner of my company and Feldwebel Jakob of 2 Company. These veteran panzer men naturally knew what a night attack on such a town would mean. Yes, we all knew what lay before us. The whole operation seemed totally senseless to me. I could not permit my people and panzers to be gambled recklessly even if it had been ordered.

At 2200hrs I was summoned to attend an operational conference at the infantry division's command post. It was hair-raising. The divisional commander had no understanding of panzer warfare and unfortunately Major D. was not the sort of man to stand up and speak his mind. My own objections to the operation were rejected by the divisional commander, Corps had ordered the attack and therefore nobody must dare speak out against it. A factor also to be taken into account was the division's shame at being taken unawares by the Russians and their panic-stricken abandonment of the town the previous night. I had a talk with Major D. who wanted to lead the attack from his command post.

Next followed agreement with the drivers of the panzer-grenadiers' armoured personnel carriers. If there was nothing which could be done to change the orders I wanted to do everything possible to carry them out with the least possible losses, for with the force we had available failure could be predicted. I also did not agree that my people should be sacrificed to the amateurism of the senior commanders. As I did each evening, I requested my supplies by radio from Abteilung 503 which, in order to reach us, would have to be brought about 50km over the snow-covered roads of the Matra mountains, for like our panzers, the large lorries could not go cross-country. Then I reported to the Abteilung 503 command post the operation ordered by Corps with an encrypted message sent in Morse: 'By Corps night attack ordered on Gyöngyös. Long live the Führer!'

This was not an expression of National Socialist sentiment, rather I wanted to indicate that we had been given a suicidal operation in which the chances of survival were not very great. Abteilung HQ understood at once and the commanding officer sent Leutnant Heerlein to the corps command post immediately to intervene. Despite that, the decision of the commanding general remained unchanged.

I slept the last two hours before the attack in my panzer, at 0130hrs I made ready and at 0200hrs started out from D.'s command post with which I had radio contact. It was pitch dark and to see anything at all we had to leave the hatches open. Unteroffizier Gärtner was commander of the spearhead vehicle, and behind my panzer came Feldwebel Jakob, then the armoured personnel carriers and the 100 infantrymen trotting along at the rear with little enthusiasm although really they ought to have been alongside the panzers.

Upon reaching the first houses we fired into the darkness with all barrels to make it seem that a major force was attacking. We raked all the streets with MG fire. The Russians had pulled back and in the glow of our flares we passed by their abandoned positions. There was a muzzle flash to the left of us – the first anti-tank gun. It fired too high and the tracer hissed overhead. One round from the leading panzer and the gun fell silent. We pressed ahead slowly and reached the water tower from where we had received fire at noon the previous day. The flares lit the street ahead of us with a pale light of short duration, and after they burnt out we found the darkness even more impenetrable. I could hardly make out Gärtner's tank, only the light shimmer of its exhaust flame. Slowly we groped our way forward.

We received a hit forward: Gärtner also reported one from an anti-tank gun. Keep calm. In the darkness we were at a disadvantage. If only the infantry would come up alongside to clean out the houses to our left and right, full of Russians. We had now penetrated about a kilometre into the town and came under increasingly heavy fire as we headed towards the town centre. Hit from the right. The Russians had set up anti-tank guns in the doorways of the houses. Therefore they were prepared and had let us come this far deliberately! We fired one explosive 8.8cm round after another into the terrace of houses, and after that the opposition began to die down. I was running very short of flares. Advancing further forward without infantry to clear the houses on both sides was impossible. Therefore I called a halt until the infantry caught up a bit. Armed with a sub-machine gun I dismounted and hurried back to the armoured personnel carriers and collected up all the flares they had before continuing further back to the infantry. Finally I found their commander, an Oberleutnant. He was helpless and had no control over his men. Then a brave Unteroffizier arrived with a group offering to at least clear out the houses either side of the panzers. Upon entering the first courtyard, the Unteroffizier in the lead, he was hit and fell dead. At the same moment the infantrymen disappeared and I stood there utterly alone. A flare fired up by the leading panzer sank down slowly and suddenly I saw a Russian anti-tank gun no more than 2m away from me. How easily that could have all gone wrong! Now the grenadiers had to leave their vehicles. Armed with sub-machine guns, hand grenades and Panzerfaust, they forced their way into every house and in bitter fighting occupied the buildings either side of the panzers. We pressed forward into increasing Russian resistance.

There was a crossroads ahead which we did not like the look of. If the Russians were so well prepared this far, what might they have got in position up there? The grenadiers were coming no further and then we came to a standstill once more. My radio connection to Major D. was worsening and in any case all I was getting from him were orders such as 'Keep attacking'. They really needed to come up and see the situation for themselves. I got out again and returned to the command post in an armoured personnel carrier.

Major D. was amazed that we had progressed as far as we had, for he was as doubtful as I had been about the sense of the operation. I explained the situation to him and made it clear that there was no purpose in going any further with it because the Russians were well prepared for us, and we could not clear out the whole town with our small battle group no more than 100m long. If the Russians had been deceived as to our size and had bolted, like our infantry the day before, then the operation might possibly have succeeded. I received his order not to continue the attack but to hold my position. With that I hoped to prevent further losses and drove back.

The grenadiers and infantry were now put under my command. I had the nearby streets cleared, but the Russians were still holding the houses. Dawn was breaking. I could see the crossroads 50m ahead of me. With more daylight our situation became less favourable. We observed the road in front of us, the houses, doors, windows, roofs – behind them all Russians tucked away in hiding. If one raised his head carelessly out of the panzer, a bullet would come whistling by. One had to take the greatest care possible. Suddenly I saw a man emerge from a house and go towards the leading panzer. He was walking slowly and I thought he was a civilian. I signalled him to approach me, and the man threw a hand grenade which he had been holding concealed, and before I could fire he had disappeared back into the house. Now the grenadiers came under sub-machine-gun fire from the rear and had to evacuate the houses we had occupied. The Russians had got behind them over the backyards. There was no denying they had guts. During this mess I received a radio message from Major D.: 'Advance again!' Were they totally nuts back there? I requested that the message be repeated before I acknowledged it. To keep attacking forward was pure madness for the Russians were simply itching for us to draw up to the crossroads. To refuse the order meant a court martial, also out of the question. I found an intermediate solution and had the three panzers rev their engines furiously and then opened fire with all barrels so that the noise of battle would be heard at Major D.'s command post. After that I reported that it would be impossible to cross the intersection. Meanwhile we had come under increasing pressure, receiving Molotov cocktails from the roofs and satchel charges from windows and doorways while Russian assault troops were working their way towards us. Unteroffizier Gärtner reported that he had damage to a track. Woe to him who lost a track here!

There we stayed for hours. Now and again I went out to the infantrymen, otherwise I would have been alone with my panzers. What we were doing here was lunacy. Whatever could be the purpose of holding this area of the town? My thoughts regarding the Higher Command were not edifying. I was just getting back into my panzer when the Russians attacked. They had worked their way up to the left and right of us slowly and suddenly opened a hail of fire on the poor grenadiers. These were forced to dismount, and suffered heavy losses doing so. Russian assault troops were also sneaking up through the side streets. In order to seal off these approaches I had the triple guns brought up. Then finally came the order to pull out. It was 1400hrs, and we had held this position for twelve hours. I covered the withdrawal with my panzers and by now there were also Russians in what had been our rear. We rolled slowly out in reverse, firing at anything that moved. With that the attack ended. So far as I remember, it was the only one in which we were unable to fulfil our assignment.

After we had re-ammunitioned and refuelled, my people rested for a while. I received new orders from Major D. Previously he had invited me to dine with him and the cognac did wonders for my nerves. So now we could get on. I had a difficult new assignment to carry out: during the night two Tigers recommissioned by the repairs group had attempted to fight their way through to me. 1 PzDiv had meanwhile discovered a route capable of use by tracked vehicles. After fording a river, one of the Tigers had become hopelessly bogged down in a sunken road. I had to retrieve this vehicle. I also had to lead my battle group back to Gyöngyöspata to form the 1 PzDiv reserve. More bad news arrived: while on the way to me the previous night Leutnant Rambow had had an accident with the tracked motorcycle and had been taken to a military hospital. Now I had no officers in my company: the Abteilung already had eight lieutenants out of action.

Before night fell I borrowed an amphibious car from Major D. and drove off for the position where the Tiger had sunk in. The car had all-wheel drive and was especially cross-country capable. It would be hard to believe the condition of the road: bottomless mud over which even the amphibious vehicle made poor progress. We had to get out and push over a number of stretches and so the journey took hours. Night fell, no moon; we drove without lights and were no longer sure whether we were in front of or behind the Russian spearheads. There was no static front line and nobody knew the whereabouts of friend or foe. Now and again we stopped and switched off the engine, listening out for the sounds of tanks or other vehicles. One always had to be aware of every possibility. Finally we got to the bogged-down panzer. The crew was working feverishly, but the recovery was unimaginably difficult. One panzer alone would not be enough.

We forced the tracks off, tried everything possible, but the panzer would not budge. I drove back to request two panzers to assist. I fetched recovery-platoon specialists from Gyöngyöspata. On the way I reconnoitred a better route there. We drove steeply downhill over narrow vineyard paths and on the other side steeply uphill, forded small brooks, and went through villages long since abandoned by German troops. The local people looked at us with frightened eyes, thinking at first that we were Russians. Back at the recovery compound I drove out with a 1-tonne tractor which was superior to all other vehicles in cross-country mobility. Gradually the recovery progressed and I could see that the panzer would eventually come free, my only worry being that the Russians might not allow us the time to complete it. Finally the remaining elements of the battle group could now set off by the newly reconnoitred route for Gyöngyöspata. I kept two Tigers with me for recovery work.

I gave orders for any bogged-down panzer to be prepared for destruction and drove back to 1 PzDiv command post to report that elements of my battle group were beyond our lines and that the way back had to be kept open for us at all costs. Therefore Division could not yet move out to Gyöngyöspata as planned. Returning to the site of the casualty I re-established radio contact and was informed that the recovery had been abandoned and the panzer destroyed. The story here was that the bogged-down panzer had finally been hauled free and was being prepared for towing when the first Russians appeared. The towing hawser was attached while under fire. The Russians had not yet got to the panzer when it slipped back and stuck again more firmly than before. Salvage was now out of the question, and with great difficulty the hawsers were removed and the panzer set alight by gunfire.

The salvage team set off on the 10km drive through enemy-occupied territory or at least No Man's Land. I went to meet them with two Tigers in order to assist if necessary: eventually we reached our own front line, which lay about halfway between Gyöngyös and Gyöngyöspata. Here a new defensive line had been established by 1 PzDiv and everybody now awaited the advancing Russians.

My battle group moved into quarters at Gyöngyöspata and the repair group immediately set to work. Next morning, 21 November 1944, a number of panzers were returned to us from the workshop. My fighting force now consisted of ten panzers. At Gyöngyöspata each crew had been allocated a house, and I had set up my command post in the well-kept quarters of the parish priest. Abteilung sent me Leutnant Fürlinger so that I no longer had to do everything myself. In the other rooms of the command post were lodged the runners and the radio-equipped armoured personnel carrier of the reconnaissance platoon, via which I had contact with Abteilung, was parked in the courtyard. In the afternoon the alarm was raised, and the Russians attacked. We were lucky and knocked out nine of them, some of them while stuck fast in the boggy ground. That evening we were all back in our quarters celebrating. There was wine in the parish cellar and every house had wonderful fruit. For the evening meal my crew prepared a goose. Next morning I sent only two panzers ahead on lookout duty: they had to report the situation to me hourly. Everybody else could rest. I frequently went to the divisional command post, also at Gyöngyöspata. That evening I reported to Abteilung some successes against enemy tanks. In the evening Major Fromme visited me and we were all in the best of moods. We dined on filled omelettes and sat together until late in candlelight.

Next morning, 23 November, we were rudely awakened by 'Stalin Organs' (multiple rocket launchers) firing into the town. In our quarters the windows shattered, very unpleasant. I found out from Division what was afoot and sent four Tigers forward. Soon I received the report that eight enemy tanks had been destroyed, and that meant twenty-five in only three days! At Division I requested the Iron Cross Second Class for several soldiers who had particularly distinguished themselves in the last few days. These were handed to me at once and I was able to pin them on the recipients shortly afterwards. In the afternoon in addition to the 'Stalin Organs' there were some unpleasant fighter-bomber attacks. The radio-equipped SdKfz 250 in the courtyard of my command post received a through-and-through hit which damaged the engine cooling system, but a replacement was sent by Abteilung within a few hours. Although I set up the Abteilung Flak platoon, Soviet ground-attack aircraft still mounted heavy raids. During one of these Gefreiter Böhler, an excellent panzer driver, was wounded by a bomb splinter and had to be admitted to the military hospital. After that he lost his enthusiasm and I advised him strongly, though his wound was nowhere near healed, to discharge himself from the field hospital and rejoin us in order to avoid being transferred to the rear. His wound had not healed by December and I took him with me to the hospital in Vienna.

That evening the 1 PzDiv command post was moved further back because the situation in Gyöngyöspata had deteriorated. I sent my own Tross back too in order not to expose them to danger unnecessarily. Only the armoured elements remained forward.

Leutnant Fürlinger and I had a very good time: we ate well, enjoyed fine wines, spent half an hour now and again in the cellar during air attacks or a few hours on lookout in the panzer. It may sound unlikely, but for us it was a period of convalescence. I went daily to Division to discuss the situation with the 1a Staff Officer, and sometimes if the situation allowed, visited the workshops to put them under pressure. This was really not at all necessary, for the senior foreman, Neubert, ensured that no time was wasted. For me he was a fatherly friend. In the spring of 1944 he had been awarded the Knight's Cross to the War Service Cross for his outstanding achievements and fully deserved the decoration. One never left him without being served an evening meal and some schnapps. On the return journey I would usually call in at the Abteilung command post in order to see how things were going. As company commander one always had concerns or requests to put to the commanding officer or his adjutant. The commanding officer spent much of his time at Corps, Division or the Army Group. Then the OKH commissions would come snooping around – people who never brought with them anything worth having.

Towards the End: The Last Weeks at the Front

I had been commanding the battle group for almost three weeks. In reality Hauptmann von Eichel-Streiber, commander of 2 Company, who was currently at Vakselly with III Workshop Platoon, should have assumed command weeks ago. It did not worry me too much, for I had an easy billet. The commander of 1 PzDiv helped out here by requesting Fromme that the battle group, for so long as it remained attached to 1 PzDiv, should remain under the command of Leutnant von Rosen. Therefore I could carry on: this was a fine recognition of my service.

Division ordered us by telephone to transfer to InfRgt 1's sector. The move there was difficult because we could not cross a small bridge and had to make a major detour through vineyards with their heavy ground. Once we were through

Rail transport from Budapest to Szolnok on 3 November 1944. This time the broad tracks were left on the panzers: the overlap can be seen clearly in this photo.

Rail transport in November 1944, from right to left, Gefreiter Stadlbauer (Jäckel's loader), Unteroffizier Jäckel (note the badge on his cap) and Feldwebel Weigl with bottle in hand. The names of the other two Abteilung members are unknown.

A wooden bridge at Szolnok, end of October 1944, erected parallel to the road bridge. Even then the weather was warm.

An 18-tonne tractor of the recovery troop and behind it a King Tiger crossing the bridge over the Danube at Szolnok. It is not certain that the Tiger is under tow: apparently one of these heavy machines was not capable of towing a 68-tonne Tiger on its own.

Around 20 October 1944, an SdKfz 250 armoured personnel carrier and Tiger 101 at the Abteilung command post at Turkeve. From left to right: surgeon Stabsarzt Dr Schramm, Leutnant von Rosen, Leutnant Piepgras, unknown, General von Nostitz, CO of 24 PzDiv, and Hauptmann Fromme.

Unteroffizier Heinz Gärtner (left in the photo), a very popular comrade and successful Tiger commander seen here with his loader/gunner Obergefreiter Helmut Klein, autumn 1944. Behind them is Gefreiter Kurt Stellzer. Heinz Gärtner was promoted to Feldwebel on 1 December 1944 and fell west of Zámoly on 7 January 1945.

Tiger 313 at a halt in the autumn of 1944. Left to right: Unteroffizier Jäckel, unknown
Gefreiter, Feldwebel Weigl and Leutnant Wagner watching aircraft, perhaps a dogfight.
The King Tiger has its turret at the 6 o'clock position.

The repairs group of 1 Company/Heavy PzAbt 503 at Polgárdi, Hungary, in November
1944. In the background the reliable 1-tonne tractor, in the foreground, the Staffel pennant
with the 'T' on its side indicates a new Abteilung insignia. In December 1944, the '503' of
Heavy PzAbt 503 was redesignated *Feldherrnhalle*.

As a result of the lack of recovery vehicles, Tigers had to take their role. Here 311, 333 and the vehicle nearest the camera in a cross-tow. Noticeable here is the build-up of mud on the panzer tracks and wheels which would have affected manoeuvrability.

A 1 Company King Tiger with Franz-Wilhelm Lochmann as radio operator. Dr Lochmann is one of the three authors of the work on Tiger Abteilung 503.

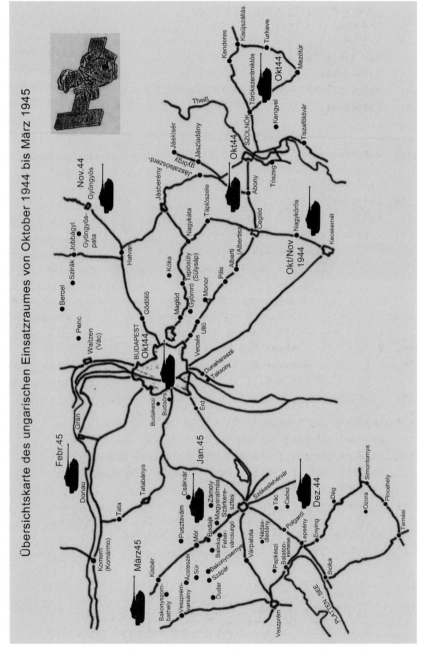

Bases and battle areas of Tiger PzAbt 503/*Feldherrnhalle* between October 1944 and March 1945 when the author's period in command was terminated by a serious wound.

Übersichtskarte des ungarischen Einsatzraumes von Oktober 1944 bis März 1945

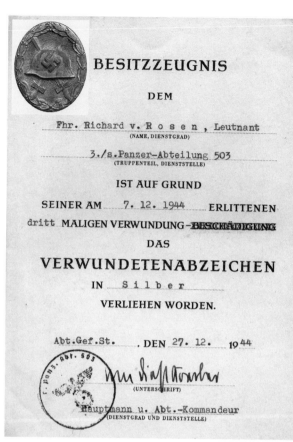

BESITZZEUGNIS

DEM

Fhr. Richard v. R o s e n , Leutnant
(NAME, DIENSTGRAD)

3./s.Panzer–Abteilung 503
(TRUPPENTEIL, DIENSTSTELLE)

IST AUF GRUND

SEINER AM 7. 12. 1944 ERLITTENEN

dritt MALIGEN VERWUNDUNG – BESCHÄDIGUNG

DAS

VERWUNDETENABZEICHEN

IN S i l b e r

VERLIEHEN WORDEN.

Abt.Gef.St. , DEN 27. 12. 19 44

(UNTERSCHRIFT)

Hauptmann u. Abt.–Kommandeur
(DIENSTGRAD UND DIENSTSTELLE)

(left) Certificate of the award of the Wound Badge in Silver to the author for his third wound on 7 December 1944. The signature is that of the Abteilung commanding officer, Hauptmann von Diest-Koerber.

(below) Tiger 314 with the name 'Annaliese', commander Unteroffizier Jäckel, under repair at Szarkereste. The advent of winter there in January 1945 brought heavy snowfall. This King Tiger with the Porsche turret is one of two examples brought out of Mailly-le-Camp (France) by the author in the late summer of 1944 under the most difficult circumstances.

The lack of sufficient camouflage materials resulted in Tiger 314 being given an emergency cover of farmyard fencing, loose boards and camouflage netting. The snow has almost melted.

Mid-January 1945: left to right: Rötz, Buhl, Stadlbauer, Niemann and Jäckel. This King Tiger was almost certainly one of the last still operational with the Porsche turret.

Certificate awarded
on 17 January 1945
to the author for the
second grade of the
Panzer Combat Badge
in Silver 'for courageous
participation on 25
operational days'.

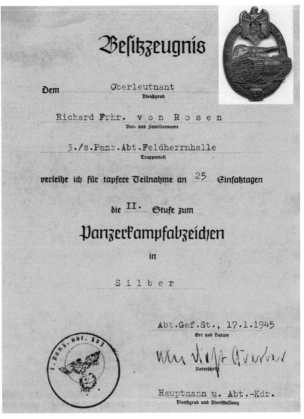

Leutnant Alfred Rubbel originally came
from 1 Company. He was in 3 Company
from December 1944 to the end of
February 1945, and then Abteilung
adjutant to the end of the war. He is one of
the three authors of the book about Tiger
Abteilung 503.

```
3./s.Pz.Abt.503                    O.U.,den 9.2.1945

            Aufschlüsselung der Kompanie.
            ----------------------------------

Kommandanten:        Richtschützen:        Ladeschützen:

Oblt.  von Rosen     Uffz. Burchard        Ogfr. Bräutigam
Ltn.   Koppe           "   Meyer             "   Deutsch
  "    Rambow           "   Niemann           "   Fellner
  "    Rubbel           "   Bechtel           "   Schneider
Obfw.  Sachs           "   Schade            "   Stadlbauer
Feldw. Kuhnert          "   Schamall          "   Stehlik
  "    Seidel           "   Urschel           "   Auste
  "    Skoda          Ogefr.Koller          Gefr. Stellter
  "    Schulz           "   Reiling           "   Schuchardt
  "    Weigl            "   Rötz              "   Vogt
Uffz.  Jaeckel          "   Klein           Pzob. Buschen
  "    Severin        Gefr. Kronenberg        "   Schöldgen
  "    Schmidt          "   Seidel
  "    Becker         Ogefr.Bauer


                Pz.-Fahrer:           Pz.-Funker:

         Uffz.  Mangels         Uffz.  Spiekermann
           "    Runge           Ogefr. Rauh
           "    Urbanski        Gefr.  Brandt
           "    Ziegler           "    Gödecke
         Ogefr. Barth            "    Liedtke
           "    Böhler           "    Niemann
           "    Braun            "    Sauter
           "    Siehl            "    Schmick
           "    Buhl             "    Schneider
         Gefr.  Eger           Pzob.  Gewecke
           "    Jung           Uffz.  Ravoth
           "    Fischer
         Pzob.  Mönkeberg
           "    Klubin
```

The personnel of 3 Company at the time when the author was seriously wounded in 1945 and forced to leave.

'Aufschlüselungder Kompanie' = Breakdown of the Company

Position occupied (page 1)
Kommandanten = Commanders
Richtschützen = Gunners
Ladeschützen = Loaders
Pz-Fahrer = Driver
Pz-Funker = Wireless operator

Ranks (English equivalent)
Oberleutnant (Full Lieutenant)
Ltn = Leutnant (2nd Lieutenant)
Oschm = Oberschirrmeister (Motor Pool NCO)
Hptfw = Hauptfeldwebel (Company Sergeant Major)
Obfw = Oberfeldwebel (Staff Sergeant)
Feldw = Feldwebel (Sergeant)
Uffz = Unteroffizier (Corporal)
Ogfr = Obergefreiter (Lance Corporal)
Gefr = Gefreiter (Trained Private Soldier)
Pzob = Probationer

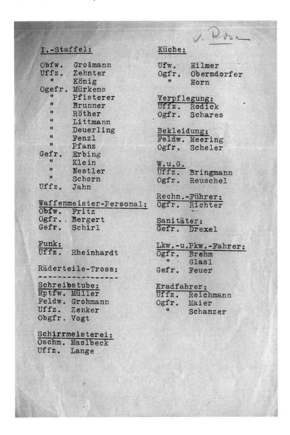

(page 2)

I-Staffel = Repairs group

Waffenmeister = Armourers

Funk = Radio room

Räderteile-Tross = Wheeled rearward services

Schreibstube = Orderly room

Schirrmeister = Motor pool

Küche = Kitchen

Verpflegung = Catering and rations supply

Bekleidung = Clothing store

W.u.G. = Weapons and equipment

Rechn.Führer = Accounts office

Sanitäter = Paramedic

Lkw u. Pkw Fahrer = Lorry and motor car drivers

Kradfahrer = Motorcyclists.

the worst, I sent Leutnant Fürlinger off with the panzers to the new operational area and drove back with the tracked motorcycle in order to apprise myself of the situation with Divisional HQ but I learned nothing precise. I reported to the command post of InfRgt 1, where I was told that my panzers were already in action. I saw from the map where they must be and hurried there on the tracked motorcycle. I recognized the panzer tracks in a field and drove for kilometre after kilometre. I thought that the advance must have made good progress despite the difficult terrain, mud knee-deep and no exaggeration. Meanwhile it had got dark and it surprised me that the panzers could have made any progress at all here. I hurried on, more kilometres, or at least so it seemed to me. I began to become ever more doubtful about the business. Never a German soldier or even a trace of one. If I hadn't had the unmistakable tracks of a Tiger in front of me, I would have thought myself to be deep behind the Russian lines. Then finally I found my troops, suddenly appearing ahead in the darkness. Leutnant Fürlinger approached me. He had a recent head wound and was incredibly lucky to be still alive. (He fell in March 1945.) He had been proceeding with the commander's hatch open since it was impossible to see anything from inside the panzer at night. At the very moment when he had bent down to say something to the gunner, his cupola was hit and he received splinter wounds to the head. Afterwards it was determined that the wounds were not as bad as they first appeared. He made his report about the attack. The company had had to advance at once without awaiting my return. Besides the panzers the Flak platoon had been present with their 2cm four-barrelled anti-aircraft guns which were also very useful in the ground attack role. The advance gone about 10km right up to where we found ourselves now. They had no panzer-grenadiers to scout ahead and Fürlinger considered it to be a miracle that I had arrived on a tracked motorcycle unscathed. He needed to go to the dressing station as soon as possible, and I wanted the panzers out of this idiotic situation right away, for to be without infantry amongst the Russians was madness!

I had a message sent to Abteilung for the surgeon, the panzers formed a hedgehog and I gave command to the most senior sergeant. Then back to the command post of InfRgt 1. They obviously felt bad about the situation and so I was authorized to pull out the panzers and radioed the order forward without delay. Previously I had telephoned Division to complain at the awful stupidity of getting the group to advance to the point where it now found itself. At midday the previous day, when I first made enquiries of Division it seemed odd to me then that, contrary to their usual practice, they had not been able to provide any precise information. As I knew now, they had not wanted to provide it, for if I had found out what this operation was like I would certainly have called it off. It was forbidden to risk Tigers except to hold up a Russian advance or make a feint to cover our own withdrawal. Tigers were irreplaceable, for at that time there were no more reserves.

I had sent the coded order to my battle group to fall back, and after it was acknowledged I set out on the tracked motorcycle to meet up with them at a certain bend in the road where a path continued across open country. The order had been acknowledged half an hour previously, they ought to have arrived in about twenty minutes. By then I had still heard no engine noises, only MG fire now and again from a part of the main front line not too far away. It was unpleasantly damp and cold. My shoes felt like lumps of clay in which I could hardly walk. This slush and mud, hardly imaginable to a city-dweller today, was nauseating. After waiting an hour I could control my impatience no longer and drove forward to meet the panzers. Once again, kilometre after kilometre, stopping now and again to listen out for the panzers. The situation was discomforting since I was only a few hundred metres from the Russian lines. I was glad to have brought a sub-machine gun along with me and held it closer. If I stumbled into the Russians here alone I would have used it on myself. I drove on, and soon reached the spot where I had found the battle group hours previously. Finally they appeared before me.

The situation was clear to me at once. Two Flak panzers, not particularly suited to cross-country travel, had bogged down hopelessly in swampy ground churned up by the Tigers. In the attempt to haul them free, a Tiger had also stuck fast. Panzers can hardly move in soft ground, as every steering movement makes them sink deeper. Furthermore it was going to be another dark night and the Russians were nearby: we could hear Russian voices very clearly from a wood in the distance. With some effort we managed to get the Tiger free, but it was damned hard work. The towing hawsers, weighing several hundredweight, had to be attached, every coupling chain was heavy, some couldn't be moved and the mud sucked our feet down. Finally all hawsers were attached, the panzers got ready to pull, and the great moment arrived when both harnessed panzers would heave together on the word of command. The bogged-down panzer moved a few centimetres forward and the tracks of the towing panzers turned crazily but achieved nothing, for they could obtain no purchase in the mud and simply ground down deeper. The two harnessed panzers escaped bogging down themselves by a hair's breadth. A metallic sound, shouts, the engines were shut down and everything fell silent. A hawser had snapped! How often it happened and another flicker of hope died! This wasn't going to work and we had to try something else though I was close to despair. It was becoming gradually clear to me that this retrieval operation was senseless, risking all my panzers to free two Flak panzers from a mudbath.

Therefore I left instructions, prepared the Flak panzers for self-destruction as a precautionary measure and drove back to the command post, arriving there at 0200hrs. They had been looking forward very much to my arrival because they were going to pull back the main front line at 0300hrs and also evacuate the village in which the command post now stood. My panzers could not possibly get back to meet this deadline: Division had got us into this mess and now they would have to deal with the consequences. They had no option but to postpone pulling back the front line in the hope that I could get my panzers free, but Division had to have completed the withdrawal by daybreak without fail, and also the panzer-grenadiers. This meant that we really had to get a move on. I downed a quick cognac with the commanding officer of the infantry regiment as a pick-me-up then I set off again on the tracked motorcycle. The situation there was unchanged. Meanwhile another Tiger had got bogged down although later recovery efforts had succeeded. I was happy to have missed it for my current nervous state was not the best. That night I was given to cursing more often than usual and carried on like a slave-driver. In such a plight one could not keep calm. It was a blessing that the Russians at least were peaceable; had they suspected how it was with us and been a bit smarter they could have wiped out my entire battle group. I reconsidered the situation and examined the possibilities of recovery from all angles before coming to the conclusion that there was no alternative. In order to bring back at least the Tigers unscathed, I had to blow up the two Flak panzers, a 24-tonne Flakpanzer IV SdKfz 161/3 *Möbelwagen* ('furniture van') with a 3.7cm gun and a 22-tonne Flakpanzer IV SdKfz 161/4 *Wirbelwind* with a quadruple 2cm cannon in a rotating turret. It was not an easy decision to make and I had to submit to a thorough enquiry later when Corps and the Army Group received the reports of their loss.

At daybreak I reached the village with the command post and received the order to transfer to Jobbaggui and report there to the command post of an SS-Division. I led my battle group back the 15km feeling wretched: such a night was harder on the nerves than a heavy panzer attack. It was incidents such as these that gave panzer men grey hair. I reported to the SS-Division: they did not make a good impression on me. We were provisionally the divisional reserve and moved into the village. I telephoned Abteilung and reported the night's events. We began the most thorough maintenance work on the panzers, outstandingly supported by foreman Späth.

Somewhat later I drove to Abteilung and had coffee with the commanding officer before heading back for a sleep, taking with me Leutnant Koppe, who had been returned to the company as platoon leader a few days previously. We got on very well together. A half-day's work ensued until everything necessary had been set in train, we had telephones connected, obtained maps of the new operational area and dealt with the trivial matters. Then naturally Feldwebel Grohmann came forward and we had to make out the operational report and see to more paperwork. The things people in the Reich got upset about: for the third time a feld-gendarmerie report from Kassel against eight men of my company who on a job to the Henschel Works there six months ago had ignored the sergeant of a patrol and failed to salute. (In the German Army an NCO had to be saluted by a man of inferior rank.) They were actually demanding that I punish these front-veterans for such a trifle. This report went into the waste-paper basket for the third time but I was convinced that within at least eight weeks I would receive an admonition. We were often burdened with crap like this but sometimes there were important things amongst it all and we had to have order. We were also receiving our field post again.

Nothing happened for four days. The front here seemed to have calmed down. Another transfer order came in. I went ahead in my VW with my dispatch riders to sort out the quarters. This nest was not up to much. The farmstead had only one room with heating and was occupied by the men, great-grandparents, grandparents, mother and child of the family. There was nothing that could be done about it, at the end of November we couldn't camp in the open and close up for warmth. Thank heavens our stay there was not long. Towards 0200hrs on 30 November a dispatch rider came from Abteilung with a written order: 'Abteilung moving to new operations area, tracked vehicles will load on the train at Waitzen (Vac). Leutnant Koppe will lead panzer elements there. Moving out immediately.' I had to report personally to the Abteilung command post, where I was advised of the new situation. After their heavy losses in the fighting east of Budapest in the last ten days of November, the Russians had reorganized and shifted the point of their main attack effort to the southern wing of our Army Group South. They had crossed the Romanian–Hungarian border, protected only by weak Hungarian forces. Fünfkirchen (Pécs) had fallen and there was nothing to prevent a quick Russian advance towards Plattensee (Lake Balaton). On 1 December 1944 the Russian spearheads had already reached Dómbovár and Kaposvár, 80km west of the Danube. By shortening the front line in the Hatvan area, 2 PzDiv and 1 PzDiv had been freed to oppose these Soviets units. 23 PzDiv had already reached the area south of Lake Balaton on 30 November and with motorized reconnaissance troops were monitoring the Pécs–Pécsvárad–Bátaszék area and the roads leading north from there. 23 PzDiv had the objective of delaying the Soviet advance for as long as possible. Heavy PzAbt 503 was now subordinated to 23 PzDiv.

Therefore we had received our movement orders. Leutnant Koppe had his job, and I reported at 0300hrs to the Abteilung command post. They were all asleep there, and so I used a sofa for the same purpose. Next morning I discussed the plans with the commanding officer. I went with Fromme to the new operational area in order to establish contact and make enquiries since it could well be my task to bring the battle group there. Our route passed through Budapest where we had time to break our journey. In the Hotel Hungaria we had a room with bath. How wonderful that was! In the evening we ate at the 'Gellert'. We had no food coupons but Hungarians at the neighbouring table helped us out. I enjoyed the atmosphere and the friendliness of the people. We met acquaintants, some from our earlier time in Budapest, others comrades-in-arms. We sat at the bar for hours. Back at the Hotel Hungaria I had a bath and then – those wonderful beds! Next morning, 2 December 1944, I drove via Stuhlweissenburg to Pincehely and one village further on found our wheeled Tross already arrived. At 23 PzDiv I took in the overall situation. The division had a sector almost 100km wide. It would only be possible to monitor it and fight delaying actions. A stop line was to be set up further on at Lake Balaton where the Russian advance had to be finally stopped. At that time the Russians were advancing 20 to 30km every day, for there was nothing to stop them. Next I went to Corps HQ. Looking for the Corps I arrived at Siófok, a charming bathing resort on Lake Balaton. Unfortunately the stay there was not restful because Russian tanks had made a surprise appearance in the vicinity and were expected at any moment. One could not say they had made a breakthrough, for there was not at that time a cohesive front line through which to break. Our defence was limited to holding strategically important points for as long as possible in order to delay the Russian advance.

On 3 December panzers of the Abteilung arrived by rail, unloaded at Balatonkenese and were driven at once to Simontornya where the Abteilung command post was located on the estate of an Hungarian noble. I got to know the baron, a fine-looking elderly Hungarian gentleman. He invited the Abteilung officers to dinner and it became an unforgettable evening for me. Our host and the baroness received us in evening dress, the table was laid with fine porcelain and glasses, flowers and candles. A footman with white gloves served drinks, then the lady of the house invited us to the table. I cannot remember the sequence of plates, after the hors d'oeuvre the baron made a speech which moved us all and we drank a toast to the old German-Hungarian brotherhood in arms. Our conversation was deliberately cultured and I remember that in conclusion there was a wonderful cake, similar to our 'Himmelstorte' at home. Just as were about to be served coffee there exploded in our very animated circle like a lightning bolt from the heavens the report by our reconnaissance platoon: the Russians had appeared nearby. I hurried out, alerted my panzers and sent out my lookouts. To be surprised by the Russians now would be extremely unfavourable. The commanding officer sent the reconnaissance platoon to make enquiries. I came back and drank my coffee. The Abteilung HQ was making hurried preparations to move out and went that same night. I remained with my battle group at the village for the time being. Our host was determined to get his family to safety. Fromme offered him Abteilung vehicles and urged him and his wife not to remain here under any circumstances. The estate vehicles were loaded up and after the first confusion everything seemed to proceed with careful deliberation. My assignment was now to secure the area for the time being and maintain contact with 23 PzDiv, for apart from my panzers there were no forces available to oppose the Russians.

At daybreak I could see the next village about 1,500m away from the windows of my command post. The Russians had got that far in the meantime. In the course of the morning there was some exchange of fire. Russian tanks had ventured out of the village, probably on reconnaissance. Upon receiving our fire they made smoke and fell back. Towards midday I was told to move my battle group during the course of the evening. About the same time I noticed that in the courtyard the estate vehicles, which had been loaded the previous night, were now being unloaded again. I went to find the baron, who declared that to flee made no sense, he would not leave his estate. His two teenage sons would make their way on horseback to relatives in Vienna with money and provisions. Shortly after that I saw them ride off. I offered the baron three of my armoured personnel carriers to take his family to safety. He was indecisive and I increased the pressure on him to go. I could sense what a difficult inner struggle he was having, it was a dramatic and, for me, a deeply moving situation. In the end he decided to stay. He had the illusion of hiding out at a hunting lodge in his woods until after the first days of the Russian occupation were over. Now I could delay my departure no longer. My panzers had returned from lookout duty and picked me up after I took my leave of the baron and his wife in the cellars of their mansion. He gave me his calling card and I wrote my home address on the back of it so that we could keep in touch after everything was over. I never discovered what happened to him or whether his two sons ever reached Vienna. It was a sadness for me that I was unable to help him, but I could not fight the war on my own. We embraced and I left.

I reported with my panzers to the commanding officer 15km away at his provisional command post, a very large manor house whose owners had fled leaving only an aged servant to protect it. He opened up to us very reluctantly. In this sumptuous, internally quite modern house I was impressed by the gorgeous bathroom and built-in bar near the drawing room. Unfortunately the bar was dry. The heating was still working, there was hot water and I took a glorious bath. What luxury and what happiness at feeling clean again! I used a British soap on a rope but forgot to take it with me when I left. I would willingly have stayed much longer in these quarters. After the servant had brought us tea and biscuits we moved out at 0400hrs and I drove the commanding officer direct to 1 PzDiv to which we were now subordinated once again. I moved into Lepsény with my battle group.

Next morning the alarm was raised and I had to take my Tigers without delay to 2 InfRgt/1 PzDiv whose command post lay 5km from Siófok. The main front line there consisted only of strongpoints. The Russians attacked constantly, hoping for a decisive breakthrough at Stuhlweissenburg. I divided my battle group: half had to advance along the highway towards Siófok where the Russians had gained ground yesterday. Leutnant Koppe led this part of the battle group. In order to relieve the infantry, the other half was to attack a village from where the Russians were making raids on our lines. I led this second group myself.

I left my medium-wave radio vehicle behind at 2 InfRgt's command post as a relay centre. It was not always easy in the unfavourable circumstances to operate a properly functioning signals network. I drove with my panzers to the position ordered, the infantry company sector. I did not like the route there in the least, in parts it was bottomless mud and difficult for my panzers to pass.

The infantry company consisted of twenty-one men guarding 2km of front, therefore the length of a football pitch each. They were overjoyed when we arrived and now felt safe. We launched the attack against the enemy-held village immediately. It confronted the infantry company sector from about 2km away. The attack went well and although we were only three panzers this was enough. We knocked out six anti-tank guns, at which the Russians decamped, and I pulled back to position the Tigers between the infantry trenches. The infantry were content.

I established contact with Leutnant Koppe and his half of the battle group. The attack had not gone so well there. An Oberfeldwebel from 2 Company had been killed. We were really depressed about it. I went on foot to the battalion command post where I had ordered my tracked motorcycle to be brought, and drove from there to the regimental command post to discuss the situation with the regimental commander, after which I was given orders to move out at 1800hrs. I had had the feeling all day that something was going to go wrong. We often had these presentiments of disaster and mostly they came true. Since there was only an hour to go until we moved back there was no point in my going forward again and instead I passed the order by radio to both halves of my battle group. While I was at Regimental HQ, my three panzers were commanded by Feldwebel Seidel, a reliable veteran. Both halves were to come now to the regimental command post. The infantry was to pull out at 2100hrs to form a new line some kilometres further back.

I expected my panzers any time after 1830hrs. Then a radio message came from Leutnant Koppe: while moving out, two Tigers had stuck fast in a swampy meadow just short of the highway. Recovery work was under way. I was on tenterhooks, for the place where Koppe now found himself was on the main front line about 100m from the advanced Russian outposts. There was no infantry available for close protection. Thus we were faced with a difficult recovery. After about thirty minutes came a new message: during the recovery work a third Tiger had got stuck fast. As if that were not enough, Feldwebel Seidel radioed me that two of his three panzers had bogged down on the path in the quagmire. I close to despair. Five panzers all bogged down together was bound to end in disaster.

After a jittery half-hour Seidel reported that his two panzers had got free. When they arrived I went with them to the spot where Leutnant Koppe's three panzers were stuck. Previously I had received the regimental commander's promise that the infantry would remain in position for as long as it took to get these panzers free. When I reached Koppe I found the following to be the situation: 20–30m to the right of the Siófok highway three Tigers had sunk fairly hopelessly into the morass. In the darkness the path was very difficult to see and the panzers had turned off only a few metres short of the highway. Every time the Russians heard an engine they fired off wildly in its general direction and the bullets whistled all around us, which naturally made the recovery work much more difficult. Before starting up an engine everybody had to take cover, for the Russians were shooting with everything they had, artillery at quite short range, mortars, anti-tank guns,

MGs, you name it. They were zeroed-in on the highway and firing blindly along it, while we had to keep on the firm ground of the highway in order to carry out the salvage work. Finally after much effort we got one panzer free and on the highway. Suddenly a barrage of fire: I took cover behind the panzer, a deafening explosion, an impact on the highway very close to me. I was struck in the face and felt something warm running down my nose. A shell splinter had cut me, how easily it could have put my eye out! I thought of my presentiment and felt relieved that now it had happened and I was freed from the nightmare of premonition. But there was worse to come.

It was past midnight on 8 December 1944 and our situation was touch and go. We had no German troops to the right or left of us and no close protection. I wanted to make one last try and got two panzers into position on the highway to heave. All available hawsers were joined together to reach the two casualties sunk into the mire 30m away, and the hawsers were just long enough. When everything was ready the order was given for all men to take cover in the panzers and then the engines were started up at an order given by radio. The Russians opened fire again, raking the highway, it was really very dangerous. Nevertheless we got one panzer free at which I was very relieved and elated. After things had quietened down a little I opened the turret hatch intending to sit up and supervise the recovery of the other panzer. At that moment I received from the rear a blow to my right shoulder and my right arm hung down limply. This time I had been hit badly: a through-and-through to the upper arm, bleeding heavily. I had received the wound from the rear, therefore the Russians must have worked their way around behind us. I gave Leutnant Koppe instructions and when a dispatch rider came by to enquire how much longer the recovery work would go on for, I went back with him and had a doctor dress the wound. I had been very lucky in that it was a pure flesh wound, the bones were intact. An hour later I was at the Abteilung command post. Shortly afterwards Leutnant Koppe also came by, as careworn as I, to report that the last panzer could not be retrieved because the Russians had surrounded the site and had worked their way up to the towing panzers. The last bogged-down Tiger had to be shot into flames but I was happy, however, that of the five which had stuck fast we had got four free. For a long while this had seemed impossible to me.

Next morning I was examined by the Abteilung surgeon, result: admission to a military hospital. I was still thinking about whether I wanted to go or not when the alarming report came in at 1000hrs that the Russians were on the point of occupying Polgárdi. The command post packed up everything in the greatest haste and a short while later we were on the way to Stuhlweissenburg. I reported myself unfit for duty to the Abteilung commanding officer and went to the Tross at Bana. There I worked through all my outstanding paperwork, such as promotions and recommendations for decorations. Feldwebel Bornschier had fallen, a painful loss for the company, I had to write to his wife. Next morning I drove to the military hospital at Komárom, taking with me Gefreiter Böhler, whose wound was still causing him problems.

We spent only one night at Komárom: next morning we were listed for a hospital train. This did not suit me since I wanted to remain in reach of my company. Therefore I drove back to the Tross at Bana and from there next morning by car to Vienna. I took Böhler with me and also my driver Glasl and Oberfeldwebel Grohmann. We had three punctures on the way and on the outskirts of Vienna a long delay for an air raid. I went first to see Leutnant Fürlinger, who was being treated as walking wounded and staying with his mother in Vienna. He took me next day to a military hospital where Böhler and I received excellent treatment. I could move about freely with my arm in a sling and enjoyed the days in Vienna. I went several times to Hitzing to visit my godmother Irene Adensamer who was very worried about the future. When the Russians occupied Vienna in mid-April 1945 she and Uncle Sander committed suicide.

On 20 December, Böhler and I were discharged from hospital at our own request. We wanted to spend Christmas with the company. I had ordered my vehicle to come to Vienna to pick us up and on 21 December we drove back. Our wounds were not yet fully healed but we ignored it. My Tross now had quarters not far from Várpalota. Very pleasant quarters had been prepared for me there in the rectory. Next morning I drove to the Abteilung command post at Berhida to report back for duty. Hauptmann Fromme had meanwhile been transferred out to the Panzer School to lecture in tactics and had already left the company. His successor was Hauptmann von Diest-Koerber. As I presented myself to him with the words, 'Leutnant von Rosen obediently reporting back,' he interrupted me and said that I had made a false statement. I had been promoted to Oberleutnant on 1 November 1944. Immediately after that he left with the panzers for operations towards Polgárdi, and after speaking to my panzer crews I returned to the Tross to save my energies for a few more days before mounting a Tiger again. On my return I found field post from my parents awaiting me. They had evacuated to the Blanquets at Rotenfels. On 24 November Strasbourg had fallen to the Allies, and since then Rastatt was on the front line. What it must be like there I could imagine only too well.

At Christmas the company surprised me with a tree and presents. Amongst other things our company shoemaker, a Russian volunteer auxiliary from Mius, had made me an attaché case from pieces of leather scraps. A touching gift, and I have it still. The 'Spiess', Hauptfeldwebel Müller, had slaughtered four fat pigs at the Tross and hung 500 sausages in a smokehouse. On every subsequent transfer we transported these sausages and the livestock maintained by the company to the new base. Müller, a baker and confectioner in civilian life, had also baked Christmas biscuits for the whole company, various sorts, with and without chocolate, with nuts or filling, almost like Café Moritz in Rastatt in peacetime! Thus every man of the company got a paper bag with biscuits and three sausages.

I wanted to spend the evening with my panzer crews. A lot of thought went into it but the situation thwarted our plans. The previous night the Abteilung had had to move to Fehervarczurgo. The Russians had unleashed a strong attack and succeeded in investing Stuhlweissenburg on Christmas Eve. Our panzers had been in the thick of it. In the evening I arrived at the Abteilung command post bringing the commanding officer a present from the company and then I celebrated Christmas with the repair group. I was not able to go forward to my panzers, and that night the company lost another, Leutnant Rambow having had to destroy his Tiger after putting seven enemy tanks out of action shortly before. To be deprived of any King Tiger was a sad loss. I was on the road until 0200hrs trying to deliver presents from the company personally, and announced some promotions, amongst them the promotion to Feldwebel of our magnificent Unteroffizier Gärtner, wearer of the German Cross in Gold.

I stayed with my Tross until 31 December 1944. On various occasions I went along the road towards the front, but more importantly I had time for my wounds to heal. I did present myself once to the commanding officer requesting that he allow me to remount my panzer but I was directed back to Tross. However, on the evening of 31 December orders came at last to take command of my battle group again. The front had receded somewhat and my panzers were at Mór, famous for its good wines and numerous taverns. The Abteilung was now subordinated to 4 Kavallerie-Brigade commanded by General Holste. It had two mounted regiments (yes, even in 1945 the Wehrmacht still had them) and a so-called heavy Abteilung with some Panzer IIIs and armoured personnel carriers. The commanding officer was Rittmeister (cavalry captain) Graf Plettenberg to whom I was directly responsible. He was also to be found at Mór with his HQ.

New Year's Eve at Mór was far from restful, for the Russians, whose trench system was in the wine-growing hills at the end of the village, were able to look down and see everything going on in our nest. Apart from short pauses when they drew breath, we lay under almost incessant 'Stalin Organ' or mortar fire. The worst time was just before midnight when the shack in which I had set up my command post rattled and shook dangerously. My men preferred to spend the night in the panzer. With Leutnant Rambow and a couple of other company stalwarts we celebrated in the shack with a couple of bottles. At midnight I dashed to Graf Plettenberg's command post and we drank to the New Year. I radioed a poem to Abteilung and thus 1945 began for us. I thought often of my family from whom I had not recently received news.

At that time I got personnel reinforcements. Leutnant Rubbel, coming fresh to us from officer training, was made leader of III Platoon in my company. This post had been vacant since Leutnant Wagner had been wounded. Before the officer course, Rubbel had spent two years in 1 Company and had had an outstanding instructor in Oberfeldwebel Fendesack. It had been his aspiration therefore to return to 1 Company. I got on very well with him, but he had the feeling that he was not welcome in 3 Company. I have to say that I saw no such signs, but was happy to have such a capable and experienced man with me. We remain friends to this day.

The New Year began with an early morning alarm. The Russians were putting very heavy pressure on the grenadiers in the vineyards and we set out with elements of the brigade for a relief attack against the heavily reinforced Hill 128 north of Mór. We made a quite good impression on the cavalrymen with this attack. Rittmeister Graf Plettenberg's heavy Abteilung and the Reiter-Rgt *von Mackensen* were to attack from the south-east and we King Tigers from the south, the two groups meeting up at the objective. On the approach my Tigers became lost – in the snow one hill looked much like another. Where was this damned Height 128? There – a heavy enemy force on a ridge. Without regard to what might be to my left or right I attacked the ridge. The Russians fled, leaving all their guns and equipment behind. We had found Hill 128 and therefore the Tigers had arrived where ordered, on time and suffered no losses. When Kavallerie-Brigade arrived we had everything under control. An entire mounted cavalry regiment attacking was an improbable sight!

My cooperation with Rittmeister Graf Plettenberg was extremely enjoyable. His 'heavy Abteilung' was an extraordinary association: the officer corps was homogenous, cultured in manner, gesture and speech. Though in action it was very weakly armed and armoured compared to us, it was at least extremely mobile! I enjoyed the distinction of being an outsider fully accepted into their circle. We carried out successful attacks together, the brilliant night attack on Arci Puszta comes to mind particularly. After a 10km advance through the woods of the Vertes mountains, we surprised the Russians so totally near Arci Puszta that this enemy-occupied town virtually fell back into our hands. I recalled my night attack at Gyöngyös. Yes, if I had had such support then, perhaps it might have succeeded.

Between our various operations I was often with Graf Plettenberg. I remember especially an officers' evening (with roasted pigeon!). In his circle the conversation was very free and frank. I learned the background and details of the 20 July plot previously unknown to me. I had never before experienced such open talk and unequivocal rejection of our regime, particularly the Nazi Party and everything connected with it. It was not just criticism, but open opposition. I felt that I belonged within this circle.

Plettenberg was a splendid officer, as was his adjutant Graf Oberndorf. That I had been fully accepted into this circle, considered as one of them and had taken part in these dangerous conversations touched me deeply and in many respects gave me release. That evening Graf Plettenberg tried to convince me to transfer into his Abteilung to lead a new company of Panthers which was being formed. It was very tempting for me to remain in this attractive aristocratic world, but it would mean leaving my own men in the lurch, who had absolute confidence in me. My decision was clear, I had to remain with my company and Abteilung where I had good and fine comrades too, and who had gone through hell with me.

My detachment to the heavy Abteilung was terminated and heavy PzAbt 503, which meanwhile had almost twenty King Tigers operational, was led into the fray by the commanding officer while we remained with Graf Plettenberg temporarily 'for cooperation'. A major offensive was being planned for the near future to prevent the threatened occupation of Budapest. We moved back to Fehervarczgurgo, and some very difficult days of operations followed. Difficult because the enemy was tenacious and the terrain dreadful. A few days previously there had been heavy snow but now there was a thaw and the mud took over. The terrain was monotonous – vast undulating plains with now and again a manor house razed to the ground. To orientate oneself in this bleak region was difficult, especially at night, and we had to move mostly by night. I experienced many unpleasant night journeys at the head of my column, although ultimately we always arrived where we had been heading.

Our orders were to capture Zámoly. The town lay well protected in a gully. The attack was difficult, the Russians dogged. We roared frontally into an anti-tank gun front and were taken under heavy fire from ahead and from the flanks. Feldwebel Gärtner's panzer received a lateral through-and-through. Apparently we were facing Stalin tanks [TN: the giant JS-2 armed with a 122mm gun, able to penetrate 100mm of armour at 2,000m]. Gärtner was seriously wounded and died on the way to the main dressing station. He had a dreadful wound in the thigh and bled to death. Another terrible loss. Later the attack was abandoned. We pulled fairly well back and spent an awfully wet and cold night in the panzer. We were hungry, frozen and dog-tired. All the many strains to which we were subjected defy description: the panic, the false alarms, bad news about panzers breaking down or bogging down or the Russians suddenly breaking through: this all played on the nerves. In the end one didn't have nerves any more and surprised oneself by what one still had the power to do. One thing was clear, the big attack across a broad front did not have the hoped-for success on the first day, the Russians being very much more tenacious than we had expected.

The next day, 8 January 1945, it could be felt that the Russians still had the initiative. Orders and counter-orders followed one after another. We were ordered to Lajamajor, but scarcely had we arrived than we were told to go back to Borbaiamajor. When we got to Borbaiamajor the order came to return at once to Lajamajor where sixty enemy tanks had turned up. Apart from some artillery and mortar fire, all was quiet there. Next morning there came an alarm and we had to proceed to Alsopuszta. Here we destroyed seven enemy tanks. A violent blizzard raged. That night too we spent in the panzer. It was cold, so we had to use the soldering lamp to warm up and we all got black faces.

The attack on Zámoly was resumed on 11 January. There had been a thaw with much slush. We rolled out at 0600hrs, and the advance was scheduled for 0640hrs after a brief preparation. Our Abteilung had committed thirteen Tigers for the operation. After rocket fire we engaged an anti-tank gun position frontally, my company being on the left flank. First we had to cross the Stuhlweissenburg–Zámoly highway, where the Russians were dug in and determined. Now we had to make a 90° turn with my left flank unprotected. Although they had ten to twelve guns in position to my left, the enemy ran for it when we attacked. We continued and then our panzer received a heavy blow – as I discovered later a through-and-through in the engine compartment. I got into another panzer. Panzers of my company were now receiving heavy hits. Together with other panzers of the Abteilung, as ordered we reached a hill from where we could operate effectively against Zámoly. At the same time Graf Plettenberg had just led his heavy Abteilung into Zámoly. Here he was seriously wounded and lost a leg, and his adjutant Graf Oberndorf was killed. From this hill Feldwebel Sachs destroyed three Russian liaison aircraft attempting to take off from a meadow near Zámoly. I dismounted to inspect the damage which my panzer had suffered, then went to the commanding officer's panzer which was not far from me. On the way I captured some terrified Russians who had been feigning death in their trench.

We had no more time to waste and got going again, the breach had to be widened. We knocked out a number of anti-tank guns and then came to a sloping vineyard beyond which it was not possible to see but apparently fell away steeply. This blocked our advance and we took up widely scattered security positions. We warded off two raids by ground attack aircraft after being bombed, but the Russians had very skilfully positioned some SU-152 self-propelled assault guns in the vineyard. These were dangerous for us since they could penetrate our frontal armour with their 152mm howitzers. We had not even spotted them when suddenly a 1 Company panzer went up in flames, killing three men, the two survivors suffering serious burns. Half an hour later the same happened to a second panzer. We withdrew a little. Apparently the crews of these guns observed us from hiding. When they saw a panzer they came into the open, aimed and fired one round, and withdrew into cover immediately. This deprived us of the opportunity to return fire and knock them out. In this terrain without cover we could find no reverse slope, we had to hold our hill at all costs and secure it, because only in that way could flank protection for Zámoly be effected. Despite small changes of position – a few metres forwards, then back, a little to the left, then to the right – it was unavoidable that the Tigers stood around in the terrain offering a large target. After another half-hour a third panzer, standing to my left, was hit, killing some of the crew. We were at a loss how to deal with these assault guns since we had no idea where they were. It seemed to me that my panzer would be next because the Russians were shooting systematically at one panzer after another left to right. I kept a sharp and concentrated lookout. Just keep calm, I told myself but it was a ghastly situation. It was approaching dusk: how I longed for nightfall! Then I saw a powerful stream of fire from opposite and at once we were hit. We were whirled about and suddenly daylight could be seen from within the panzer. We had received a through-and-through, the engine had had it. I shouted 'Abandon!' and in five seconds the whole crew was out.

Thank God they all made it: only the driver had been wounded. After taking him along the path to the dressing station I returned to the panzers. Darkness was falling, protecting us from further losses. I still had two panzers intact. I went on foot to the commanding officer's panzer for a short situation conference, then crept my way back with a crew member carrying a sub-machine gun. The panzer had not caught fire, and we had orders to bring it back. We made it ready to tow, that is to say the engine and drive train were disconnected in the interior by removing a number of screws, then the towing hawser was attached. Meanwhile I stood guard with the sub-machine gun. This was more for moral support than effective defence. Once darkness fell, a 1 Company panzer towed the casualty away under the Russians' noses. Now I saw how lucky we had been again: a large area of armour had been penetrated yet we had only one man wounded.

Of the thirteen panzers which had set out that morning from Abteilung, by evening we had three still operational. 1 Company had seven dead, while 3 Company just one man wounded. Two panzers were write-offs, the remaining Tigers, some of which had received serious damage, could be recovered and brought to the rear. In one of these towing manoeuvres Leutnant Heerlein the Abteilung adjutant was wounded. The day had brought the Abteilung heavy losses as against the success of reconquering Zámoly. Losses inflicted on the enemy were twenty-one tanks and self-propelled assault guns, twenty anti-tank guns, three aircraft and a multiple rocket launcher destroyed. We headed back to Alsopuszta.

Next morning I drove with the commanding officer to the Abteilung command post at Bodajk. There I received my appointment as company commander, until then I had only been company leader. The appointment was only made possible by my promotion to Oberleutnant. It did nothing to change my duties but after a definite time as 'commander' one could be promoted to Hauptmann. To that extent this appointment was an important event. Now I had a couple of days to rest. The Abteilung surgeon attended to my wound, not yet fully healed, and I attended to my company's panzers, ensuring that they emerged as quickly as possible from the workshop.

The next few weeks we operated in the Fehervarczurgo–Zámoly–Stuhlweissenburg triangle, the purpose being to protect the narrows between Lake Balaton and Lake Velencer, mostly by attacking the enemy where they broke through. Stuhlweissenburg changed hands several times. On 10 February Budapest capitulated. The two attempts to relieve Budapest made either side of Lake Velencer got very close to the Hungarian capital but in the end our forces were not strong enough. We had good results, destroying numerous Russian tanks, assault guns and anti-tank guns. Our losses were kept within acceptable limits and in this period the company had no fatalities. If the number of Tigers operational was large, the Abteilung would be led by the commanding officer, and the three companies by their respective commanders: if the number fell, they would be assembled into a battle group led by one of the three company commanders. The leadership changed every seven days so that if everything went according to plan, after seven days of operations I would have a rest. Of course, it did not always work out that way and then I would have to spend longer in the field. The panzer crews often got periods for rest as nearly all panzers went into the workshop from time to time to repair battle damage or technical defects. Then they would remain with the panzer.

The general war situation was by now causing us great concern. I had in my company some Silesians and East Prussians who had serious worries for their families once the Russians had crossed the Reich borders in the East. Some got news that their families had been evacuated, others had received no field post for weeks. This uncertainty was intolerable. I knew the family circumstances of my men. They came to me with their problems, but in these cases my hands were tied. Married men always got preference when it came to handing out leave passes. If happy or sad tidings were received from home there was always special leave no matter how the situation stood with us. It now happened much more frequently that soldiers had to be given leave if news came that their family had been bombed out. When these soldiers returned to the company one had to take a special interest in them. The more tragic the circumstances became in the homeland, the more the company became a constant factor, a kind of 'substitute family' for the men. Here one felt understood and supported by their comrades. What they told us about the homeland was generally not good, the war had taken over all aspects of life. The loudest mouths were those who had never experienced the front, and so one would be happy to be back 'at home' with the gang. I also had concerns. I had heard nothing from home for several weeks but I knew that my parents were at Rotenfels. But what was it really like? What had become of my brother Wuller after the bombing of Dresden, of which we had naturally heard? Thus every man had his cross to bear.

On orders of the highest, the Abteilung was renamed Heavy PzAbt *Feldherrnhalle* and we were integrated at the same time into Panzerkorps *Feldherrnhalle*. We thought this was nonsense. We preferred to be 503 and within the unit continued to refer to ourselves as such. 503 was now a Waffen-SS Heavy PzAbt, and so around

5 February 1945 it was rumoured that we were to be pulled from the Front. To where was unknown for the time being. On 12 February the Tigers began loading at Mór and we arrived at Panzerkorps *Feldherrnhalle* which was preparing to play the leading role in destroying the Russian bridgehead on the Gran. Here our Abteilung was subordinated to Reichsgrenadier-Division *Hoch und Deutschmeister*. The first transports arrived on 15 February at Perbete, and the Abteilung set up at Csuz. Because insufficient rail transporters were available, 3 Company had to wait until empty wagons came back from Perbete to Mór. Therefore my company did not load until later. I used the time at Mór to try its wonderful wines. We made visits to the winegrowers and were soon able to distinguish the better wines of the southern slopes from the others.

The Russians had established a major bridgehead over the Gran, a tributary of the Danube, which presented a constant threat to the German Front and Vienna. In order to remove it a force was assembled consisting of our Panzerkorps, a Waffen-SS Panzerkorps and the Leibstandarte *Adolf Hitler*. The attack was to begin on 17 February 1945. The Abteilung had twenty-two battleworthy Tigers, but only a few from 3 Company. The attack began well, but then the commanding officer's panzer received a hit on the side of the turret. Because Hauptmann von Diest-Koerber was forced to navigate from an open hatch at night – as did all panzer commanders – he was seriously wounded in the back of the head by a shell splinter. Leutnant Heerlein took over leading the attack, and the commanding officer was taken by an armoured personnel carrier ambulance to the rear and was treated later in the Luftwaffe hospital at Pressburg (Bratislava). Hauptmann Wiegand, chief of the supply company and the oldest company leader in the Abteilung, came forward to take command. I did not take part in this attack because most of 3 Company had not arrived at Perbete in time. Now, on the morning of 18 February, they were ready and could get involved in the Abteilung's attack.

At daybreak we advanced along the railway line to Kis Nifalu as an Abteilung. After three hours the village was in our possession once we had broken through strong anti-tank gun and tank fronts. The artillery gave us outstanding support. I had their advanced spotter as sixth man in my panzer, therefore I could tell him directly what I wanted and he then passed it on to his batteries as a radio message. The artillery laid smoke into the village forcing the Russians to decamp. Their defence had begun to totter: after mopping up we pushed on and were soon confronted by a minefield. In order not to lose time I dismounted and cleared a path myself for the panzers and defused wooden chest- and tar-mines as I had been taught in 1943 at Tolokonoye by the pioneer Oberfeldwebel Baumann. In half an hour I had defused fifty mines and then we passed through without damage.

We reached our first intermediate objective and came across only weak resistance. Meanwhile we had progressed a good distance behind the Russian lines. A new order now came from Division. After decoding it we thought initially there had been some mistake and requested a repeat: but no, we had a new objective to aim for about 20km from where we were now, and it was getting dark. Therefore we advanced, always cross-country, occasionally running into enemy tanks. Open fire, hit, press on. The most difficult task was to navigate through a pitch-dark night. Towards midnight we came to a very swampy area which caused us difficulties. Some distance away we saw to our left white flares going up, the signal for 'German troops' and we heard the typical engine noise of German panzers. After another hour we succeeded in making direct contact with the Leibstandarte *Adolf Hitler* which had made its way here from the north with forty to fifty panzers. At first we approached them but then received an order from Division to halt. This was in the Muszla area. Hauptmann Wiegand went to establish contact with Division while I waited with the panzers for several hours for our supply which arrived at 0400hrs with the longed-for field kitchen. The food was cold, only the coffee was hot. Towards 0700hrs I arrived at Köbölkut as ordered with the panzers. Here Hauptmann Wiegand was waiting for us with new orders. We had to liberate two villages, but apparently the Russians had got wind of the presence of Tigers and decamped and we fulfilled the mission without meeting significant resistance. Here we would have liked to pause awhile, but new orders kept us going.

This time our advance took us through mountainous country. It was a strain, particularly for the drivers who had had no sleep for twenty-eight hours. The pre-spring sunshine made up for it somewhat. Towards evening we got to our new objective, much longed-for, but we had to make a night attack on Kemend straight away, therefore no sleep. The terrain before us was difficult, numerous deep gulches had to be crossed, and in darkness when contact with the enemy had to be expected at any moment, making it doubly unpleasant.

We had already driven through the Russian lines. They had been abandoned, which gave me an uneasy feeling. After crossing a very difficult gorge we came to a broad elevated plain with an upwards slope. We could only guess our direction of advance, therefore we went forward slowly. It was clear to me that our main difficulties would not present themselves until daybreak. If we reached Kemend during the night, we would be left totally to our own devices after dawn for the entire area could be easily seen from the higher ground on the other bank of the Gran where the Russians had positioned themselves. We would not be able to receive supplies or reinforcements during daylight. This was something to worry about later, for our advance was still progressing and the Russians were too quiet for comfort.

Suddenly we came across mines laid to the left, right and ahead of us. We were already into a minefield whose borders could not be determined. We began attempts to clear them but they had been laid carefully and were totally frozen-in besides. There was no room to manoeuvre and we finally had to accept that we had come to a dead end. We worked feverishly to change the damaged sections of track, this setting off other mines in the process. Since we could not proceed through the minefield our only option was to withdraw for now it had begun to get light. The calendar read 20 February 1945, my last day on active service.

We had just pulled back to the gorge when at first light we had the Russians at our throats. Their tank attack was skilful but in tank combat we were still a little superior to them. Towards midday the situation quietened down and Hauptmann Wiegand drove back to the command post. I left two panzers on watch ahead and went back 2km up to a quarry in order to give the crews some rest. Every two hours the two panzers ahead were to be relieved. I stretched myself out on the rear of my panzer, enjoying the warmth of the engine below and the sun above, and fell asleep. A little later the enemy artillery fired on precisely this little spot and shell splinters shattered my left elbow.

I noticed this while half asleep and did not fully come to my senses until I found a surgeon working on my arm. He applied an emergency dressing and I was conveyed by armoured personnel carrier to the command post at Köbölkut where Dr Büry looked at the wound. They were all very concerned about me. Leutnant Koppe now took over command of the company and I discussed everything with him which needed to be done. They had given me a shot of morphine and this held off the pain.

I reported myself unfit for duty to Hauptmann Wiegand and drove to the workshop where I had my evening meal with Oberleutnant Barkhausen. Then I was returned to the Tross at Tardosked in the more comfortable Mercedes of the commanding officer. We arrived there around midnight, expected by the 'Spiess', Hauptfeldwebel Müller. Thanks to the morphine I slept well. Next morning in the orderly room I dictated some important things I wanted to see to myself, promotions, decorations and the like, then summoned the company Feldwebels to take my leave of them. The company was fallen in, less those men on active duty forward, in order for me to make a parting speech, short because I had begun to feel weak and my dressing was soaked with blood. In closing I told my company what I firmly believed at that moment: 'In three months I shall be back with you!' Then I shook each man by the hand and was driven in the commanding officer's car to the Luftwaffe hospital at Pressburg.

(right) Hauptmann Wolfram von Eichel-Streiber, 2 Company Commander of Heavy PzAbt 503, accompanied the author to the Luftwaffe military hospital at Pressburg in February 1945.

(below) Wounded men and a Red Cross nurse enjoying the spring sunshine on the balcony of a military hospital.

10

Military Hospital and the End of the War (February–July 1945)

Hauptmann von Eichel-Streiber accompanied me to Pressburg. My commanding officer, Hauptmann von Diest-Koerber, was also at the Luftwaffe hospital there and I was admitted to his ward. Not much could be done with me the first few days. Because of the large wound and swelling it could not be put in plaster. The wound was treated twice under anaesthetic so that splinters of shell and bone could be removed. There was much discharge matter. I was given daily injections of morphine, and was always asking for more, but the dosage could not be exceeded to avoid my becoming addicted. After a few days the commanding officer was discharged at his own request. I had been able to dictate my letters to him and he helped me so far as necessary. The letters in which I informed my parents of my wound never arrived. The last field post they received from me was dated 17 February 1945: the French had occupied my home province of Baden before my letters from hospital arrived.

I became very bed-ridden. The doctors were at a loss, for without a plaster cast the bones would not knit and because the joint was shattered the ends of the upper and lower arms could not unite. The arm remained badly swollen and suppurating. There was often talk of amputation but the doctors there did not want to risk doing it. As soon as I was able to travel they would send me to a hospital in Germany. At that time my company had a pause in operations and so from time to time a vehicle would arrive with visitors. One afternoon at the end of February I received a surprise visit from Hauptmann Eichel-Streiber wearing a solemn face, followed by 'Spiess' Müller and Feldwebel Sachs and the hospital surgeons. On behalf of the commanding officer, Eichel awarded me the German Cross in Gold. Müller had brought a lot of drink and cakes he had baked personally, and acorn coffee in thermos flasks. More and more people joined our happy throng, and we all drank a toast to me so often that I needed no painkillers for the rest of the day. I received humorous cards from the company signed by everybody and a very kind letter from the commanding officer which pleased me greatly. They remain of great value to me today.

In the evening I was visited by the German envoy in Pressburg, Minister Hanns Ludin, who had held the test for my SA-riding certificate in 1939. In 1941 he had become an SA-Obergruppenführer in the diplomatic service and was hanged as a war criminal at Bratislava in 1947. He stood at my bedside and congratulated me, then read my name on the clipboard at the foot of my bed and asked, 'A son of the old Rosens of Rastatt?' When I confirmed it he recalled how during his fortress confinement at Rastatt he had been invited to lunch at our house on many Sundays. Next day he sent a young female secretary from the consulate with two bottles of champagne.

A few days later I was scheduled to be transferred by hospital train to Germany. Fortune smiled on me again. In mid-March the Army Group consultant surgeon, a professor at Greifswald University, came on a routine visit to the hospital. He was available to all military hospitals in the Army Group's area in order to advise on difficult cases and if necessary take them on himself. He had been shown four such cases at Pressburg. After examining me he operated at once and so saved my stiffened arm. Now he fixed my arm at a 190° bend using a chest, upper and lower arm plaster cast which kept the wound area open and by hooks reaching into the wounds fixed the bones in this position. This gave them the chance to knit together again.

At the end of March the Russians were dangerously close to Pressburg. I was brought out on the last hospital train to leave the town and after crossing the Reich border on Easter Sunday went into a military hospital at Gars on the River Inn on 3 April 1945, and transferred three days later to the military hospital at Haag/Inn because better surgical treatment was available there. The well-known Professor Frey of Munich was chief surgeon and so I was in the best hands. I had lost weight over the preceding weeks and my plaster cast had begun to rub, therefore windows were cut into it for access to the suppurating wounds.

Naturally I followed the course of events from the various Fronts: in April a large town or city fell every day. It was entirely obvious that the end was near and not even a miracle could stave off our total defeat. On 20 April, the Führer's birthday, Goebbels made a speech of praise which ended, as did all those made over the years, with the sentence, 'May he remain for us what he is to us and always was: Our Hitler!' I remembered this phrase very clearly because in seventh grade at High School I had had to deliver Goebbels' birthday speech from memory. At the time we thought it was rubbish, but upon hearing these words again on 20 April 1945 in this situation I could only shake my head and marvel at how people had been taken in by it for all those years. On 1 May the Special Bulletin came reporting Hitler's death, kept back from us for twelve hours, and that he had reportedly 'fallen in the Battle for the Reich capital'. Finally, I thought, finally it's over and we can put an end to this pointless butchery. Make it quick, for better an end with horror than horror without end.

Some days previously my plaster cast had been cut off. It was a long procedure before I was finally peeled out of my breastplate. The bones had knitted together but the wound looked much as before. Now that the cast was off I could carry my arm in a sling. The wrist was stiff and the shoulder far from flexible. I dressed myself for the first time and took a walk through the village but was happier when back in the hospital. Every day the improvement continued: only the elbow required a heavy dressing because it was still ejecting small splinters of bone, which was good.

On 26 April the patients were given the choice of remaining at the hospital until the Americans arrived or being released at once to the location of one's choice. I elected for the latter. I thought that Tegernsee would be a bit more lively than along the Inn and requested transfer to a hospital there since the wound still required attention. I didn't know then that my Aunt Britta was at Rottach on Tegernsee but I was aware that the Boschhof with my cousin Brittchen Erlacher must be somewhere near. I was given my documents, medical records and rations for the journey and after hanging my pack on my belt I left. Public transport had been suspended, no trains or buses, so I had to hitch-hike. There were many Wehrmacht vehicles about, however, and so I had no problem getting a ride but lacking a map I landed up at Brannenburg on the Austrian border towards midday, not what I had hoped for. While awaiting another lift I met some Frenchmen from the French Legion [TN: i.e. who had volunteered to fight for the Germans] who were not sure where they should be. Poor lads, they really had backed the wrong horse. That evening I got to Tegernsee, a glorious spot. Nature undisturbed, unwrecked!

I reported to the main military hospital and was directed to a former boarding house, the 'Bayernheim', now an auxiliary hospital. Half the patients were officers and I shared a triple room with two junior lieutenants. I took two days' leave and hitch-hiked to my cousin Erlacher on the Boschof at Beuerberg. There I also found my Aunt Lilly from Karlsruhe and through her I received the first recent news about my parents at Rastatt.

Next morning I was awoken by my relatives at 0600hrs and informed with excitement that a certain Hauptmann Gerngross had carried out a putsch in Munich with the intention of surrendering the city to the Americans without a fight. The putsch had been quickly put down but then, on the Boschhof at any rate, there was great anxiety about the future consequences. As a member of the Wehrmacht I had to make myself scarce as quickly as possible and so I hitch-hiked back to Tegernsee. On the Boschhof I had been told that Aunt Britta was in Rottach and Uncle Kurt at Schloss Tegernsee which had been converted into an overspill hospital. I visited him that same afternoon. The wound he had received at the Front in 1915 broke out again occasionally and now he lay with nine other men in a large, fairly miserable ward and was surprised and pleased to see me, cordial and kinsmanlike. We exchanged news and before I left he telephoned Aunt Britta at Rohrach: 'Do you know who is here with me? Richard!' Aunt Britta's own son Richard was a medical officer with the troops in Kurland and she had not heard from him for a long time.

As can be imagined, the correction of this dreadful misunderstanding was awkward. Next day, a Sunday, I accompanied Uncle Kurt to visit her. It was a glorious spring day with many people like ourselves taking a promenade on the shores of the lake. Everybody was expecting peace and the faces, at least in this

Captured German troops being searched by an American soldier.

peaceful setting, were hopeful. It was very pleasant to have re-established contact with the family. Aunt Britta was just the same as always and seemed to have got over yesterday's upset.

Then the war overtook us again, and on 30 April the Americans arrived in Munich and were expected at Tegernsee any day. They advised their presence with some mortar fire which landed in St Quirin, therefore close by.

From our balcony we saw Sherman tanks advancing very slowly and cautiously along the lakeside road towards Wiessee although there was no German opposition. We had binoculars and gave a running commentary on this show. That morning I wrapped my pistol in oily rags and dug a hole for it below an imposing tree so that I could retrieve it later. Probably it is still there today. Towards evening it was rumoured that the Americans were already in Tegernsee. Next morning we were all ordered to our rooms and an American doctor went with our senior surgeon from room to room and had the individual cases explained to him. An American soldier was posted at the ground-floor entrance to the hospital and we were prohibited from leaving, and no more visits by relatives were possible. A German soldier from Alsace was taken off and appeared two days later wearing French uniform. I gave him a letter for my parents in the hope he could deliver it in the French-occupied zone, but it never arrived.

On 8 May 1945 the military capitulation came into force. It had been expected for days since it was inevitable. No more war, though not yet quite peace, but no air raids, no shooting, no deaths and no new mutilations. Now we had the prospect of life without fighting, without danger, and perhaps one day peace would really come. Tegernsee was lit up again in the evening and it was bright around us after the years of blackout to which we had grown accustomed. But there was mourning for the many who would not experience this day, and worries about one's comrades-in-arms also increased. Which of them had come through it? Were they all now in Russian captivity? Would one ever see them again?

I now spent much time with Major Hannibal von Lüttichau and an Oberleutnant von Linden from the Foreign Office. The days confined in the hospital were long, and we often played skat or poker. The three of us discussed things a lot. I found it heavy going having to condemn what was past day after day. Suddenly everything here was no longer German but 'Bavarian'. I did not like that at all. Linden, who had contacts and wanted to enter the Bavarian administration, called me the 'bronze rock'. The nurses were no longer from the German, but the Bavarian Red Cross. There were still no newspapers and the radio was in the hands of the American military. Much of what we heard was considered to be propaganda. We still knew next to nothing of the dreadful things which had accompanied the war. Of the Holocaust and the extent of the concentration camps we, at least, had no knowledge and when we discovered the facts found them at first so unbelievable that it needed time before we could open our eyes to these horrific scenes.

Our time was fully taken up by what lay ahead, what plans had to be made and taken in hand for the future. Before, the military had done one's thinking for one to a certain extent, but now one had to think for oneself and was responsible for oneself.

In mid-June everybody was interrogated by American officers, most of whom were German Jews. Family, occupation, membership of Party organizations, time as a soldier, etc. were asked. The interrogators knew the German circumstances exceedingly well, and so their questions were precise and one had to answer exactly. I was required to take off the big bandage from my left arm to prove that I did not have my blood group tattooed under my armpit as was done in the SS. It was all finished on 25 June and, so far as medically possible, everybody was discharged. In the morning at 0800hrs we had to fall in in front of the main hospital at Tegernsee in order of rank, then the names were read out quickly and each individual had to step forward to receive his certificate of discharge. It gave him his freedom and he could go home. The ceremony ended and five men were still standing there, myself amongst them. We had no idea why we had not received our discharge papers and were very disappointed. Then two jeeps drew up and we were told to get in.

We were taken to a giant prison camp at Bad Aibling. It consisted of some administrative barrack huts, otherwise only large pens to hold 200 to 300 prisoners each, without any protection against the weather and surrounded by barbed wire. There was no grass, the ground was trampled underfoot, soft and muddy. Once in the camp we were ordered to remove the national insignia, shoulder straps and collar patches from caps and jackets. Now one was just prisoner 'XY'. The food was a miserable offering of very watery cabbage soup with specks of fat. For the night one sought somewhere dry: there was no blanket, only the clothes one stood up in. The days were not summery June and warm, the weather was unseasonal and it rained a lot. I met Unteroffizier Gramlich from my company. He had been here several days and knew the drill. He could not tell me anything about the company, which he had left some time before, for he had been scooped up in the campaign known as *Heldenklau* (clawing-up heroes – selecting men off the street as fit for the front) and was to have become an infantryman. How he finished up at Aibling I cannot remember.

Now came the same interrogation as I had already gone through at Tegernsee. This one was more impersonal and unpleasant, but I got my discharge certificate. Meanwhile those who lived in the zone of French occupation were separated out and next day, my 23rd birthday, loaded on a Dodge lorry and taken off. Our driver wanted to talk and asked who spoke English. I joined him in the cab to show him the way to Tuttlingen in the French zone. On the way we passed through Munich. The destruction was indescribable. Some burnt-out ruins were still standing but then we came to blocks of streets where everything had been razed to the ground left and right of us and great mountains of rubble stood either side of the thoroughfare. Where were the people who had once lived here? We saw few of them on the street. It would be generations before it could all be rebuilt. Then we came to districts where the trams were still running: the destruction on the outskirts of the city was less, but it still looked appalling.

Our route went through the countryside, past neat undamaged villages and small towns in which life seemed to be normal. About 1700hrs we arrived at Tuttlingen. I enquired the way to the camp. 'Make sure they don't keep you there! Every day transports leave here for France.' That was all we needed, to stay prisoners, and prisoners of the French, to boot. It seemed to us laughable that the French considered themselves one of the victorious nations: after all they had declared war on us and we had overwhelmed them totally in less than two months. This and similar thoughts ran through my mind as we came to the French prison camp. Our driver accompanied us to the barrack hut where our papers were examined and the French endorsement stamped on them. This served at the same time as an authority to proceed to one's hometown, without it one could not leave for one's home address. When we had all been processed and returned to the lorry, our kind driver said that next day he would be driving back via Stuttgart: if anyone wanted to go there with him they were welcome aboard. Departure was at 0900hrs. That was wonderful for me, for connections from Tuttlingen into the Rhine Valley were very troublesome and I hoped that from Stuttgart I would be able to take a train. We looked for somewhere to spend the night, Caritas or the camp of a similar charity. It was my first night of freedom, my first night as a civilian, for now I was no longer a prisoner of war. We were also warned here if possible not to show ourselves in the city: the French couldn't be trusted, they just kidnapped people off the street at will. What I saw of their military at Tuttlingen did not inspire much confidence either.

Next morning, a Sunday, our lorry arrived at 0900hrs on the dot and took us to Stuttgart. We were set down at the last tram stop and we took our leave of our driver, who had been so helpful and friendly to us, with much thanks. I had the impression that he had sympathy for us. I can't remember in which suburb of Stuttgart we found ourselves. We stood around rather lost in a church forecourt, the bells rang and the people left mass. They were all dressed in their Sunday best and in holiday mood. We discharged soldiers must have made a pitiful impression. People came up to us, spoke and invited us to their houses. In a few minutes we were all amongst friendly people sharing their Sunday lunch with us. They gave us good advice: 'Don't take the tram through Stuttgart. At the Schlossplatz junction they take off anyone who looks like a former soldier. They do just what they like and we have no rights. Take the train the long way around the city to Zuffenhausen. The railway stations are still in American hands and the French can't touch you there.' I followed this advice, got to Zuffenhausen without a problem and had to wait on the station platform for several hours until a goods train left for Karlsruhe. We arrived there at midnight, not at the main station but at Karlsruhe-West. There was curfew from 2200hrs, therefore we had to stay at the station. I curled up and slept with many others in a goods yard. Tomorrow I would definitely be home!

As early as allowed I walked across the city to the main station to ask about trains. The next train for Rastatt would not be leaving until the afternoon. I strolled around the streets: even here there was much destruction but Munich looked a lot worse. The Americans were in Karlsruhe, so one could move about without fear. The border between the US and French zones of occupation ran through Durmersheim between Karlsruhe and Rastatt. It was a proper border with barriers across the street and checkpoints. The passenger train left for Rastatt at 1700hrs. When I went through the ticket barrier there I asked the railway official how things were in Sibyllen-Strasse. 'Everything is still standing,' was the comforting answer. I crossed the rail installations, the Ludwig Wilhelm-Strasse and then turned into our Sibyllen-Strasse. It was an indescribable feeling, this return home, after everything that lay behind me. I recognized my Mama from afar, shopping for the evening meal at the Kolonialwaren store and she came towards me. How tired she looked. Then she recognized me and we hurried to meet: 'Son, I can't believe you're back home!'

I cannot describe how moving this moment was. Mama took me by the hand, we went through the house and garden to the rear gate. 'Erich, Richard is home!' she called out as we went up to the veranda and Papa – I can still see this clearly –

jumped up and unable to speak came down to me. His face lit up, a rare occurence after years of worry, difficulties and humiliation. How thankful I was to be back home with my parents, knowing at last that they had also survived. Reading these lines, the reader can perhaps empathise with my feelings of happiness.

BESITZZEUGNIS

DEM

Frhr. Richard von R o s e n , Oberleutnant
(NAME, DIENSTGRAD)

3./s.Panzer-Abt. Feldherrnhalle
(TRUPPENTEIL, DIENSTSTELLE)

IST AUF GRUND

SEINER AM 20. Februar 1945 ERLITTENEN

fünf MALIGEN VERWUNDUNG – BESCHÄDIGUNG

DAS

VERWUNDETENABZEICHEN

IN G o l d

VERLIEHEN WORDEN

Abt.Gef.St. DEN 27. 2. 194 5

(UNTERSCHRIFT)

Hauptmann u. Abt.-Kommandeur
(DIENSTGRAD UND DIENSTSTELLE)

Certificate of the award of the Wound Badge in Gold to the author for his fifth wound on 20 February 1945. The signature is that of the Abteilung commanding officer, Hauptmann von Diest-Koerber. Von Rosen was very fortunate to have survived the wound.

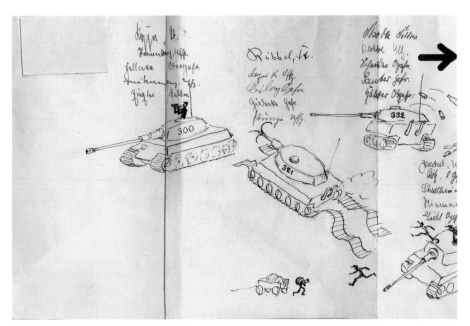

(**above, facing page top, and below**) When the author was at Pressburg military hospital at the end of February 1945, Leutnant Linsser sketched the subsequent adventures of Tiger Abt 503/*Feldherrnhalle* and had everybody sign it. This unique document has been preserved in three parts. Please follow the arrows!

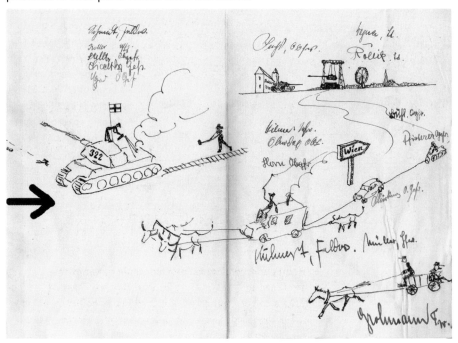

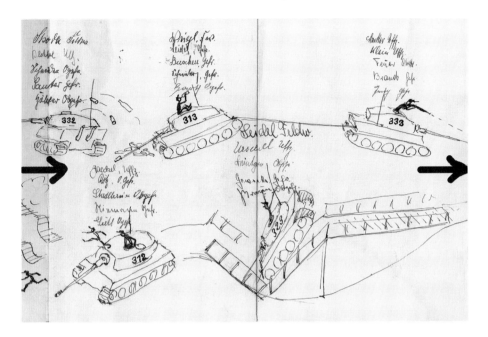

'Hearty congratulations from the whole company to Oberleutnant von Rosen on the award of the German Cross in Gold.' Leutnant Linsser painted a fair copy on the cover page of the congratulations card. Below it another original called 'the Reflection' by the men.

Another card with congratulations and best wishes for his recovery sent to the author by
Erich Fürlinger of 1 Company. Fürlinger fell a few days later, on 27 March 1945. The
text of the letter reads: 'Dear Richard, My heartiest congratulations on the award of
the German Cross in Gold. Come back to us sound very soon. With happy greetings as
vigorous as ever. Erich.

Abteilung Commanding Officer Hauptmann von Diest-Koerber confirms the award of the
German Cross in Gold to the author on 28 February 1945, being the copy of a telex dated
13 March 1945.

Abschrift vom Fernschreiben vom 13.3.45.

Pz.Kps.FHH./IIa.

Das Deutsche Kreuz in Gold wurde am 28.2.45 verliehen an:

Oberlt. Frhr. v. R o s e n , Kp.-Chef 3./s.Pz.Abt.Feldherrnhalle.
Verleihung ist bekanntzugeben (Verfg. OKH/PA/P 5e 1/Staff.Nr.
2010/45 v.6.3.45).
Zusatz: Die Auszeichnung und Besitzurkunde werden nachgereicht.

    Oberkdo.d.H.Gr.Süd/IIa
    i.A. Grell,Oberst

    Für die Richtigkeit der Abschrift:

    Hauptmann u. Abt.-Kdr.

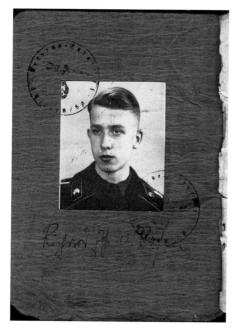

Inside page of the author's *Soldbuch* with details of promotions.

Sketched title page of the Abteilung newspaper for 1945 advising the change of designation from Heavy PzAbt 503 to *Feldherrnhalle*.

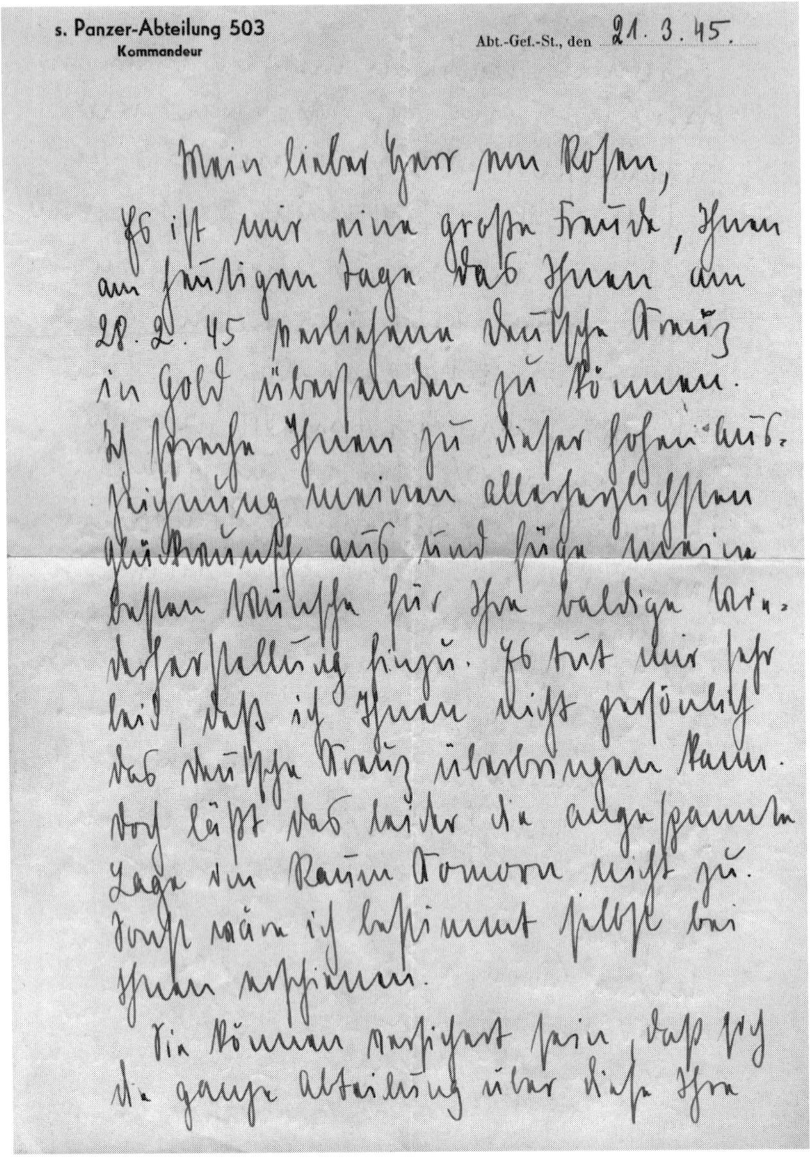

s. Panzer-Abteilung 503
Kommandeur
                                                    Abt.-Gef.-St., den **21. 3. 45.**

[Handwritten letter in German cursive]

A cordial letter from the Abteilung commander von Diest-Koerber to the wounded author: 'My dear Herr von Rosen, It is a great pleasure for me to be able to send you today the German Cross in Gold awarded to you on 28 February 1945. I express my heartiest congratulations on this high decoration and add my best wishes for your speedy recovery. I very much regret that I am unable to bring the German Cross to you personally. Unfortunately the difficult situation in the Komorn area does not permit me to, otherwise I would certainly have come to you there. You may rest assured that the entire Abteilung rejoices at this award merited many times over, and that we all have the wish that you may

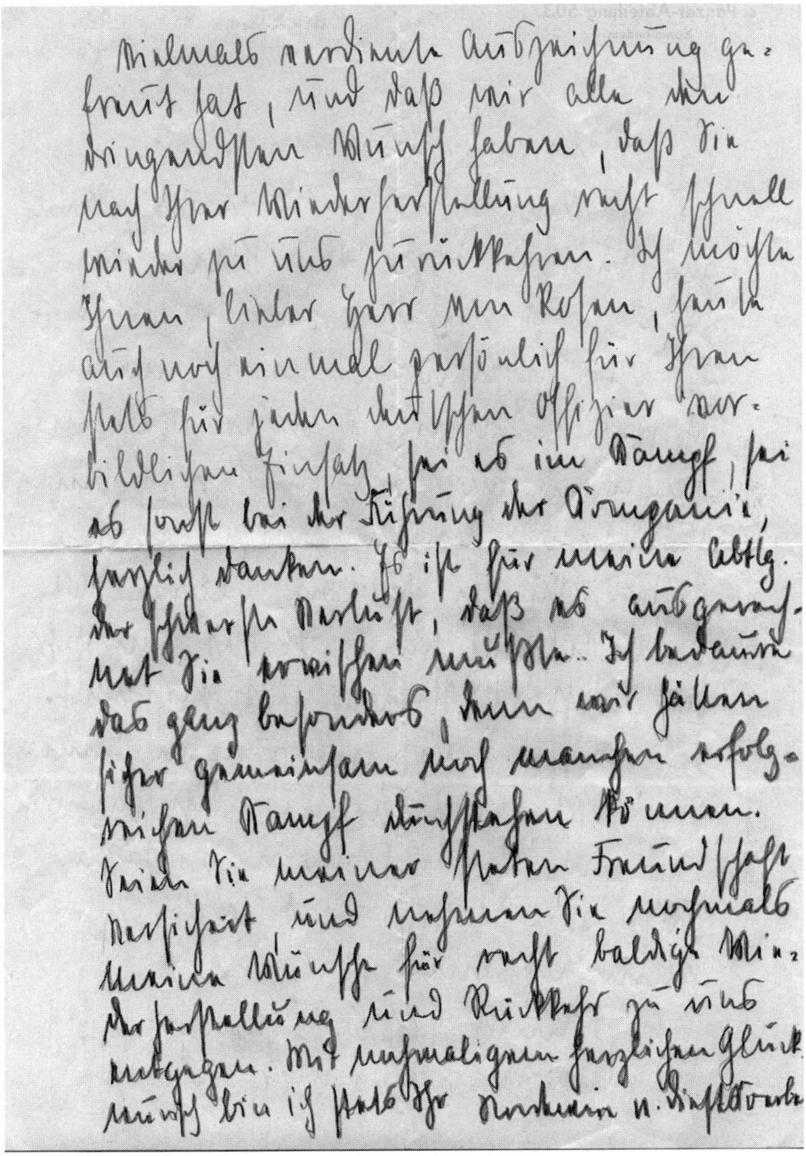

[illegible] verdiente Auszeichnung gebracht hat, und dass wir alle den dringenden Wunsch haben, dass Sie nach Ihrer Wiederherstellung recht schnell wieder zu uns zurückkehren. Ich möchte Ihnen, lieber Herr von Rosen, heute auch noch einmal persönlich für Ihren stets für jeden deutschen Offizier vorbildlichen Einsatz, sei es im Kampf, sei es sonst bei der Führung der Kompanie, herzlich danken. Es ist für meine Abtlg. der schwerste Verlust, dass es ausgerechnet Sie erwischen musste. Ich bedauere das ganz besonders, denn wir hätten sicher gemeinsam noch manchen erfolgreichen Kampf durchstehen können. Seien Sie meiner steten Freundschaft versichert und nehmen Sie nochmals meine Wünsche für recht baldige Wiederherstellung und Rückkehr zu uns entgegen. Mit nochmaligem herzlichen Glückwunsch bin ich stets Ihr Nordewin v. Diest-Koerber

return to us very soon following your recovery. I would like to thank you personally, dear Herr von Rosen, for your constant exemplary conduct, be it in battle or in the leadership of the company. For my Abteilung it is the most difficult loss to bear that we lose you of all people. I regret it quite especially for we would certainly have gone on to achieve many successful results in common in the field. You are assured of my constant friendship, and I ask you to accept once more my wishes for your speedy recovery and return to us. Once again, my heartiest congratulations. Yours, Nordewin von Diest-Koerber.'

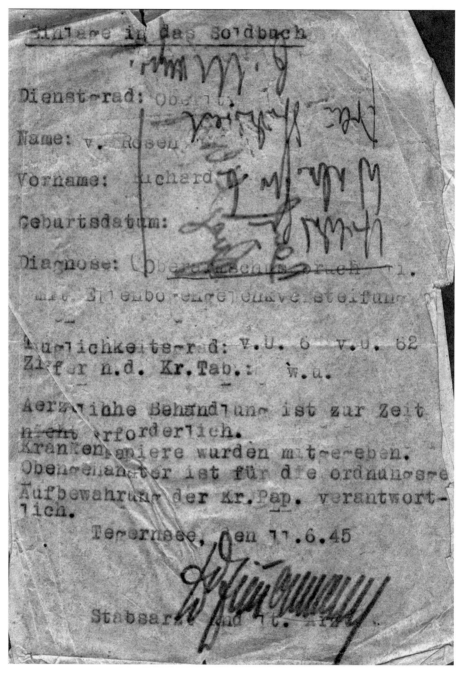

A post-war entry in the author's *Soldbuch* regarding his medical condition, Tegernsee, 11 June 1945

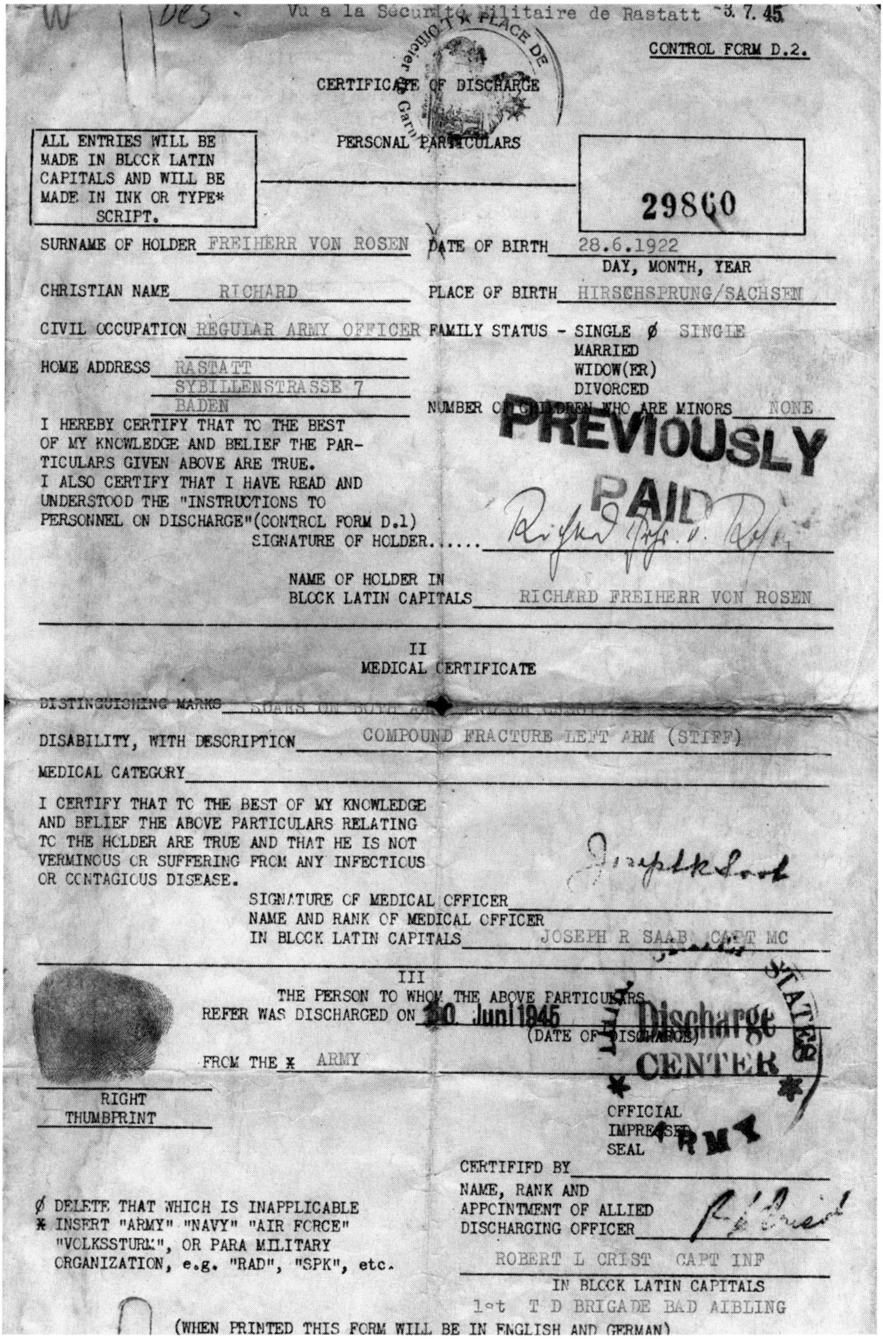

Vu a la Securité Militaire de Rastatt ~3. 7. 45

CONTROL FORM D.2.

CERTIFICATE OF DISCHARGE

PERSONAL PARTICULARS

I

ALL ENTRIES WILL BE MADE IN BLOCK LATIN CAPITALS AND WILL BE MADE IN INK OR TYPE* SCRIPT.

29860

SURNAME OF HOLDER FREIHERR VON ROSEN

DATE OF BIRTH 28.6.1922
DAY, MONTH, YEAR

CHRISTIAN NAME RICHARD

PLACE OF BIRTH HIRSCHSPRUNG/SACHSEN

CIVIL OCCUPATION REGULAR ARMY OFFICER

FAMILY STATUS - SINGLE Ø SINGLE
MARRIED

HOME ADDRESS RASTATT
SYBILLENSTRASSE 7
BADEN

WIDOW(ER)
DIVORCED

NUMBER OF CHILDREN WHO ARE MINORS NONE

I HEREBY CERTIFY THAT TO THE BEST OF MY KNOWLEDGE AND BELIEF THE PARTICULARS GIVEN ABOVE ARE TRUE. I ALSO CERTIFY THAT I HAVE READ AND UNDERSTOOD THE "INSTRUCTIONS TO PERSONNEL ON DISCHARGE"(CONTROL FORM D.1) SIGNATURE OF HOLDER......

PREVIOUSLY PAID

NAME OF HOLDER IN BLOCK LATIN CAPITALS RICHARD FREIHERR VON ROSEN

II
MEDICAL CERTIFICATE

DISTINGUISHING MARKS SCARS ON BOTH ARMS AND LEFT UPPER THIGH

DISABILITY, WITH DESCRIPTION COMPOUND FRACTURE LEFT ARM (STIFF)

MEDICAL CATEGORY

I CERTIFY THAT TO THE BEST OF MY KNOWLEDGE AND BELIEF THE ABOVE PARTICULARS RELATING TO THE HOLDER ARE TRUE AND THAT HE IS NOT VERMINOUS OR SUFFERING FROM ANY INFECTIOUS OR CONTAGIOUS DISEASE.

SIGNATURE OF MEDICAL OFFICER
NAME AND RANK OF MEDICAL OFFICER IN BLOCK LATIN CAPITALS JOSEPH R SAAB CAPT MC

III
THE PERSON TO WHOM THE ABOVE PARTICULARS REFER WAS DISCHARGED ON 30 Juni 1945
(DATE OF DISCHARGE)

FROM THE x ARMY

RIGHT THUMBPRINT

OFFICIAL IMPRESSED SEAL

CERTIFIED BY

NAME, RANK AND APPOINTMENT OF ALLIED DISCHARGING OFFICER ROBERT L CRIST CAPT INF
IN BLOCK LATIN CAPITALS
1st T D BRIGADE BAD AIBLING

Ø DELETE THAT WHICH IS INAPPLICABLE
* INSERT "ARMY" "NAVY" "AIR FORCE" "VOLKSSTURM", OR PARA MILITARY ORGANIZATION, e.g. "RAD", "SPK", etc.

(WHEN PRINTED THIS FORM WILL BE IN ENGLISH AND GERMAN)

The author's discharge certificate from US captivity. The corresponding French release was issued later.

Group photo of the reunion of former members of Tiger Abteilung 503 in Bassum from 12 to 14 August 1955. 1. The author. 2. Alfred Rubbel 3. Franz-Wilhelm Lochmann 4. Rolf Fromme.

Some participants in the reunion of August 1958: the author third from right, Dr Franz-Wilhelm Lochmann third from left: below, in the checked shirt, Alfred Rubbel.

11

Home Again

Rastatt under French Occupation

That beautiful July evening we sat for hours on the veranda, looking out over our blossoming garden. I could hardly believe that I was home again, no longer having to go back to the Front, seeing my parents alive, if visibly older and careworn. How many were denied this pleasure. Even my parents had come to life again. Their greatest worry, how and whether I would get through the last months of the war and the capitulation, had been shed. I was back home, if with a mutilated arm, but otherwise hale and hearty, determined to let nothing get me down.

There was so much to tell, for so much had happened in the time in which we were out of touch. The last letter my parents had received was sent shortly before the operation at the river Gran in mid-February 1945, therefore a few days before my last wound. None of my letters written during my time in military hospital, given to various messengers, had arrived. There had been no proper postal service for months. My first question was about my brother and sisters. At the Russian advance, Wuller had fled from Dresden to Oberbärenburg and married Ruth von Quast there. That he had survived the horrific bombing raids on Dresden I had found out while in Hungary. Aja was in Sweden: there was no news from her but we believed she would be safe in a neutral country. At that time we did not know that she had been interned and deported. Elisabeth was working as a nursing assistant in a military hospital at Baden-Baden and was happy to be of service in this way. She had finished her schooling at Spetzgart. This was all good news. But on the other hand my mother's brother, Uncle Willy Seidlitz, had been killed at Eisernach on 31 March 1945 in a fighter-bomber attack, and my mother's elder sister Aunt Mary Schöne, after losing Bernhard, had also lost Konrad and Gottfried in the last months of the war. Three sons fallen, how could one bear that? Oskar von Löwies had also fallen, my brother-in-law to whom I owed so many thanks.

It had been in September 1944 that I had last spent a day at home. Up to that time Rastatt had still been spared air raids, but soon afterwards in the autumn of 1944 the Allies' Western Front moved up rapidly. Strasbourg fell in November and heavy fighting raged along the western banks of the Rhine in Alsace from December. The Front ran along the Rhine and was thus only about 10km from Rastatt which became a front-line town. The first air raid did severe damage to the area around the railway station and the town came frequently under enemy artillery fire. My parents had left the house in Sibyllen-Strasse unattended and found shelter at Schloss Rotenfels. They took all they could carry on bicycles, leaving everything else behind. Nobody could predict that this situation would last into the spring of 1945. At first my parents could cycle to and from home to collect valuable items from the cellar and return with a rucksack-full. Papa compared himself to a man on an island whose wrecked ship lay offshore but could be reached on the ebb tide. Later German soldiers were billeted in the house and then in March came the French occupation. Initially my parents dared not venture to Rastatt to look after things. Besides plundering troops with loose trigger fingers, whole gangs of displaced persons released from camps, mostly Poles and Russians, roamed the district making everybody uneasy. The great Rastatt hospital had to be cleared out for them; they set up in it and made it the base for their criminal operations. When my parents returned to Sibyllen-Strasse for the first time they found the house still standing but all ground-floor windows broken. Inside it looked as though a hurricane had hit it. Instead of using the toilets these vandals defecated in the rooms or the drawers of the furniture. There were some art connoisseurs amongst them, however, for several of the valuable Impressionist paintings, the fine bronze statuettes by Meunier, porcelain from Reval and the old family silver not locked in the two house safes had been stolen or destroyed. Papa told me that he had thought the house could not be made habitable again but Mama got to work on it and gradually every room was cleaned and cleared out. Missing items of furniture such as the sofa and chairs had found their way into other neighbourhood houses, carried there by soldiers.

Gradually life began to get back to normal. There were no longer any German authorities, the rule of law was in the hands of the occupying troops. The French had installed a mayor, an old Communist, who had survived the Nazi period and had now set up a kind of town council with others of like mind. Lord of the town was a French colonel given the title of Military Governor. The real lord of the manor was a small lieutenant from Alsace by the name of Schaefer, head of the

Sûreté Nationale. He exercised police powers and his German informers supplied him at his HQ, the Villa Mayer, with persons to be interrogated and often tortured. Rastatt was in the hands of French and German Communists and many personal scores were settled. There was no German jurisdiction and not until December 1945 was the establishment of an Inferior Court permitted. Until then my Papa was unemployed. Just as well that it was summer and one could live on the veranda or in the garden, needed no heating and had the produce from the garden. In the French-occupied zone, food rationing was particularly harsh, only 800 calories per day being allotted. Food production and trade in the Rastatt area had collapsed totally and long queues waited outside shops. There was no bread or potatoes. In summer it could be tolerated but what when winter came? Papa once wrote to an acquaintance:

> Healthwise we are not badly off, but we have in prospect an evil winter since we can only heat one room and as regards food we are staring famine in the face. I am in the same situation as yourself and others, and my memory fails me. My eyes are suffering from the poor rations lacking any fats. I cannot see anywhere any prospect, no matter how remote, that we old people will know better times. On the contrary, it will get worse. An incapable government at the head, and the prevalent will to crush us underfoot on the part of the occupation forces, of whom the most hated are the French.

At first I was just happy to have my own bed in my own room. I still had no thoughts about the future and how I could make a new life for myself as a civilian not under military compulsion, in a civilian occupation. I was happy that I had the last five years behind me with good conduct, but the fate that might have befallen my comrades caused me great unease.

On the first morning home I awoke early. The sun shone into my room, I went to the window and drank in the old familiar surroundings. Here there was no destruction, here everything seemed peaceful, everything was unchanged and remained just as I remembered it. My first problem was what to wear. The old clothes I still had no longer fitted. Until my call-up I had worn short trousers. Then I found something or other: shirt and trousers sufficed, it was still summer after all. I had no shoes, though.

I went with Papa to Bernhard the glazier. Each of us carried a leaf of casement window: they were very heavy. Window glass was unobtainable, but a substitute was so-called wire glass, thin glass on a wire fabric which could be rolled but was not very stable. Even this was scarce so that there was little point in making window frames, and the existing frames we boarded over with plywood. For the immediate future I would have enough to do keeping the house wind-proof, but I at least could relieve Papa of the heavy physical work.

I still carried my wounded left arm in a sling: the wound had not healed and was still suppurating small bone splinters. Every day I went to have it re-bandaged at our old fortress prison, converted into a civilian outpatients' department after the hospital would no longer treat Germans. I met some old acquaintances from school and the Jungvolk. It was appalling to learn how many had fallen in the last months of the war. Many of my good friends would never be coming home. When I came across their parents I almost had a bad conscience that I had come though it almost unscathed.

On the first day a French officer stopped me in the street to check my discharge certificate. As a former active officer I had had to register at the office of the local commandant and report every Saturday morning. I was forbidden to leave Rastatt. There were numerous minor irritants. For example, you had to step down from the pavement into the road if a French officer came towards you, and doff your cap in salute. Or: before the town halls of the smaller communities, flagpoles were set up with the French tricolour, likewise as you went past one you had to doff your cap as a salute to the flag. One day Papa cycled through one of these Rhine villages in order to collect something from a fisherman and he failed to salute the tricolour in front of the town hall. A French sentry stopped him, he had to dismount, go back and walk past the flagpole cap in hand. The French were a laughing stock, but it was humiliating all the same.

The French had loudspeaker vans drive through the streets of the town to announce the latest regulations instigated by the Military Governor. Yesterday all sewing machines had to be placed on the doorstep at 0800hrs, a couple of days previously all thigh- or riding boots had to be handed in. All radios had been confiscated in the first days of the occupation. Ours had been taken, but it was no great loss. It only broadcast the French occupation news which nobody believed anyway. We still had no newspapers: it would be still some time before the occupation force issued the necessary licences. Thus we remained without news as in other occupied zones of Germany and fixated on our intimate circle.

Naturally the aversion to the French occupying force grew constantly. Drunk with the arrogance of their 'victory' and hate-filled intention to humiliate us,

Everywhere in the areas reconquered by the Allies in 1944–5 even civilians became involved in the capture of German soldiers.

every sensation of liberation was suffocated. But now the by-word came to be: caught together, be hanged together. We learned constantly and at every turn that the will of the French 'victors' was not pacification but collective punishment, the repression and dismantling of Germany. From the very beginning what we experienced was not liberation but defeat, total and our own fault. We had had no illusions but whoever dreamt of ethics, morality and a reformed way of living was soon disappointed. Destruction, hunger, hopelessness, four million dead, ten million prisoners and missing: all laws, lawful claims and contracts without validity. Nobody was spared it, we all had to bear the consequences. But there had been much more destroyed: the desertion of so many who had been *'Volksgenossen und Volksgenossinnen'* – a National Socialist term for all male and female members of the *Volk* and Blood. One now experienced denunciations, originating from a desire for revenge against colleagues, neighbours, supervisors and 'the rich' – an indescribable degeneration of the spirit. It was all the foreplay for the denazification process which followed it. In the French Zone it was mostly the Communists who settled old scores against 'the class enemy' going back to 1919 and on through the Nazi years. The French occupation force was also thoroughly infiltrated by Communists. The troops here were mostly newly formed units made up of former Resistance fighters into whose ranks the French Communist Party had placed a large number of its adherents. Thus it was not surprising that the German Communists, and all who now claimed to be so, received special treatment.

All this bore down heavily on the people in such a small town as Rastatt. Nevertheless the revival began: gallows humour, plans and a wish for culture. A good book, good music after long deprivation, a good sermon – one longed for them. Life then consisted of barter and improvisation. Black markets developed in which mainly displaced persons offered food and other luxuries not to be found in the shops. Gradually one felt that this immediate post-war period was almost passably tolerable so long as one kept hoping for improvement. The hand of the French occupation authority lay on all our everyday affairs, and soon we saw that their uniforms and vehicles merely replaced the 'golden pheasants' [TN: slang term for the brown-uniformed Party officials] of the Nazis.

I had been home three weeks when one morning the loudspeaker vans drove through the streets. Interspersed between French marches the following order was broadcast: All former soldiers had to report the day after tomorrow for registration at Camp Malschbach near Baden-Baden bringing their release certificate, rations for two days and a blanket. This set the alarm bells ringing as far as I was concerned. We had often seen how the French kidnapped released prisoners of war from the streets and deported them to France. Here there were no rights and no law. The purpose of this new French registration was not clear but some underhand business was suspected. I had a short talk with my parents and we were all agreed that I should disappear as soon as possible. The same day I crossed the green frontier into Karlsruhe in the US Zone. From there I rode goods trains for thirty-six hours to Tegernsee. The US Zone was run more correctly, and I felt more secure here with my US release papers. Aunt Britta arranged a room for me at Rottach at the Thomahof with Frau von Liebermann in the neighbourhood, where I spent the next three weeks. My wounded arm was still in a sling and I was not up to looking for work.

I went wandering in the mountains, bathed in the lake and recovered from the strains of the preceding years. At the town hall I received ration coupons enabling me to have a cheap basic dish at a restaurant every day. In between I spent three days at Kreuth in the clinic with my cousins Heinz and Richard May who carried out a minor operation on my grossly swollen left arm and extracted the remaining splinters of bone. Then I felt I should return home. I had no idea what I was going to do when I got there, but it was clear to me that I had to make my mind up soon about which trade or profession I should follow. Many opportunities were not available to me as a former active officer, but in the various zones of occupation the regulations tended to be widely different. After all my experiences so far I saw that the British Zone looked the best.

First I hitch-hiked to the address in Nuremberg of my former orderly room sergeant Grohmann. From him I heard how at the end of the war the company had found itself in the northern part of Czechoslovakia. Always retreating and under heavy pressure, at the time of the ceasefire PzAbt 503 lay between the American and Russian lines. Because the Americans declined to accept the surrender of troops on the far side of the demarcation line, the Abteilung's commander Hauptmann von Diest-Koerber released all the men from their obligations and recommended that they attempt to cross the American lines in small groups and head for Reich territory. To that end every man received his military pass, pay and rations. Grohmann had succeeded in getting back with a few men of the Abteilung, how the others had fared he did not know. In fact a third had got home, but the remainder were caught by the Americans and handed over to the Russians where they spent many years in captivity. Leutnant Koppe, who commanded 3 Company after I was wounded, was not released until Christmas 1955.

Back at Rastatt I was happy to learn that during my absence nobody had enquired about me and therefore I seemed to have a clean slate. My Rastatt comrades-in-arms had all been hauled off to Malschbach camp but all came back home. Papa told me how he had also been obliged to surrender himself for Malschbach although he was 65 and had not been in military service for thirty years. He had been an officer, however, and apparently that was enough. This time I spent only a few days at home: I wanted to get to the British Zone and seek its better opportunities. Therefore I set off via Düsseldorf to Essen, where I met my former company leader Walter Scherf. Other stops I made were at Hanover, Bremen and Hamburg. I spent the nights in station bunkers, ate in communal kitchens, hitch-hiked on ramshackle lorries or atop the coal on goods trains. A curiosity: even on goods trains tickets were inspected, the conductor climbing over the loads, wagon to wagon. My ticket was my release certificate for my story was always that I was on my way home from captivity. I spent some time with Aunt Ebba at Closter Lune near Lüneburg, bringing her news from home and helping out with her chores. There was still no postal service at that time, and so receiving any news about relatives was always a happy event.

I made enquiries at the universities of Gottingen and Hamburg but no possibility existed for a former active officer to become an undergraduate. If I could have got accepted anywhere I would probably have studied Law which I thought would offer me the best prospects of employment once qualified. At many stations on my list I had an address to go to: if not I could request the address for a given surname at the residents' registration offices. In this way I met many men from my former Abteilung on my trip. Each would know two or three other addresses so that soon I had compiled the first list of Abteilung members. That was the beginning of an association which we expanded and was to last to the present times.

At the beginning of October 1945 I returned home to find the situation unchanged. As for my own future, I was no better off than when I started. My sister Elisabeth had finished her nursing duties at Baden-Baden and applied to the Agricultural Technical College at Stuttgart-Hohenheim for a training position as an agricultural assistant. In those days this is the type of thing one could expect to happen: Elisabeth had taken my bicycle to scout around locally for food from farms and had been quite successful. On the way home some Poles blocked her way, threw her off the bicycle and made off with both bicycle and vegetables. The return of Elisabeth was so overdue that we began to be anxious for her, finally she turned up on foot, shocked and outraged. She had actually got off lightly, for rape was common then, not only by Poles and Russians, but also by French colonial troops.

One night some shadowy figures visited our garden again and stole the last of the fruit on the trees. Papa went to the Russian bureau at the former hospital and complained in Russian. He was actually successful, and a sign was nailed on our front door in Cyrillic script: 'Entering this property is forbidden, a Russian family lives here.' After that we were left in peace.

Meanwhile my other sister Aja had also come home. The Swedes had interned her as an undesirable alien of the 'German Academy' (Goethe Institute) and then deported her to Lübeck. Now she was home, and had plans to work as a secretary in Bremen.

12

A Prisoner of the French

In mid-October five Frenchmen made a sudden appearance in order to conduct a house search. While the family was locked in the dining room, they ransacked the house and left everything in chaos. We were unable to imagine what it was all about and only much later discovered that my father had been denounced. They were searching – in vain – for incriminating material. When they came to my room on the upper floor, the Frenchmen found a photograph with the panzers of my company on the Champs Élysées which apparently upset them. They also discovered my paperweight, a defused French mortar bomb and confiscated it. They made a very close inspection of my books before they left. Half an hour later they re-appeared to arrest me. I was taken away and locked in a cell at the jail on Engel-Strasse. I can still hear the rattle of its keys in the lock. A stool, a table, a folding bed, a toilet. Milky glass in the small, barred window blocked the view outside although I could just see the sky through a small slit. A naked bulb provided dim lighting. I sat on the stool, considering the situation. Besides the French controllers at this jail were some German prison staff who provided a support service. The door opened and a German official entered, asking my name and the reason for my arrest.

'What, you are the son of the Inferior Court Magistrate von Rosen?' He shook his head, left the cell and returned with two bedsheets and a blanket. 'In the morning when you wake up, leave these under the mattress at once so that the French don't see them.' It did me good to have met this friendly man. In the evening I received my washing kit and some underclothes left at the prison gate by my parents. I spent three days in that cell without the French taking any interest in me, no interrogation, no questions, nothing. I was left alone. I thought about what books they might have confiscated from my bedroom. As I saw it, there had been nothing compromising in my bookcase. When I had been the prisoner of war of the Americans my mother had taken out anything which she thought might be considered National Socialist.

They fetched me on the fourth day. Escorted by an armed soldier I was walked through the town to the former fortress prison. I knew it well, for in earlier times it had been our Jungvolk hostel. The French had now set up in this large building what they called a '*camp de concentration*' with 100 inmates, all minor Party functionaries from the Rastatt area and a couple of harmless people who had been denounced. Herr Kappler, a former engineer at Mercedes Benz in Gaggenau, and Herr von Blanquet from Rotenfels, a friend of my parents, were also there. I was shown to a bed in a dormitory of twenty men. The camp was guarded by Spahis (Algerian-Moroccan cavalry). They were friendly to us since they had the same feeling of being repressed by the French as we did. At night we were locked in our large communal cell with a bucket, which by morning was filled to the brim. All prisoners had to work, and were led in small squads each morning to the various workplaces. Because I still had my left arm in a sling, I did not do manual labour. Visiting hours were from 1500hrs to 1700hrs on Saturdays. One's relations came to the camp gate, then the prisoner was called and could talk for five minutes through the barbed wire fence. Visitors were allowed to bring underwear, food and reading material. Mama always had something tasty for me from the butcher or baker. I asked for English-language school books for the periods when I sat alone in the cell. This annoyed the French, who though I should be learning French. I read Galsworthy's *Forsyte Saga* which I had started at home. Mama brought me the second volume. A Spahi looked them over at the camp gate and asked her what type of book it was. When she said it was by an English author, it was confiscated. 'England many Jews. Jews no good.' No comment.

Meanwhile the French had set up a military tribunal at Rastatt. The presiding judge, Colonel Braman, visited our camp and asked to be presented to each inmate.

'*Voici, mon Colonel, c'est le fils du Baron von Rosen.*' (And here, Colonel, this is the son of the Baron von Rosen.)

'*Oh, mais pourquoi vous êtes ici?*' (Oh, but why are you here?)

He had a long conversation with me about my service during the war, my period as a PoW and the reason for my present remand. He showed me the scars on his head which he had received in a German concentration camp, which I replied by showing him the wounds on both my arms.

His escort said, '*Laissez-le, il est et il reste un Nazi.*' (Let him be, he is and will always be a Nazi.)

To hear this from a French mouth made me grin. I was not going to let them grind me down. A few days later I received orders to pack my things accompanied by the explanation, *'Vous n'êtes pas un prisonnier politique, vous êtes un criminel.'* (You are not a political prisoner, you are a criminal.)

Therefore I was returned to the jail on Engel-Strasse where I was offered work in the kitchen. In order to avoid the monotony of the single cell I accepted willingly. With two much older prisoners on remand, I had to get up before breakfast each morning to heat the large kitchen range, peel the root vegetables and assist in the preparation of the thin soup served at midday. One of my two companions was awaiting judgment for illegal slaughtering, the other had killed his wife with a letter opener at Gernsbach. She had been having an affair with a Frenchman. He made a point of saying that he had stabbed her thirty-five times which was proof that it had been a crime of passion and he wanted me to put in a good word with my father. Such cases did not fall within my father's jurisdiction, however. Once we had cleaned the kitchen in the afternoon we did not return to our cells, under the pretext of having to do more work later, but stayed in the kitchen playing skat. Should a Frenchman appear unexpectedly, the cards would vanish like greased lightning and we would get busy. One Sunday afternoon this happened quite suddenly, and Colonel Braman appeared in the kitchen showing his wife and daughter the jail. Our shout of 'Attention' rang out particularly loudly and we stood at attention. Braman told his wife who I was and after an astonished 'Are you?' I received the sympathetic looks and encouraging smiles of both women. I felt like an animal at the zoo. Next evening Braman visited me in my cell to inform me that I was to be brought before the military tribunal on 22 December and wanted to know which books had been found in my room during the house search. I gave him a few harmless titles, but at that time even military literature was as illegal as that of the Nazis. Next day I received my writ of summons and the indictment: 'Possession of military literature and ammunition.' Papa let me know that he had got me a lawyer. That was comforting. After our last conversation I had the impression that Colonel Braman was well disposed towards me.

The military tribunal was held in the Rastatt château in the rooms where the Inferior Court used to sit. An armed sentry made sure I didn't escape and delivered me to the court. In the waiting room I found my papa and to my great surprise my brother Wuller. He had come the day before from Dresden across the green demarcation line in company with his wife Ruth.

The trial was public. There were eight other cases, most of them breaches of the pass regulations, being out after curfew and similar crimes. Then came my case. I had only a brief talk with my advocate and was surprised by his lack of interest. My name was called and I stood before the judge's desk. An interrogation was begun using an incompetent interpreter. Several times I had to object when my denial of this or that was turned by him into an admission. Then it was the turn of my advocate who mentioned in his pleading Conrad Rosen, Maréchal de France. Then I was led out and the next case called. I waited outside until the verdict was ready. As a mitigating circumstance Colonel Braman mentioned that I had become a soldier at the age of 18 and had fought bravely for my country, been wounded five times and was a descendant of a Maréchal de France. The sentence: four weeks' imprisonment, my period on remand to be counted so that I was free at once.

'*Vous êtes libre,*' were the last words and I left the courtroom very relived. I thought I would be able to go home immediately but the French overseer explained that I had to serve the present day out and would have to wait until the morning for my discharge. The cell door slammed behind me once more. More fun and games? In the middle of my darkest thoughts I was called into the court office where to my surprise I found Colonel Braman completing my discharge papers. While I stood waiting he snapped to my guard, '*Apportez donc une chaise pour le Baron de Rosen!*' (Bring a chair for Baron von Rosen then!). The man had to obey – what satisfaction! – for this was one of the most hated of the French and had kicked the seat of my pants the day before.

Colonel Braman then accompanied me home and on the way told me how unpleasant he had found it to have me before his tribunal, but the High Command at Baden-Baden had ordered him to make an example of me. Originally they wanted to prove that I had been active as one of Himmler's 'werewolves' but this had been going too far. 'I hope I find you in agreement with the solution I found,' he said. Therefore there were decent Frenchmen.

This experience was the beginning of a less emotional and more just assessment of our neighbouring country for me. We arrived home, and when my father opened the front door Colonel Braman said to him simply, 'Herr Baron, here is your son.' Without any further explanation he offered us both his hand and disappeared into the darkness of the still unlit street.

At this point I must digress. In 1964 I was General Staff Officer to the C-in-C Allied Troops in Central Europe based at Fontainebleau. By chance I discovered that ex-Colonel Braman lived nearby. It was a joyful reunion under quite normal circumstances, and a friendship evolved which lasted until his death. He was a great man and contributed much to my better understanding of the French people. In my post-war career I worked, with some intervals, a total of twelve years in France attached to Allied Staffs, in the École Supérieure de Guerre and finally as Military Attaché at the West German Embassy in Paris. Over the years my family and I got to know and love the country, gained French friends and thus became protagonists for Franco-German cooperation and friendship.

To return to my tale. The day after my discharge was Christmas Eve. We had a tree lit with a few burnt-down candle stubs. We needed no presents, for the greatest present was to be all together, having all survived the war. Aja was also there. We sang together the carol 'Silent Night' and never before had I sung with so much gratitude and confidence the last lines of the song, 'Christ the Saviour is here.'

Leutnant Richard Freiherr von Rosen.

Epilogue

I was 17 years old when the harsh facts of life entered into my carefree and happy youth. The war arrived, pitiless for us all. It left its mark on me. When it ended I was 23, and had spent four and a half years either at the Front or in military hospitals. As a young man I was not hard, but I had to learn to be, at first with myself and later, as an NCO and officer, towards others. I had to give orders which sent many of my men to their deaths. That was not easy to come to terms with. So why did we fight? It was our obligation by law and the Fatherland was in danger. For my generation the term 'Fatherland' still meant a lot. In France, Great Britain, the United States and many other countries that is probably still the case. One felt called to do one's duty no matter what the circumstances might be that had brought it about it, or provoked it. Our conscience then was not the conscience of today. That was only a part of my motivation, however. The other part was the urge to prove myself. For that reason I never did anything then of which I am ashamed today. My education and predisposition helped me find the right way. I have to make it clear though, that at no time was I called upon to make a decision against my conscience. I had a lot of luck in those years, above all in outstanding superiors who led and impressed me, and perhaps protected me too.

I fought alongside eighteen million German soldiers. Four million of them failed to survive the war, amongst them many of the companions of my youth. At the end of the war the balance looked like this: most of the large cities had been razed to the ground by British and US bombing. This resulted in the deaths of 800,000 people, women, children, pensioners. Almost every family had members to mourn, soldiers and civilians. The provinces in the East were removed from the Reich territory and their populations, and about twelve million people were forced to flee, or were driven out. What made the defeat unbearable, however, was the knowledge that the victims were killed for an unjust and highly criminal cause. How much bitterness was there in this depressing vision? If the first months after the end of the war were dedicated to preserving those who had come through it, to the struggle against hunger and cold and also to inner seething against the humiliations inflicted by the occupying Powers, then came something additional. Slowly we awoke from a trance-like state to become conscious of an infernal hatred for those who had forced us into this misery.

From the end of November 1945 the major German war criminals were arraigned at Nuremberg before the International Military Tribunals. Now the twelve Hitler years came back chapter by chapter, all the guilt and horror. From the prosecuting advocates we learned the cruel truths. It was a bitter and nasty awakening.

I understand if my readers cannot see that only a fraction of the population knew the details of the Nazi plans to persecute and exterminate. I refer specifically to the Holocaust. Daniel Goldhagen's assertion that the German nation consisted of 'willing executioners' shows a complete misunderstanding of the situation. Certainly the discrimination against the Jews was generally known, as were the deportations, and there was no revolt against it. It was always explained that these were resettlement measures. The systematic extermination was a state secret and only those immediately involved were informed. The broad mass of the population knew nothing of 'the Final Solution'. The leadership had kept quiet about it, knowing well that such cruelty would find no understanding, not to mention no support. Today I know that the systematically programmed crimes committed by the regime and its supporters are unparalleled in our history. I also had believed in Germany's 'just, clean war' against the background of my own experiences at the Front, until my eyes were opened. I am convinced that it was the same for most young Germans blindly drawn into war. Shame, regret and a certain fatalism were the consequences for those who fought for it and suffered for it, and that was almost everybody.

Richard Freiherr von Rosen
Kreuth, September 2012.

Richard Freiherr von Rosen – Military Career

Born	28 June 1922.
25 Oct 1940	Recruit, Pz ErsatzAbt 35 in Bamberg.
5 Nov 1940	Officer cadet (Fahnenjunker) course, PzRgt 35.
20 Feb 1941	Gunner, 1 Company/PzRegt 35.
1 Mar 1941	Gefreiter (Private, trained soldier).
1 Jul 1941	Fahnenjunker-Unteroffizier (Officer cadet-corporal) (promoted for bravery in the field).
1 Oct 1941	Training staff, PzErsatzAbt 35, Bamberg.
25 Feb–30 May 1942	Officers' Course, Panzer Troop School, Wünsdorf.
1 Jun 1942	Fahnenjunker-Feldwebel (Sergeant), and immediately promoted to Leutnant.
1 Jul 1942	Half-platoon leader, 2 Company/Heavy PzAbt 502 (later redesignated 3 Company/Heavy PzAbt 503).
15 Jan 1943	Platoon leader, 3 Company/Heavy PzAbt 503.
15 Sep 1944	Company leader, 3 Company/Heavy PzAbt 503.
1 Nov 1944	Oberleutnant and company commander, 3 Company/ Heavy PzAbt 503.
28 Feb 1945	Awarded German Cross in Gold.

War service decorations:

Iron Cross First Class
Iron Cross Second Class
German Cross in Gold
Panzer Combat Badge, Stage II
Wound Badge in Gold

1 Jul 1952	Entry into Department Blank, Bonn.
10 Jul 1952	With West German Delegation at the Conference for a European Defence Community (EVG) Paris.
1 Oct 1954	Official in Charge, Section Panzer Grenadier, Department Blank.
1 Jun 1955	Transferred to NATO HQ Europe (SHAPE Paris) as Official in Charge, Land Forces.
16 Nov 1955	Commissioned into Bundeswehr in rank of Hauptmann.
2 Jan 1958	Company commander, PzBat 13, Schwanewerde.
1 Apr 1959	Company commander, PzBat 74, Seedorf.
1 Jun 1959	Leadership Academy, Bundeswehr: 3 General Staff course.
1 Oct 1959	École Supérieure de Guerre, Paris.
1 Oct 1960	Promoted to Major.
1 Jul 1961	Until 9 Jan 1964, G.1 Officer, PzGrenDiv. Sigmaringen.
10 Jan 1964	Until 30 Sep 1966, G.3 Officer to C-in-C, Allied Land Forces, (AFCENT, Fontainebleau).
9 Aug 1964	Oberstleutnant (Leutnant-Colonel), General Staff.
1 Oct 1966	Until 18 Jan 1970 CO, PzBat 294, Stetten am kalten Markt.
19 Jan 1970	Until 31 May 1972, Official in charge, German Federal Ministry of Defence, Bonn.
31 Mar 1970	Oberst (Colonel), General Staff.
1 Apr 1972	Until 30 Sep 1976 Commanding Officer, PzBrig 21, Augustdorf.
3 Nov 1975	Brigadegeneral (Brigadier-General).
1 Oct 1976	Until 31 Mar 1980 Defence Attaché at West German Embassy, Paris.
1 Apr 1980	Generalmajor (Major-General): West German chargé d'affaires to the C-in-C, French forces in West Germany.
30 Sep 1982	Retired.

Post-war Decorations:

> Bundeswehr Cross of Honour in Gold (Ehrenkreuz der Bundeswehr)
> Officier de la Legion d'honneur
> Commandeur de l'Ordre National du Mérite

Thanksgiving

During the three years of its existence a total of 310 soldiers served in 3 Company/ Heavy PzAbt 503. This was three times its set strength. The turnover was relatively high through death or wounds. Two officers, twenty-two NCOs and thirty-two men fell in this period. Only twenty-seven graves of company members in military cemeteries are known at present to the Volksbund für Kriegsgräberfürsorge (German War Graves Commission).

When the war ended in 1945, the company was stranded between the American and Russian lines. A few men, including the Abteilung commander, made their way in long overnight walks through the Bavarian woods to Germany. The bulk of the Abteilung, amongst them most of the officers, were held in the US prisoner of war camp at Wallern.

Contrary to the international conventions, after a few weeks all prisoners from the Abteilung were handed over to the Russians. How many died in captivity cannot be determined. Leutnant Koppe, who led the company after I was wounded for the fifth time, was a prisoner for ten years before the intervention of Federal Chancellor Adenauer brought about his release.

In the post-war years all who were fortunate enough to survive those terrible years worked to rebuild for the future. Contacts were only made sporadically. In later years, gradually a list of eighty-six surviving members of 3 Company was drawn up. Nearly all had gained a firm foothold in civilian life. Many trades and professions were represented amongst us: from worker and employees, from mechanic and artisan to independent salesman, farmer, attorney and vineyard owner. Five ex-company members served in the Bundeswehr after 1955, and three generals in three different armies. Besides myself, a general in the Bundeswehr, one of my very good Unteroffiziers became a general in the Volksarmee of the German Democratic Republic (he died before the reunification).

A panzer man from the Alsace is said to have become a general in the French Army, but he has avoided all contact with us, although the report comes from a source regarded as totally reliable. Another ex-company member became an Oberst in the Volksarmee. After the reunification he found his way to us and I had many very interesting conversations with him about our varied pasts.

About forty former company men attended the first reunion at Bamberg in 1976. They came with their wives, and it was almost a family affair. The initiative came from former members. Up to 2008 we met almost annually, but at each meeting there would be some whom we had to mourn. At the time of writing in 2013 there are still five former 3 Company members alive, all over 90 and no longer able to attend a reunion.

I am very grateful to my comrades of PzRgt 35 and Heavy PzAbt 503. After so many years they helped me to confirm facts and provided additional information. Much previously unpublished pictorial material comes from these sources.

I would also especially like to thank Jürgen Achatz. His father was one of the veteran panzer men of PzRgt 35. He survived Stary-Bychow as I did but was taken prisoner by the Russians there. Especially valuable to me were his additions which I added to my own diary kept over this period. Jürgen Achatz made me a very generous gift of the material a few years ago which inspired me to compose my war experiences.

The timetables added to the text are taken from:

Volks-Ploetz, *Auszug aus der Geschichte*, 3rd edition, 1979.

1939-1945: Der zweite Weltkrieg in Chronik und Dokumenten, Wehr und Wissen Verlag, 1959.

Other Greenhill Books Include:

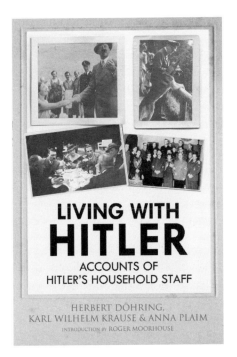

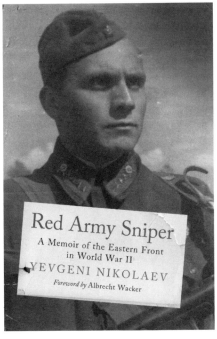

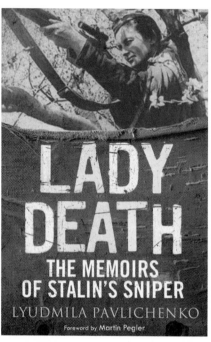

LADY DEATH

THE MEMOIRS OF STALIN'S SNIPER

LYUDMILA PAVLICHENKO

Foreword by Martin Pegler

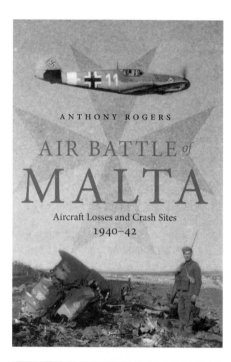

ANTHONY ROGERS

AIR BATTLE *of* MALTA

Aircraft Losses and Crash Sites
1940–42

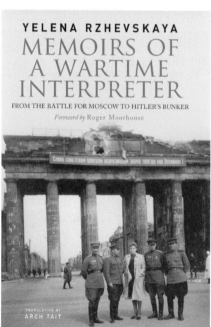

YELENA RZHEVSKAYA

MEMOIRS OF A WARTIME INTERPRETER

FROM THE BATTLE FOR MOSCOW TO HITLER'S BUNKER

Foreword by Roger Moorhouse

TRANSLATION BY
ARCH TAIT

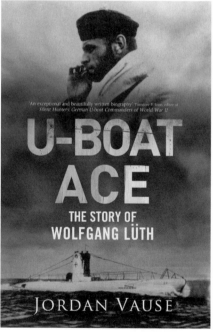

'An exceptional and beautifully written biography' Timothy P. Mulligan, author of
Silent Hunters: German U-boat Commanders of World War II

U-BOAT ACE

THE STORY OF WOLFGANG LÜTH

JORDAN VAUSE